Wolf Hustle

Wolf Hustle

A Black Woman
on Wall Street

CIN FABRÉ

DIALOGUE BOOKS

First published in Great Britain in 2023 by Dialogue Books

First published in the United States of America in 2022
by Henry Holt and Company

1 3 5 7 9 10 8 6 4 2

Copyright © 2023 by Fabre, LLC

The moral right of the author has been asserted.

A CIP catalogue record for this book
is available from the British Library.

ISBN 978-0-349-70395-4

Printed and bound in Great Britain by Clays Ltd, Elcograf S.p.A.

Papers used by Dialogue Books are from well-managed forests
and other responsible sources.

Dialogue Books
Carmelite House
50 Victoria Embankment
London EC4Y 0DZ

www.dialoguebooks.co.uk

Dialogue Books, part of Little Brown, Book Group Limited,
an Hachette UK company.

For my mom, Oline, whose advice follows me, always. *Sendy, respect yourself and others will, too.*

"Piti piti, zwazo fe nich li"
Little by little, the bird builds its nest

Haitian proverb

Introduction

T HE HUSTLE HAS ALWAYS BEEN WITH ME. ONCE I DIS-
covered the stock market I became infected with the
delirious joy that comes from a successful speculative
trade, a short, an initial public offering (IPO), all the bells and
whistles that have the power to get you dirty, filthy, abominably
rich (and, by the same token, the power to get you to terribly,
horribly, heart-attack-inducingly lose everything). That's when
Wall Street became my hustle.

There were drugs everywhere, cocaine and quaaludes, sex,
too, of course, but the drug I can still feel coursing through my
veins to this day is the energy of the Pit. It was palpable the second you walked into the building—the air itself was electrified
with frenetic action and the thrill of making money. Or at least,
the promise of it. The shrill cacophony of phones ringing and
voices calling out, the booming laughter exploding at a crude
joke, the tang of anxious sweat hanging under our noses—it
all coursed through me, pushed me to work harder than I ever
had in my whole life. It was intoxication and agony. I took in
the dysfunction, tried not to let it decay who I was as a person.

When you hear about the wolves in finance, you probably
envision the Jordan Belforts of this world—and the tales of
the crazy hours they worked, the antics they got into off Wall

Street with their ties discarded and hair no longer neatly slicked back. Away from their significant others, out in the Hamptons or in a hotel room, bottles upon bottles of Dom, mountains of snow, thousands of dollars thrown around carelessly, sometimes crumpled up or burned just because they could. It's all true. I was there, and I witnessed it. I took part in some of it, too. But these wolves—many of whom built (and lost) vast personal fortunes at the expense of others—were part of an exclusive club. You know the one I'm talking about—the boys' club. Specifically, one made up of white men. I wasn't part of that club. As a Black woman on 1990s Wall Street, I certainly wasn't supposed to be there. I refused to accept that. Why couldn't I have a seat at the table? If I wasn't going to receive an invitation, I was going to keep showing up until a seat was made available for me. None of these men—some coming from humble backgrounds, most well-to-do, all equipped with the inherent privilege that comes from being a white man, a valuable currency in itself—had faced what I had. I showed up to the boardroom every day with an "I-have-nothing-to-lose" mindset that was as strong as a white man's privilege. Disadvantages? I WAS the advantage, and I would use everything I had to achieve success.

The money, the drugs, the parties, the sharp suits, the fast-talking brokers—that's part of the story, sure. But it's not the whole story. As is often the case, history (and pop culture, for that matter) has gravely overlooked the voices of those who don't check certain boxes. Nobody knows the part of the story in which a daughter of Haitian immigrants, who grew up in the Bronx projects, broke into Wall Street to become one of its youngest Black female stockbrokers, landing clients worth hundreds of millions. And frankly, that part of the story is much more interesting.

∽

I would have found my way to the stock market one way or another—you can believe that. But my introduction to the bull and bear came from, of all people, an awkward high school student named Ali—we'll get to him in a moment.

Eyes always on the ground looking for the gleam of a quarter or a nickel fallen from someone's pocket onto the sidewalk, remorselessly looting cash from my dad's hidden stash, I always burned to make money, to hoard it, save it, and spend it. You see, in lieu of outward showings of affection, my parents placed their love in things, my mother proving her love for us children by paying for our tuition, our clothes, our housing, my father demonstrating his lack of love by selfishly spending only on himself. Money was currency not only in the wider world, to buy movie tickets and Nikes and schoolbooks, but a channel through which to funnel our deepest emotions, our lusts, loves, and ambitions.

So it really can't at all be a surprise that I was enterprising, to say the least, constantly drawing schematics in my head, planning various get-rich-quick schemes as a kid, first so that I could buy candy and shock my tastebuds with sugar and carbs, indulging in addictive pleasures like Chicco sticks, Red Hots, Boston Baked Beans, Now & Laters, and chalky bubble gum. Later, it was so I could save to buy a car, which I saw as the ultimate path to freedom, a way to escape the confines of my life, which mostly consisted at that time of yelling parents and dark bedrooms.

At thirteen, I became a tutor, assisting elementary school kids twice a week with their homework, helping them understand addition and subtraction, multiplication and division, which I'd mastered long ago to best be able to determine how much bang for my buck I could get at the corner bodega near our house. I made six dollars an hour, which was popping for 1989.

But it was a couple of years later that quiet, stocky Ali opened my eyes to the fact that there was an entire world in which men and women—mostly men—existed solely to hustle and were held accountable for making bank. I knew I could fill that role. I could do it with my eyes closed.

At that moment in time, my hustle was lunch tickets. The target? Queens Vocational Technical High School in Long Island City. If you've been to Long Island City recently, you might think of sleek high-rise buildings, where families and well-to-do yuppies live with their domestic partners and designer dogs, shopping at tastefully appointed Foodcellar Market or, better yet, ordering their groceries in for the doorman to receive on their behalf. Muscled, smooth-skinned young people with management titles and 401(k)s, whose sights are set on conquering Manhattan, which they can see from their twenty-fourth-story balconies. You know the type.

The Long Island City of my youth wasn't that. Not even close. There wasn't even a Starbucks to be found. Can you imagine? Just a beat-up coffee truck with coffee, black or with milk. Not a latte to be seen for miles.

Back in the early nineties, Long Island City was a piece of Queens that very few people had heard of—it was all abandoned factories, rusted-out cars, and cracked pavement. There was nothing glamorous about it; its gentrification wouldn't happen until years later when developers realized they could make the waterfront area sexy and jack up the price of everything infinity-fold. I do admire their eye for opportunity. Everyone's gotta make a buck, and they saw an opening.

Well, when I was in high school, there was a diner that all the students hung out at before first bell, there was a Mickey D's that kids went to after school for greasy fries and McFlurrys, and there were a few nondescript bakeries, feeding out bread and other baked goods in trucks for supply elsewhere, probably in better-to-do neighborhoods. And that was about it. Not much else existed in the area, apart from my school, Queens Vocational Technical High School, and another vocational high school nearby that taught, of all things, aviation mechanics.

Queens Vo prepared you to work in blue-collar jobs across

various industries. If you went there, you were likely not considering college after graduation. For many in attendance, completing high school was a feat in itself, as many dropped out because of unplanned pregnancies or to work full-time to help their families out. The areas of focus were cosmetology—mostly Black girls and Latinx girls did cosmetology; plumbing, medical assistance, computer technology, electrical installation, electronics technology, and business. Most of the guys at the school picked electrical or computer tech, and the few white girls in school and some Latinx girls did business. I also chose business because I felt that I could pick up practical skills that would help me hustle in whatever career I chose.

Apart from learning our vocation, we also had math, art, science, social studies, English, and gym class, but our vocational classes dominated our time. Which is how I came to know Ali, who was also in business. He might not otherwise have interacted with me—he was a fierce introvert—but I was curious to know more about him, particularly because he always seemed to be flush with cash. Besides, I liked quiet people—they were good listeners, and I was always running my mouth, in need of someone to offer an occasional head nod or an "oh, yeah" to accompany my verbal flow. Ali had a seriously cool car with constantly blaring speakers that had to have cost him a pretty penny. And he often participated in my lunch ticket hustle when I could pin him down.

Let me break it down for you. At Queens Vo, we didn't have nice things. We didn't have a gym. We always had to exercise outside, rain or shine, even in the dead of winter. We didn't have a cafeteria, or even a real kitchen—only an auditorium, where the lunch ladies would hand out simple hot lunches, usually a microwaved cheeseburger wrapped in foil accompanied by a carton of chocolate milk. We'd take this to the auditorium and balance our lunch trays precariously on our knees while sitting on folding chairs, the cold seats biting in winter and searing our asses in summer, smacking us when we stood up if we didn't move fast enough. Lunch tickets cost one dollar. If you were really poor, you could notify the lunch ladies that you needed assistance and you could get your lunch for free, but most kids chose not to do that, perhaps to avoid public embarrassment, and instead would fork over a buck to get lunch. I saw my in there.

If you were to ask me whether stealing is a crime, I'd have to put that right back on you. Who's doing the stealing? Are they economically disadvantaged? Are they stealing from someone or something that has historically benefited from their labor, underpaid or not paid at all?

What I'm trying to get at is, as cliché as it sounds, there's a lot of gray in this world and seeing things in stark black and white isn't always the way to do it.

Or maybe I'm just trying to soften what I'm about to tell you. You be the judge.

I stole from my school and I didn't feel a shred of guilt doing it. I took six lunch ticket books from the front office by distracting the lunch coordinator, then sliding the little stapled booklets into my backpack one day. They fit right in, as if they should have been there and were taking their rightful place nestled among my notebooks and textbooks. It was easy and felt right.

I sold these tickets right back to the kids who would have bought these same tickets from the school. Instead, they bought them from me. Why did they do that? They weren't getting a discount—I would never sell myself short, come on—and they weren't getting any extras, like dessert, thrown in. So why did they buy from me?

I honestly think they liked fucking over the school. I know I did.

They also may have liked the transaction as much as I did,

crinkled and worn dollar bills exchanging hands in return for the little slips of paper that would buy them a burger or a sandwich or some other mediocre lunch item.

Maybe they wanted to support me—they knew and respected a hustle when they saw one. Or maybe it felt like some kind of illicit deal—it probably felt good doing something wrong.

All I know is that kids bought tickets from me every day, and my proverbial nest egg grew. Sometimes, kids even handed me their lunch tickets that they hadn't used, which meant I'd make a couple of extra dollars a day.

I usually sold ten tickets a day, which meant ten dollars, more if students gave me their unused tickets. I'd walk the lunch line, up and down, like a trench-coated scalper hawking game tickets. I'd forfeit my own lunch ticket in order to make an extra buck (I'd often eat my friends' leftovers that they didn't want or I would be one of the few to claim free lunch) and it went really well for a good chunk of time.

But an eagle-eyed lunch lady had spotted me trawling the line one day and reported me to the principal, Mr. Serber. Lunch ladies were always looked down upon by the administration, and I hoped that they'd keep their mouths shut, would sympathize with me over the Man, but nope, it wasn't meant to be.

Mr. Serber, a white, middle-aged man with a comb-over, small beady eyes, and a hawkish nose, awaited me in his cramped office. He shut the door and sat me down opposite his desk. His own chair made a sad exhale as he sat and steepled his fingertips, looking over them at me. He sighed, as if the weight of the world were on his shoulders, and then he chose not to see the budding entrepreneur in front of him.

"I have been made aware that you are selling lunch tickets, Ms. Fabré," he said, his eyes narrowed, looking at me.

It never entered my mind to lie to him here, though I had

no problem lying to adults. I simply didn't see anything wrong with what I was doing. After all, I was charging face value—I wasn't even hiking up the price. I confirmed to Serber with a nod of my head. He let out another weary sigh. He almost seemed disappointed that I had let the truth escape so easily, but I was a seasoned pro, from years of practice at confession having attended Catholic school before coming to Queens Vo. He took a moment to regroup, then picked up his interrogation.

"Well, how did you come into possession of these ticket books, then?"

Yikes. He must have known about the missing books.

I told him part of the truth—that friends gave me their unused tickets and I resold them. No harm, no foul.

He dropped the "F" bomb.

"Do you know that what you are doing is a *felony*?"

At the time, I didn't know what the word meant, so it didn't scare me. Looking back, I don't exactly love that he was trying to criminalize me, a young Black girl.

I let him drone on for a few minutes about right and wrong before it felt like the torrent was reaching its end. I assured him that I wouldn't do it again, and he let me out of his office with a stern warning. Of course, the next day I was back in business, and the day after that, I landed in the hot seat with Serber again. This time, he sighed and theatrically rubbed his face.

"Ms. Fabré, are you still selling lunch tickets?"

I gave him the wide-eyed stare that I sometimes used to disarm adults, and vehemently told him I wasn't, that kids were continuing to come to me looking for tickets, and that I was turning them away as quickly as I could. You could practically see the halo hanging over my head in that moment.

Serber delivered a righteous speech, then shooed me away with another warning. Like any good businessperson faced with a challenge, I pivoted, selling tickets outside of the auditorium, away from the prying eyes of those cawing lunch lady crows.

I was a charismatic seller, offering those reluctant to buy from me promotional freebies with no supposed catch. Of course, there was a catch; the catch was that I then guilted them into purchasing tickets from me, obligating them to be customers.

One afternoon, I spotted Ali, an easy target when I could manage to get to him, as he usually had cash and could be persuaded to part with it without too much difficulty on my part. Ali was a weird guy with weird mannerisms—he was so soft-spoken that you always had to lean in to hear whatever it was he was saying. He was painfully tall and sported a mustache, which was an impressive thing to be able to grow successfully in high school, but which also meant that he stuck out like a sore, or rather hairy, thumb. Plus, the mustache made it impossible to read his lips, so most kids had a hard time communicating with him. He never started conversations with anyone, and he had very few friends. When he did choose to say something, he always looked nervous, his eyes darting around, as if he was worried he was about to be overheard giving away classified information. I half-suspected that Ali was an undercover cop, an adult gathering secrets about the student body like in *21 Jump Street*. All that said, Ali was ahead of his time and very mature. I knew if he opened his mouth, it would be to say something that I should listen to.

Our school was tiny—my graduating class had only about two hundred people—so I made it my duty to get to know everyone. Ali tolerated my presence because I wouldn't allow anything else—I would force conversation upon him and he would generally oblige with some short, soft-spoken remark.

That day, as I was making my rounds, I saw Ali towering over everyone else, waiting for lunch. This was a rare opportunity, as he usually ate greasy-spoon food at the diner around the corner from the school. I wanted to see what information I could mine from him, so I couldn't pass him up. I made a bee-line toward him.

As I locked eyes with Ali, I saw a wary look pass over his face. He knew all about my hustle, and had paid for tickets, I suspected, just to get rid of me. I didn't mind—as long as he bought from me, I didn't care what his reason was. He cut me off before I could begin my spiel in earnest.

"You have change for a five? 'Cause I know you're gonna ask me to buy a ticket," he said softly.

I grinned. A fellow business person, getting right down to brass tacks. I liked it! I made change and we exchanged money for the lunch ticket.

Coolly appraising him, I asked, "Ali, how could you afford to buy your car and those stereo speakers?" For that level of profit, I couldn't think of much else that would be possible for kids in our world other than selling weed, or maybe working a part-time job for *years*.

Ali explained that he'd been speculating in the stock market and had made a tidy profit recently. He decided to treat himself with the stereo upgrade.

I looked at him blankly.

"What's a stock market?" I'd never heard of it, was suspicious of it, wanted to learn everything I could to see if I could take advantage of it for myself.

Ali was incredulous—he couldn't believe that I'd never heard of the stock market, that I was completely unfamiliar with terms like the Dow and Wall Street and NASDAQ. It was all foreign to me—until that point, I just wanted to be able to buy enough candy so I could get a sugar high and not fall asleep in English class.

That day, Ali gave me a crash course on the stock market,

explaining about buying and selling, holding and shorting, stocks and bonds. He shared that he held a joint account with his dad and, with the guidance of an investment adviser, had a profitable portfolio.

I was instantly hooked—I could feel the irresistible pull of the market even when filtered secondhand through Ali. This sounded like a far better way to make money than selling drugs or working long hours at some menial labor job. Ali parted ways with me by telling me that the more money I invested in the market, the bigger the return would be. He conveniently forgot to mention the other side of the coin: losses.

But the few hundred dollars I'd saved from my lunch ticket business weren't enough to put into the market if I wanted a considerable return. And my parents certainly wouldn't be giving me any money to invest—my mother didn't trust banks and hid all her savings in various places around the house, while my father had never handed out more than a quarter to any of his children (he didn't have a favorite among us—he was his own favorite, of course).

From that day, I vowed to find a way into the stock market. For now, all I could do was continue to hustle, so I put all my energy back into my lunch ticket biz.

My "regulars" had it good—I was a generous salesperson, offering credit if they were short on some days. They'd often run up tabs, then pay me in lump sums later. I ran a neat ledger in my head and kept track carefully of who owed me what. I knew who was good for it, and I didn't often make judgment errors, choosing to work with those who I knew would cough up cash when I asked for it.

But there's always going to be someone who tries to take advantage of your generosity, who will lean on you until you're forced to teach them a lesson and show them who's boss.

Alicia was that person for me. Also in the eleventh grade, she was so pale that you could see the blueish-purple of her veins underneath her skin.

She owed me a whopping twelve dollars and had started dodging me when she saw me. But I knew she wasn't cash poor—she was buying soda and pretzels from the snack lady who sold us all sugar-loaded snacks. I couldn't let word get out that I was soft on clients. I wouldn't let her make a fool out of me.

So I confronted her before science class while she was gossiping with a friend at her locker. It was truly a cinematic moment as I puffed myself up and asked, "Hey, Alicia, where's my money?"

She looked at me and rolled her eyes before continuing her conversation.

I couldn't have that. That kind of attitude after I'd shown her such kindness and let her run up her tab to an exorbitant twelve dollars? This was disrespectful and I could not, for the sake of my business, tolerate it.

I leaned between her and her friend, forcing them to halt their conversation. "Excuse me—I asked you a question," I said to her in a soft, dangerous tone.

Alicia was annoyed—but not as annoyed as I was. "Why are you bothering me, Cin? I told you I'll give it to you when I have it."

What I did next surprised even me. I grabbed Alicia by her neck and threw her against the wall, hard. I stared into her eyes, which were now clouded with fear, and I stood up straight.

"I want my fucking money," I told her, my face inches away from hers.

I was still squeezing her neck, so she only offered a small, short nod in response. Her feet dangled, as I had lifted her off the ground with my throw. I wouldn't have been surprised if she had pissed her pants at this point.

I released her suddenly and she crumpled to the ground before jumping up and running off, her friend already long gone.

Where did that come from? I'd always been a peaceful person and rarely engaged in fights throughout elementary school and junior high, even though there'd been plenty of opportunities. The only times I'd fought were against bullies when they provoked me: once I threw a chair at a kid's head, the other time I grabbed a bat to swing at a kid who was taunting me but was nabbed by a teacher before I could inflict any damage. Was I turning into my father? He'd always been physically and verbally abusive to our family and I had loathed him for it. I didn't want to be anything like him—he was a monster. But this experience felt strangely empowering to me. Clearly, doing nothing about Alicia's debt yielded no results, but the threat of an ass whupping sure gave me what I wanted, and quick.

The next day, Alicia didn't come to school. But she returned the following day and paid me back without further protest. She averted her eyes, refusing to look at me, and quickly handed me two fives and two singles, which were sweaty from her tight grip, before she murmured something about how she had to go. She beat a quick retreat before I could say anything to her. But she actually continued to buy lunch tickets from me, which I allowed her to do, as her debt was erased, and I didn't see anything wrong in accepting her money (though I never extended her credit like I had before. I had learned a wise lesson here).

This moment with Alicia had given me an undeniable, electric thrill, but I was also, at the same time, horrified by it. What did it mean to snap like that and feel such little guilt toward Alicia? Was I going to turn out like my dad? Did the fact that I was worrying about this signal that I *couldn't* be like him? After all, he relished his monstrousness, delighted in it, and had only become worse as the years ticked by. In the coming decade when I was on Wall Street, not sure if I liked who I had become, I would return to this moment again and again, slamming Alicia into the wall, remembering the vein in her neck pulsing rapidly against my palm while I held her by the throat.

Who was I? Who did I want to be? Who could I become?

Chapter 1

FOR MANY, "THE AMERICAN DREAM" IS AN EMPTY phrase—not a dream so much as the half-conscious state that's found between sleeping and waking. It's that wait at the bus stop, shifting from one foot to the other; that intake of breath before the doctor pierces your skin with his needle; that 3–2–1 countdown on New Year's Eve. You're stuck. The bus never comes, the needle never plunges, the New Year never arrives.

For some people, the dream deferred is a bitter surprise. They believed this burnished, time-worn ideal, believed their family and friends who said the sky's the limit, believed in the red, white, and blue promise of America, with its picket fences and green grass freshly mown. Others never subscribed to such a belief in the first place, knowing that they'd wind up disappointed, with nothing to show for their efforts except cuts and bruises . . . or worse.

Where you fall on this spectrum of believing in the American dream could very well be correlated to what you think of the phrase "pull yourself up by your bootstraps." Hell, if you want to be efficient, take the rest of the phrase away and leave yourself with just "bootstraps"—when else is that word *ever* employed, except in relation to making the case that marginalized people and their communities should just, well, you know . . . pull 'em up! Seriously, I bet you can't think of a time in which you heard or used the word "bootstraps" in another context. Go ahead, I'll wait.

Many are indoctrinated into the hazy optimism of stars and stripes through the lens of their parents. I was no different, I would come to find out. In 1973, my parents came to America from Haiti looking for a better life for themselves and the children that they knew they would bring into the world. In the United States lay the glittering promise of wealth, of social advancement, of nice boots and their straps. In Haiti, they saw nothing but their past selves staring back at them like ghosts— both dissatisfied with how far they could go in Haiti, both united in their belief that America would provide them with fertile opportunity.

Haiti, the Pearl of the Antilles, so beautiful, once a cash cow for its former colonizer, France, which knew it as Saint Domingue. That was not its first name, and France wasn't even the first colonizer of Haiti. Before France, there was Spain— that genocidal maniac Christopher Columbus knocked into the island in 1492 on the *Santa Maria* and thought he'd arrived in India or China. He dubbed it Hispaniola and matter-of-factly set about enslaving the island's original inhabitants, the Taíno people, who had migrated to the island long before from South America, and who had named it Haiti, meaning "the land of the high mountains."

In a letter to Luis de Santángel, Spain's *escribano de ración* to monarchs King Ferdinand II and Queen Isabella I—a.k.a. treasurer, a.k.a. sugar daddy to Columbus—Columbus wrote of the Taíno, "They never refuse anything that is asked for. They . . . show so much love that they would give their very hearts." That's a mighty convenient viewpoint for you, Chris, but okay, sure.

Colonizers gonna colonize, though. Columbus wasted no

time claiming what was not his to claim in the name of Spain and, in short order, enslaved the Taíno people, treating them so sadistically that it's estimated up to fifty thousand of these Indigenous people committed suicide, diving off cliffs or offing themselves in any other way they could, to avoid forced marriage, slavery, rape, torture, murder, and other mistreatment by Columbus and his men. Many who didn't die by murder or suicide were killed off by the diseases that the colonizers unknowingly brought with them.

There is no precise number to be given for how many Taíno died at the hands of Columbus, his men, and their germ warfare—the prevailing notion is that almost all were wiped out by Columbus's genocide, with only a fraction surviving and/or intermarrying and having children with the colonizers. When Spain ceded Haiti to France in 1697, this "extinction" was also a convenient argument to justify French colonizers bringing over enormous numbers of enslaved people from Africa to work the land, much of their labor used to farm the sugarcane and coffee plantations they established there.

Most of the enslaved people the French colonizers brought over to Haiti hailed from Central and West Africa. West African culture in particular was instrumental in influencing Haitian vodou, which many Haitians to this day intermingle with the Catholicism brought over by the Spanish and French—my family was no exception here.

The French were making a killing (literally . . . the life expectancy of an enslaved person during this time was shockingly low—twenty-one years) off of the labor of African enslaved people, gorging themselves on the profits from the aforementioned coffee and sugarcane plantations that the Africans worked; in the 1700s, Haiti was one of the richest colonies in the world. The French were greedy, though, and they couldn't let a good thing be, could they? By the late 1700s, they had brought close to six hundred thousand enslaved people to the island, and whites were outnumbered twenty to one.

I know I'm good with numbers, but it certainly doesn't take a Wall Street genius to understand that those odds clearly were not in France's favor. In 1791, Toussaint Louverture—former enslaved person and the first Black general of the French army (get it, guy!)—and other brave Black folks kicked off the Haitian Revolution, which must have been a real pain in the ass for France, given that they were already dealing with the French Revolution and all. I'm going to bet there were some heads apart from Marie Antoinette's that rolled for not being able to contain the Haitian uprising. Twelve years into the fighting, short, smelly handed Napoleon Bonaparte had to concede defeat to Louverture's successor, Jean-Jacques Dessalines, who pronounced Haiti to be a free nation on January 1, 1804. Oh, and while Dessalines and his crew were at it, they abolished slavery, becoming the first country in the world ever to do so, not to mention that they were the first state ever to be established by a slave rebellion. A bloody birth, to be sure, one in which the country was delivered after a long labor, and the doctor needed to slap it on the butt to start it squalling, but eventually, red-faced, it did, and the name on the birth certificate was now the Republic of Haiti, or *Repiblik d Ayiti* in Creole, which, along with French, became the mother tongue for Haitians.

Do you feel transported back to school where you're doodling idly in the margins of your notebook or etching feverish declarations of love into your desk while keeping an ear open in case the teacher calls your name? There's a point to this history lesson, I promise.

See, after the Haitian Revolution, France pulled some real shady shit: In exchange for recognizing Haiti's independence, France required Haiti to pay France 150 million francs (about $21 billion in today's currency), which was more than ten times the annual budget of Haiti. By comparison, the United States had a few years earlier paid only 15 million francs for Louisiana, a swath of land much larger than tiny Haiti. The thinking was that France needed to be compensated for its loss of revenue stemming from its slavery. Yes, you read that right—the people who had been enslaved were forced to pay their enslavers for their enslavers' profit loss.

The result? Starting in 1825, Haiti was forced to tax its citizens severely to even begin to pay off its debt, which—get this—with interest from the loans it was forced to take from French banks, wasn't paid off until 1947, a whopping 122 years later. Public infrastructure—from hospitals to schools to roads to bridges to sources of drinking water—was constantly underfunded, and Haiti was unable to develop in ways that other, more financially unencumbered countries could, what with that debt hanging over its head for nearly 150 years. But tell me again how you think people should just pull themselves up by their bootstraps. If *this* isn't an argument for reparations against slavery, then I don't know what is.

Other countries, like the United States and Germany, paternalistically insinuated themselves in Haiti's politics—for their own benefit, of course—over the years, and the government has been more often than not in upheaval, making the path to prosperity for Haitians that much more difficult. Since declaring its independence, Haiti has been through thirty-two coups! (In case you're wondering, that's a lot.) Today, Haiti remains one of the poorest countries in the Americas, and it ranks 145 out of 182 countries on the United Nations Human Development index. Not great. Many Haitians strike out from their homes in an attempt to create better lives for their families—it's one of the only means of egress from a life of poverty.

Which brings us back to Mommy and Poppy.

My mother was born in a small town in the northeastern

part of Haiti, before her parents moved the family to a farm on the "good" side of Port-au-Prince ("good" meaning wealthier here). The second oldest of eight children, Mommy rarely spoke about her siblings or her parents or life before New York, so what I know of her childhood and early adulthood is pieced together from the brief reminiscences that I could pry from her. When I was young and would ask her what she was like as a kid—*Did you wear barrettes in your hair like me? What was your favorite song? Why didn't you like your family?*—she would usually frown and say, "It doesn't matter," before hurrying off to complete some joyless adult task. But every so often, she would let down her guard and her eyes would soften, and it was during these rare moments that I could see her remembering the deliciously sour smell of rum mash in her nostrils or the feel of the Caribbean sun on her face.

By American standards, my mother's family was very poor—you might even say destitute, without necessities like plumbing that Americans always take for granted. But in Haiti, the family was considered solidly middle class. They had livestock and farmed sugarcane, and they even had workers farming the land for them, whom they either paid in cash or, if the workers preferred, in alcohol (always rum) or other supplies, like food or clothing. In a country as cash poor as Haiti, many people lived this way and got by through bartering, whether it was for services, labor, or goods. They might occasionally have household help as well—in Haiti, there was always someone worse off than you, willing to work for almost nothing.

But most of the time, Mom and her seven siblings maintained the house and helped their parents with chores while the staff did the harder work of farm labor. The farmhouse was large—five whole bedrooms—but with such a large Catholic family, there were inevitably younger siblings who'd be forced to share a room if not a bed. Ermilienne Jacquet was the oldest daughter, then came my mother, Oline, then Johnny, the first son, then Thonine Fleurantin, Elcie Francois, Hermite, Frito Lapomarede, and the baby of the family, Paulette, who was eighteen years younger than Ermilienne, the firstborn.

Even though they were situated in the lush, neon tropics of the Caribbean, the house was constantly plunged in darkness because the farmhouse had no electricity. When needed, they would use kerosene lamps and eat dinner by a flickering, oily flame, swinging the same lamp in front of them to cast shadows in hallways and down stairs to use the outhouse at night. And while she had one, Mom preferred not to use her chamber pot, opting for the outhouse instead, because she knew she would have to muck out the sloshy contents of the pot the following morning. In their family, the various functions of their bodies were kept strictly secret, never to be openly discussed, and Mom vastly preferred a tiptoed walk outside in her nightgown to admitting that her body had base needs that would require the service of a chamber pot.

Any nighttime wanderings were made a little less scary by the fact that the family allowed their chickens and roosters to come into the house as they pleased, and the hens would often roost indoors. Soft clucks permeated the night, which Mom and her siblings found comforting, helping to stave off the terror of the darkness just a bit. The chickens' presence was especially welcome in the early mornings, as each kid would be assigned to cook breakfast once a week, and in order to successfully pull it all together before school or mass, they would have to rise in the dark and head to the kitchen, which was outdoors, with only the chickens for company.

Meals were simple and often relied on the bounty of the farm or the river nearby. It goes without saying that rice and beans were a staple. So, too, was legume. Haitian legume varies per household, with cooks often very protective of their recipes, which they hand down from generation to generation. A thick stew made with vegetables and usually some kind of protein, our family's legume had spinach, lima bean, and eggplant in it, and meat when we could get our hands on some. On the farm, they'd often add pork to their legume; in New York, my mom would add smoky bacon in tribute.

Other favorites included fried goat, cow's tongue, pigs' feet, and roast chicken—Haitians are never scared of using offal and innards—meat of any kind is precious and not to be wasted. Food was usually spiced aggressively, most often with Scotch bonnet pepper and warm spices like cloves. In many Haitian dishes, "epis" is used as a base; think of it like a Caribbean sofrito. Most often made with green and red bell peppers, onion, garlic, cilantro, parsley, and oil, it can also be used as a marinade or a pesto-like topping. In Haiti, epis is ubiquitous in households, and my mother's family kitchen was no exception. Traditionally, mortars and pestles were used to pulverize the ingredients, but now many people, including my mother when she would make it in New York, simply use a blender. I do like to think of my mother as a small child, pounding epis ingredients in a mortar and pestle by moonlight, surrounded by her hen friends, maybe a little lonely, maybe finding peace in this simple act.

The family was also treated to the tropical harvest of the trees on their land, able to pull at will a mango, a guava, or an orange from a nearby tree, or stoop to pick up a hairy coconut fallen to the ground. My mother loved mangoes, in particular, and they're my favorite fruit, too. Whenever she was hungry she would run to the closest mango tree and snap off a yellow jewel from a heavy branch. Small and sweet, the Haitian mangoes were always juicy, and Mom would peel the mango messily with her hands, letting the juices run down her chin as she happily ate its tender meat.

Sometimes the family would eat fish that they had caught

from the nearby river, some flash of silver that they'd managed to catch with a net or a pole and a worm they had dug up from the rich, brown soil of the riverbank. More often than not, they would eat fish on Sundays, as the children were required to clean their clothes in the river before mass once a week. My mother or Ermilienne would often cook the fish, as they were oldest and could roast the fish over an open flame until its skin was crisped and the flesh delicately flaky. Sometimes they'd make patties, which in Haiti are a general term for any kind of chicken, beef, fish, or vegetable mixture encased in pastry.

Breakfast eaten, surplus laundry pinned and dripping on clotheslines, the family would then head to mass on Sunday mornings, seven kids in total (one died as an infant), all wearing their best, newly washed and pressed dresses or suits (probably their only—even though they were considered middle class, they still didn't have much extra for nonessentials).

Catholicism is omnipresent in Haiti, and a majority of Haitians identify as Catholics. Catholicism was first brought over to Haiti in the early 1500s by the Spanish, then strongly reinforced by waves of incoming French priests and monks, who set up parishes and orders all over the island, and who established Our Lady of Perpetual Help as Haiti's patron saint (does anyone else find that funny?). Catholicism has never supplanted the tradition of vodou; in fact, Haitian vodou is the product of the blending of West African religions (Yoruba in particular) and Catholicism. As a result, many devout Catholics practice vodou with equal reverence, seeing no conflict between the two. And while many people who don't know much about vodou think it's "black magic," any Haitian knows that vodou is only evil if you intend to use it for such. Vodou, as my mother and her sisters believed, actually gave women strength to endure what the world had doled out for them as females, with all the particular pains that being a woman might bring them.

This is why Mom and her family went to mass with strict adherence, praying the rosary with fervor. It's also why they believed in the power of Bondye, the deity who created the universe, and made offerings of food and other gifts to various *Iwa*, spirits who are sometimes compared to saints or angels in Christianity. Their family had First Communion and Reconciliation ceremonies; so, too, did they have ceremonies with *oungan* (priests) and *mambo* (priestesses) to channel and communicate with the *Iwa*.

On weekdays, Mom and her siblings would leave the farm to go to private school in town. While old people like to claim the hardship of walking to school in inclement weather (*In my day we had to walk miles in the snow!*), my mom and her siblings really did have it tough: They would have to find the shallow spots in the river and wade barefoot to the other side of the riverbank to get to school. When it rained particularly hard, which wasn't uncommon, the river would swell and its banks would flood. Adult volunteers would take shifts ferrying the children on their backs to or from school if the flooding wasn't severe. If the rains came while they were at school and it was particularly bad, they'd have to stay the night with relatives in town. And if the rains had flooded the banks while they were asleep before school, they would have to stay home and help their parents with chores.

Haiti's school system was woefully underfunded. To fill the gap, many private schools, often associated with Catholic parishes, sprang up to serve children. So even though the school she went to was private, it wasn't particularly exemplary. And she was lucky—many caregivers couldn't afford books or uniforms so many kids never got the opportunity to go to school.

That said, the school, which was run by stern nuns who had free rein to hit students, did teach English, which was not entirely common back then. Most schools—and households and communities—spoke in Creole, or occasionally French. But Mom and her siblings learned both French and English at their school, and, as a result, my mother, Oline, was incredibly vain about it. Even though she never finished high school, she always felt that she was better than others, this attitude even extending to members of her own family. This was partly due to what she viewed as her superior education. It was also, sadly, due to her own colorism. Her parents were both Black, but her father, my grandfather, was from a region called Fond-des-Blancs (in French, this literally translates to "white background"), about four hours from Port-au-Prince. Fond-des-Blancs is home to many people of Polish descent, whose ancestors had been soldiers in French regiments but who switched to fight for the Haitian Revolution against France, and who, in recognition for their service, were awarded Haitian citizenship by the new Republic of Haiti. As such, many people in Fond-des-Blancs are lighter-skinned than others in Haiti; some even have blue or green eyes. My grandfather was light-skinned, while my grandmother was not. Oline was light-skinned and was contemptuous of everyone, or almost everyone. While she didn't like her, she did cede a little bit of respect to her sister Paulette, who was also light-skinned. This attitude is what undoubtedly drew my mother to my father, who also was originally from Fond-des-Blancs.

In the wake of the hideous manipulation and abuse my father directed at my mother and us, it's hard for me to view my father in a positive light. But if I try hard, I can sometimes squint and see a version of the man my mother fell in love with.

Mom was maybe sixteen or seventeen when she met "Fab," as everyone called my father—the timeline for when, exactly, their lives came to intertwine is uncertain, as my mother was incredibly secretive, and she never told her family, or me for that matter, when they actually met, or how. So all that I can do is imagine how their meeting first played out. . . .

Passing by the sherbet-colored houses in town, maybe my mother spotted Fab first, impressed with his good looks, enjoying the cut of his suit. Or maybe he saw her on her way to school, her shoes damp from putting them back on after crossing the river. Was she preoccupied with her own thoughts and he called out to her to get her attention? Or maybe his roving eyes up and down her body were enough for her to sense him and for her to catch his glance. Maybe she flushed with pleasure at attention from such a rakishly handsome guy. Maybe, as she was beautiful herself, she was used to such notice and he had to wheedle with her to stop, to speak to him for a moment. Was she worried that she would be late for school, and would face a nun's wrath for her tardiness? Or was she swept up in the immediate romance of it all, the idea of school and how she might miss it never crossing her mind?

I don't know the answers, but I do know that even if she made it to school that day, there was another day that she didn't return. She never finished school, and, given that my grandparents wanted their children educated, I suspect that Fab's romantic attentions had something to do with it.

When my mother was twenty years old and Fab was twenty-five, they decided to get married. My grandparents were fully on board with Fab—he was charming and so handsome, and after all, he was from Fond-des-Blancs, which counts for a lot in Haiti.

A rare black-and-white photo of the two on their wedding day shows Oline in a white wedding dress, all beads and lace and elegance. Her hair is in a glorious bouffant, and a veil frames her face, resting lightly like wisps of cotton candy around her shoulders. She gazes at the camera with heavily lined eyes, unsmiling but not unhappy looking, with her hands clasped over her heart, her wedding band shining from her ring finger. Fab stands slightly behind her, his arms encircling her waist possessively. He looks sharp in his gray suit and tie, and a slight smirk dances on his face. He looks away from the camera as if he has gotten away with something and he knows it.

And he has, hasn't he? He has managed to marry into a family of much higher social standing than his; he has secured a beautiful bride who doesn't suspect that he has a much darker side yet to be revealed. He hasn't shared with Oline the extent of hardship he has faced growing up—how his mother had four children with different men out of wedlock, something so incredibly scandalous that it made it difficult for her to get work. That his father died in a bus accident so couldn't contribute. That his mother couldn't afford shoes for her children so he went barefoot. That there was rarely enough food to feed the children, certainly not multiple times a day, so his mother often went without, and her children had only rice, with not even beans to accompany the meal. When Fab was eight, his mother could no longer afford to keep him and his brother and they were sent away to live with an aunt, a move that invisibly but indelibly marked Fab for life and seemingly affected his every action and viewpoint moving forward.

He hasn't told his new bride the whole truth about how he was fired from his most recent job, that he has come to the end of the line on career opportunities in Haiti and that there may be some people unhappy with him, some who might wish him harm if he stays. He has borrowed—and will never return—money from his wife's family and called an uncle in New York, one who says he can help Fab and his wife stateside, if Oline will only put her trust in him, put her trust in the American Dream, as he has.

And so she does.

Chapter 2

AMERICA, LAND OF THE FREE, HOME OF THE BRAVE. That's what we sing so patriotically, right? Well, there is land here, though I don't quite know how you'd classify it as "free" in a nation first stolen from Indigenous people, then built upon the bodies of those who never tasted freedom. Doesn't seem very brave to me. If I'm being honest, though, I do have to admit that the line *is* catchy. Francis Scott Key, a fat-cat lawyer and part-time poet who penned the poem "Defence of Fort M'Henry," which was later repurposed for our country's national anthem, was a slaveholder from a rich Maryland plantation family, surprise surprise. I guess that gives us some insight into whom he deemed legitimate to count as free and brave, though.

I suppose that what I'm trying to get at here is that beauty is in the eye of the beholder. For my parents, the sights and sounds and smells of New York City were the most intoxicating they'd ever had the fortune to experience. The city pulsed with the energy of opportunity, of betterment, of upward mobility, and that, to them, was far more beautiful than anything you'd find ensconced in some airless museum.

And what were they breathing in? The starry lights of Broadway, showgirls and show tunes, slick glass office buildings and

Michelin restaurants, foam-flecked ferry rides to see the Statue of Liberty, stately Park Avenue, fresh bursts of greenery in Central Park?

Ha, no.

When my parents entered into the United States, passports officially stamped, they didn't have a romantic first glimpse of New York City that they recounted to us children in hushed tones of nostalgia, telling us of postcard views of the city from the airplane, of the ground rushing to meet the sky. No, they were shuffled in from Miami and then immediately decamped to a tiny, cramped apartment in Harlem, which my mother's uncle helped them secure.

When they opened their eyes in the morning, casting upward glances at their cracked ceiling, the thump of music could be heard from open windows and passing stereos on the streets. Muffled conversation and tired floorboards could be heard both above and below them. Outside, they sailed over oceans of concrete, making port at corner bodegas for small necessities. They really did feel as if they were in Francis Scott Key's land of the free, liberated and able to shape their lives however they saw fit.

To them, America was the greatest country in the world and New York City was the greatest city in the world.

"If you can make it here, you can make it anywhere," my mother would recite to me in a singsong voice when I would complain to her as a child. I didn't understand my parents' unwavering reverence of the city when all I could see of it, seemingly for miles around us, were projects, brick and asphalt and bars on windows.

"Sendy," my mother would say in her heavy Haitian accent, "you can become a millionaire here. You can do anything you want here!"

This wouldn't stop my grousing, but it didn't faze my mother. She would simply shrug and say, "Someday you'll see."

Soon after arriving, my father found quick work driving a yellow cab, zipping around the city, picking up and dropping off Hasidic women with shopping bags, briefcase-toting men, hippies in fringe, Black Panthers, grandmothers with bent backs. The back seat of his cab represented a diversity not present in their own neighborhood of Harlem. The Fair Housing Act passed in 1968 had little effect on the city in the seventies, with many landlords in Manhattan still refusing to rent to Black people outside of Harlem and other poorer neighborhoods. And middle-class Black folks were leaving in crashing waves for better-quality housing in the Bronx, Queens, and Brooklyn. The Harlem race riots had erupted in 1964, not too long before, and tensions remained high. Crime in Harlem was high, too, and police precinct officers in Harlem at the time numbered around one Black officer per six white officers, which certainly didn't help to ease the racial tensions, which were boiling over.

Things weren't great in Harlem because of systemic and institutional injustices, corruption, and, you know, plain ole, stare-you-in-the-face-and-spit-on-your-shoes racism.

Fab and Oline weren't overly concerned with these issues, though, Oline thinking she was above it all, and Fab so narcissistic that his definition of equality meant scamming both Black and white folks. They had other things on their minds.

For Fab, it was about memorizing the ins and outs of the city streets, figuring out how to overcharge customers through long routes and incorrect fare rates while charming their pants off so they'd give him the biggest tip possible. Determining by sight who would pay and who might stiff him, regardless of who was first in line on the corner. Ear always cocked for the doormen at the hotels and residential towers who would release shrill whistles into the air, signaling for Fab to slow down and stop for a hopefully rich, and, barring that, inattentive fare. He learned how to navigate the nauseating stop-and-start traffic of the Big Apple and made his own worthy contributions to the incessant noise of the city, pressing down on his horn whenever he felt like asserting himself in the vast sea of yellow cabs on the street. It was in driving a cab that he learned how to be his own kind of businessman, perfecting how he said things, not what.

Meanwhile, Oline was enormously pregnant with my oldest brother, doing what she could to ready herself for the birth of their first child. She less nested so much as furiously roosted, buying diapers on sale, clipping coupons for savings, packing her meager hospital bag. Even though she was hustling, pinching pennies wherever possible, money was tight. Fab wasn't exactly being a bountiful provider to his wife and child to be—somehow much of the money he made off driving the cab seemed confusingly to drain from his pocket by the time he made it to their walk-up for the dinner Oline was still dutifully cooking each night, usually something inflected with spice and the memory of Haiti. This unfortunate empty-wallet trend, she would realize too late, was destined to repeat itself for years to come.

In 1975, less than a year after they arrived in America, Oline gave birth to a son she named Glifford. She delivered him at Harlem Hospital. I honestly don't even know if my father was present for Glifford's birth. My mother—who was almost always angry at him for something, usually deservedly so—would regularly tell us that he didn't give a damn about us kids and that he most certainly didn't visit her in the hospital for two out of the three deliveries she had, all at Harlem Hospital. Maybe he did manage to make it to the first one—maybe he even played the part of concerned husband, ushering Oline out the door of their apartment before comically rushing back in for the forgotten hospital bag as if he were in a sitcom with a laugh track.

Instructing her to breathe, while forgetting to breathe himself, tripping to open the car door for her, telling her that they were almost to the hospital while snatching worried glances at her every few seconds, careening around on the road like a madman in the taxi while my mother clutched her swollen belly, calmer than him. It's nice to think about him being by her side, dabbing her sweaty forehead and telling her to push while she swears in Creole at him (*Fèmen dyol ou enbesil! Shut up, you imbecile! Tèt zozo! Dickhead!*), him taking it in stride, knowing it's all worth it when he gets to hold his son for the first time, the troubles of the world falling away as he looks into Glifford's eyes, knowing immediately that he would lay down his life to protect this tiny, blanketed bundle.

Yeah . . . It's a nice scene, but I highly doubt that happened. In the seventies, birth in the hospital was only just beginning to be viewed as a family event—fathers usually stayed outside the delivery room; the stereotype of the pacing father-to-be in the hallways of the hospital usually held true, though I'm skeptical that Fab would have been anxious enough to pace. In the unlikely event that Fab expressed any interest in entering the delivery room, my mother would have refused him—no way would she ever have allowed him to see her in such a state of naked vulnerability like that. (She never even said the word "pregnant" out loud when we were children—I don't know what she thought Glifford and I were thinking when she was eight months pregnant with Philip, our youngest brother, never once acknowledging her altered state, but she certainly never shared with us.) I doubt that Fab would have voiced such a desire, though. After all, this wasn't even his first child, nothing to get too excited about when you already have one. Oh, what was that? Yes, you heard right. He conveniently forgot to tell my mother he had fathered a son, Silvio, in his early twenties, in

Haiti. She wouldn't learn about Silvio until years later. Perhaps it didn't matter to her anymore because Silvio was one of *several* children Fab had had out of wedlock.

Regardless of whether Fab was present for Glifford's birth, my mother recuperated from the delivery as quickly and efficiently as possible, getting out of the hospital as soon as she could so as not to incur more charges than she needed to.

As soon as she was able, Oline took little Glifford back home to the little Harlem apartment, bathing, powdering, and diapering him while Fab stayed away for increasingly longer periods of time, citing a shortage of passengers as the reason for his absences. By now, my mother had a better sense of who Fab really was, his Mr. Hyde replacing the Dr. Jekyll my mother first thought she knew. I'm sure, too, that the subtle-as-an-elephant clues he dropped at home—the rum on his hot breath, the foreign perfume lingering on his clothes—also gave her an idea of some of what he was up to when he wasn't with her.

As a newly arrived immigrant sidelined at home with a baby, Oline must have been at least a little lonely. She had no friends to speak of at the time, she had left her family and her way of life back in Haiti, and her husband had increasingly become a stranger to her. Not to mention that Glifford was a disconcertingly quiet baby, his silence becoming a trademark of his personality for his entire life—he never seemed to fuss, and Oline must have felt, at times, like even he didn't need her, content as he was to lie in his crib and grab at his toes, spitting soft bubbles.

She wouldn't be remedying any of this in Harlem, though. She wouldn't get used to shopping for shoes at Florsheim's on Amsterdam Avenue, and she wouldn't have to swat away the pamphlets that the Muslim Brotherhood liked to pass out. She would no longer pass by the many churches in the neighborhood

adorned with signs that yelled out, "GOD IS ALIVE!"; "DOPE IS
DEATH MANY DIE EVERY DAY JESUS SAVES HEALS AND DELIVERS";
or "IN TIMES LIKE THESE, CHRIST IS WHAT YOU NEED!"

Instead, she would soon have a brand-new life to adjust to
because three things happened to her next, all in dizzying suc-
cession: she became pregnant with me, Fab was shot, and a new
home awaited them in the Bronx, a whole world away.

Chapter 3

OLINE BECAME PREGNANT AGAIN, ONLY A SHORT while after giving birth to Glifford. It likely didn't come as a huge surprise to her. As devoutly Catholic as Oline was, she certainly was not using birth control. Neither was abstinence an option—Fab was still hungry for his bride, even if the space beside her in their bed often remained cold, Fab out in the middle of the night to God knows where.

While my mother was preparing to give birth to her second child, baby girl, me, Fab was always away, ostensibly driving his yellow cab nights and mornings to sock away cash, though likely leaving room for plenty of other underhanded dealings away from the eyes of his wife. Even though they had only been wedded a couple of years, Fab and Oline's marriage was on rocky ground. What trust they had in each other had very quickly dissipated, ground out by hard living, infidelity, and lifelong emotional and physical trauma. These were two beings who were determined to succeed in life, yes, but who had both already been through more than most ever would in a lifetime, resulting in constant clashes, the two oil and water, unable to merge or find common ground.

What ensued was one long-fought battle that would last for years—with both at each other's throats, both convinced that the other was out to get them, both practicing vodou to safeguard against one another's black magic. After my father convinced my mother to take out a life insurance policy with himself listed as beneficiary, my mother reported to me that, in consultation with an *oungan* in the Bronx, my father had secretly sprinkled Haitian itch powder in my mother's car in an effort to get her to crash her car and kill her so that he could cash in on that fresh, juicy policy. In retaliation, my mother vigorously stuck pins in her vodou doll. The doll, a stand-in for my father, was a faceless brown figure about six inches long, which my mother had made out of some sort of rough material, maybe burlap. Whenever my mother felt that my father was using vodou against her or even us kids, which was fairly often, she would mumble angrily to herself and stick another long, sharp pin into the doll in an effort to counteract his ill effects. There were *a lot* of pins in that doll.

With Glifford underfoot and another baby on the way, Oline desperately wanted to leave Harlem behind, as so many other folks in the neighborhood had done in recent years, escaping for safer territory and better housing. Fortunately, she didn't have long to wait.

Oline fervently believed in God's salvation, and it likely felt like a miracle come from on high when Oline and Fab received the news that they had qualified for subsidized housing in the Bronx. As soon as they arrived in New York, my mother's uncle had advised them to apply, and they'd been on the waiting list for about a year. Did they know anything about the Bronx? Nothing much except that this semi-helpful uncle lived there and it was *not* where my father was shot. Good enough for them. Not to mention that they would be relocating to a two-bedroom apartment with an eat-in kitchen and views of a park for only sixty-five dollars a month (roughly equivalent to three hundred eighteen dollars today). Compared to their current one-bedroom, this was a palace and a steal.

Packing up their few belongings didn't take long—Oline threw some pots and pans, clothing, and diapers into trash bags, leaving behind anything that they couldn't carry or fit into the cab. She and Fab unceremoniously said goodbye to Harlem and hello to the Bronx. They would push forward in search of a better life no matter what it took.

When Afrika Islam was rocking the jams
And on the other side of town was a kid named Flash
Patterson and Millbrook projects
Casanova all over, ya couldn't stop it

-From "South Bronx" by Boogie Down Productions

I hate to break the news to you, but if you didn't live in the Bronx, particularly the South Bronx, during the era that gave birth to hip-hop artists like KRS-One, D-Nice, and DJ Scott La Rock of Boogie Down Productions, you're an outsider and you'll just *never know* how certain facets of life can play out, to your benefit, perhaps, but most definitely to your detriment. Chances are, if you're reading this, you probably *are* that outsider and your references for the Bronx are limited to *A Bronx Tale*, *The Warriors*, and J-Lo's bop "Jenny from the Block." It's okay—I'm not judging you. Not too much, anyway.

It was hard living in the South Bronx; it was a life I actively tried to escape, one that I did escape, though many were not that lucky. Many died far too young, others lived but never left. The South Bronx has gentrified over the years—I hear in recent years, some boutique hotels have even moved in—but it is still blighted in many areas by urban decay, by the fires that frantic people burned to better their lives, the thick smoke from those fires a choked symbol of their desperation. It is still the poorest borough in New York City and, in some parts, represents the most abject poverty in the country. But I don't want to paint a picture of hopelessness—that's too reductive and just not accurate. The Bronx is also full of life, of color and sound, and, above all else, resilience.

The year my parents moved to the Bronx was the year that I was born—1976; it was less than a year later that the World Series pitted the Yankees, my own Bronx Bombers, against the Los Angeles Dodgers at Yankee Stadium, and Howard Cosell was incorrectly credited with saying, "Ladies and gentlemen, the Bronx is burning." He never actually said that—journalists messed it up, and the line stuck. But the phrase stays with me because I have always felt like I was born with a fire raging inside me, the flames licking my chest, curling around my heart and making me burn bright.

My ambition has always devoured all of the oxygen in the room so that I can grow bigger, sparking to catch and expand hungrily beyond the neatly kept boundaries that polite society says that I shouldn't cross. Fire keeps no borders and neither do I. I am not afraid to burn those who cross me—it is how I have always lived my life, whether it is scrambling to sell lunch tickets to make a few dollars in high school or surpassing the expectations of the good ole boys in the boardroom. A fire is always in motion, and I've never stopped moving forward.

It's always felt fitting, then, that my parents made a life for themselves and for us in the Bronx. My parents knew very little about the borough, but they were sure it was better than where they had been. They knew that the Bronx Zoo was here, Yankee Stadium was here, that morning show host Regis Philbin had grown up here, a random fact that they would often repeat with reverence in their voices, not for him personally, of course, but for how far he'd managed to travel outside the geography of his upbringing. Turns out he had grown up in the East Bronx, a nicer enclave, but still, look what he had made of himself!

Even though the Bronx was generally considered a step up from Harlem in the seventies, the South Bronx, where we lived, was poor with a capital "P." Overwhelmingly, it was Black and Latinx families that settled here, often cramping too many people into too-small apartments, sometimes with as many as four generations in one household. Instead of trees adorning the streets, garbage dotted its sidewalks and highways. Yellow smiley face plastic bags and those ubiquitous Greek-style blue paper coffee cups caught the eye in place of flower beds. It would always be in your best interest to wear shoes in case you had some crazy notion to go barefoot because broken glass and smeared dog shit littered the streets, not to mention those suspicious-looking uncapped soda bottles that you never wanted to kick over; if you did, there was a good chance you'd get a drenching of some drunk's piss on you, not Sunkist. The garbage cans placed at irregular intervals throughout the neighborhood were usually overflowing with trash and paired with piles of black garbage bags beside them.

But it hadn't always been like this. Following World War II, with soldiers returning home, there was a demand and subsequent boom in public housing construction across the five boroughs, including in the Bronx. Veterans were given priority for affordable housing, including in the Lester Patterson Houses, which completed construction in 1950. We called it the "Patterson Projects," "Patterson," or even just the "PJs."

Part of the New York City Housing Authority, Patterson comprised—and still does to this day—fifteen buildings, either six or thirteen stories high, with a whopping 1,791 apartments total, spanning over seventeen acres and 748,000 square feet.

In the beginning, Patterson was fairly diverse. After-school programs and night classes were readily available for its residents, with some subsidization offered for kids' extracurriculars like music. But with an influx of drugs in the 1960s, made worse by the increased popularity of heroin in the 1970s and crack in the 1980s, white flight occurred, leaving the vast majority of people in Patterson either Black or Brown. At the same time, public funding and blue-collar jobs for young people were drying up in the South Bronx, leading to increased crime and harsh policing in the community.

When Fab and Oline found themselves moving into Patterson, the neighborhood was rough, rougher than it had ever been. It wasn't uncommon to hear gunshots ring out and to see patrol cars passing by with overwhelming frequency, police stopping to throw someone onto the hood of their car. At Patterson most people didn't want to contact the cops unless they absolutely had to.

The prevailing view in the neighborhood was that the local cops couldn't be bothered to actually help you in a crisis—they were much more liable to beat you or cart you off to jail for some small infraction. As a result, folks learned how to handle issues themselves, dealing with disputes on their own and meting out their own justice. The times that my mother *would* call the police on my father who was abusing her yet again? The cops, almost always the same two guys assigned to our building, would take their sweet time in arriving, and when finally they did make it to our home, you could see the contempt in their eyes, a look flashing between the two that said, *"Them again?"*

Oline also became well acquainted with another pair of cops who were assigned the street beat in the neighborhood. At the time, her hustle was selling merchandise on the sidewalk that she bought wholesale and marked up: giant teddy bears, children's bicycles, candy, water, seat covers made of wooden beads, fruit-scented air freshener trees that I loved to huff. Glifford and I were involved in her hustle, too—we'd spend nights helping Oline assemble the bicycles, a strange little family assembly line. My favorite part was sticking the iridescent streamers to the handlebars of the girls' bikes, which were always pink or purple.

Eventually, Oline's hustle grew to the point that she employed neighborhood kids to hawk the candy and water on major avenues. She hired a teenager to oversee her child gang and he'd collect their earnings at the end of the day and deliver it all to Oline, who would then frowningly pay back a small sum to the teen to allot to her young employees.

But before Oline had expanded her operation, it was mostly a one-woman show (Fab would occasionally pop up to assist her, then later it would be Glifford, who would eagerly help her set up folding tables on the sidewalk and carefully arrange the merchandise for passersby). She tried to rotate locations as often as she could because she didn't have a license to sell goods on the street. Unfortunately, the cops would inevitably show up and confiscate her merchandise despite her desperate pleas. I always knew when they'd nabbed her because she'd come home early in the afternoon, fuming and mumbling in Creole under her breath. Whenever this happened, I'd give her a wide berth.

Eventually Oline wised up, and after yet another confiscation, she quietly made some kind of murky deal with the cops. I never knew the specifics of her agreement, but it was obvious she paid them off in some way because they left her alone after that, their eyes seeming to skip over her sidewalk operation when they passed her on the street.

I personally was not afraid of the cops—I thought that the men and women in blue were meant to serve and protect us. That's what my parents taught me and what TV showed me, regardless of what was happening in the streets. My best friend's dad was a cop, and some of the kids I grew up with in the hood ended up becoming cops to serve the same people and neighborhood in which they grew up. The ones I'd encounter just a few years later would also often let me go with a warning after they nabbed me for racing recklessly on the road. I also think it had something to do with me being a good talker—I was almost always able to get myself out of deep shit with people who weren't my parents.

The elevators in Patterson, which constantly smelled of piss, would often break down. There was an octagon-shaped glass plate on the elevator door, so people could see if the elevator was trundling its way up from a lower floor. In summertime, if you got stuck in the elevator, and there was no one nearby to help you, you would break the glass for air as it would get so stiflingly hot and suffocating, likely with a whole crowd of people stuffed together, trying not to faint from the oven-like conditions in that tiny box. You think we would call 911 to help us out? No. We'd wait until someone else in the building needed to use the elevator and figured out it was stuck. Then they would grab a few people to help us climb out. The plate was broken more often than not, and the sharp crunch of glass was always underfoot so you had to be careful or risk slicing your feet. I had no idea any of this was abnormal—it just seemed like a minor, everyday nuisance to put up with, and I'd sigh and roll my eyes if I needed the elevator and it hadn't come after five minutes. Stuck again.

And what about Nixon's war on drugs? Yeah, the war had come to Patterson, though I wasn't aware of the constant parade of drug deals that took place in the front and back of our building. I had no idea that the murmured conversations and slap of hands exchanging baggies for money was anything out of the ordinary. My mother, in her own way, tried to protect me without clueing me in to what was going on.

"Sendy, those men you see on the stairs? Leave them be.

Don't look at them, okay? Go up, up, up quickly, okay? Come right home."

It became a game for me, banging open the building door and racing up the stairs to our apartment as fast as I could, my flip-flops slapping the concrete, the men in the stairwells teary blurs out of the corner of my eyes. Running up the stairs every day, I actually felt incredibly safe, even if my mother felt otherwise. There was community to be found here—people would leave their front doors open, music blasting from stereos, which intermingled with the cooking smells of whatever that night's dinner would be—pernil or fried chicken or whatever was on sale at the Western Beef grocery store around the corner.

Our building at Patterson was small—six floors—so everyone knew everyone else and their business. And it always seemed to me like everyone I saw had a grandma who lived with them. The grandmas were somewhat interchangeable—they all wore long house coats and fuzzy or netted slippers, their hair always in pink foamy rollers. I don't think I ever saw a single one fully dressed. Whenever I'd say hello, the grandmas were sweet to me, asking me how my brother and I were doing. I had no idea of the shouted conversations in *their* homes—I wanted a grandma to live with us, to soothe me, make me feel loved, one whose chest I could lay my head on. If I couldn't have that, maybe even a different family entirely, one that wouldn't yell or hit or drink. Did that even exist?

Families didn't come and go often because once you got an apartment in the projects, you just didn't leave. Where else could you get a two- or three-bedroom with an eat-in kitchen for under a hundred dollars a month? That's one of the insidious ways the system kept people down.

For all the violence and crime, though, there was always a loose sense of camaraderie present. Passing a stranger by on the street, you might catch their glance and exchange quick nods before going about your day. What that nod was meant to convey was, "Hey, I see you, we're in this same shit together."

For better or worse, Fab and Oline were in this shit together, too; they had tied themselves to each other, each the other's albatross around their neck. Soon after officially becoming Patterson residents, Oline, taking another quick trip back to Harlem Hospital, gave birth to me, which meant that she had yet another ragged thread knotting herself to Fab.

It's funny what you might piece together about yourself when you pause to consider your first memory. What do you recall of your first shred of consciousness? Is it of your mother cradling you, all warmth and sweetness and light? Maybe it's a birthday party or some other small marvel. For me, my earliest memory is an inkblot of fear, of fragmented darkness. Around two years old, I dimly recall standing in my crib, clutched by terror because I had seen a fleshy hand reaching into the crib as I groggily awoke from a nap. I remember shrieking for my mother and it felt like ages until she rushed in, shushing me, assuring me that whatever was frightening me was the product of a bad dream, turning on the lights to dispel the dark, haunted corners of the small room I shared with Glifford, my brother. Had I seen anything? Maybe, maybe not. Regardless, I believe it is solid evidence that there was negative energy festering in our home, following Glifford and me, and later our younger brother, Philip, around, invading our thoughts and experiences.

In our building, there were eight apartments on each floor—four at the front of the building, then the elevator and an incinerator, then a cluster of four apartments in the back of the building. Our apartment, which was much larger than the one-bedroom in Harlem that Fab and Oline first occupied, was at the back of the building and it was a cheerless place. Next door to us was Ms. Jefferson, a teacher at the daycare center I went to for preschool and, later, for after-school care, and her niece. My mother didn't let us interact with our neighbors much—she was suspicious of everyone and trusted no one—but the few times I peeked into Ms. Jefferson's place, I saw that she had a much fancier apartment than we did. It always amused me to know that Ms. Jefferson had a life outside of the school. When I was very young, I thought that the teachers lived at the school together, as I lived with my family at Patterson. When I was a little older, it was still very strange to have my home life and school life intersect like that. If you don't know what I mean, just think of when you were young and you ran into your teacher at the grocery store in the wild—probably an awkward and fascinating experience at the same time, seeing your teacher doing real-person things like bagging potatoes or studying the ingredients list of a soup can when, in your young mind, she existed in a bubble, living to grade papers or to stand in front of the blackboard and drone.

We were situated on the fifth floor, which, again, because the elevator often broke down, meant that we were usually forced to trudge up many dark flights of stairs. Our apartment opened directly into our kitchen, the floor of which was covered in mismatched tiles of linoleum. Being poor, utilitarianism was the priority, with decor coming far behind, so whatever was on sale or within easy reach meant that's what we would end up with, courtesy of NYCHA, the New York City Housing Authority—thus the patchwork of mismatched linoleum tiles in the kitchen. That might also be why our kitchen was puzzlingly only half-covered with wallpaper, like the installer had taken a smoke break and never returned to finish the job. It was a look, all right. The kitchen was also safeguarded by White Jesus—my mother had placed a framed portrait of a long-haired Caucasian Jesus to watch over us. He looked less like our lord and savior and more like a stern hippie babysitter in robes.

"Sendy, Jesus is always watching," my mother would often caution me. At the time, I actually thought he could see everything I did. It certainly felt that way—Jesus's eyes would creepily follow me around the house wherever I went, discouraging me from any mischief I might get up to, which I inevitably did anyway.

As out of sorts as the kitchen may have appeared, it was large and we had enough space to fit a kitchen table and chairs where we kids would eat, that is, before we were allowed to graduate to the dining room table in the living room.

Our front door was outfitted with heavy-duty locks and a custom-made steel bar, all of which my mother had sprung for despite the extra cost because she didn't want any intruders coming in. Plenty of robberies and break-ins happened in the neighborhood and Oline was not about to let that happen to her and her brood. When I was older and my mother allowed me to go outside unattended, I, too, wasn't allowed to intrude, as she didn't trust me not to lose the keys for the extra dead bolts because those keys were expensive to duplicate. I would have to hope that Glifford, as the Keeper of the Keys, would be home when I came back from school, or that he would have eaten lunch at home and left the door unlocked before returning to school so that I could get inside. Otherwise, I'd have to wait for someone with a key to come home and let me in. I wasn't exactly a latchkey kid.

Our living room was also a sight—our deep-red couch was encased in clear plastic, as any Haitian mother would dictate, to avoid dyes from clothing or unlucky spills from clumsy children staining the furniture. The thick plastic would always make me sweat, and in the summer, it was torture to peel myself off the couch if wearing shorts, which I inevitably was, as I was almost always guaranteed to leave some skin behind—at least, it was painful enough to feel that way. My mother had also demonstrated a rare bit of Haitian pride by hanging a painting of

Haitian farmers working in the fields, perhaps as a reminder of the hard work that she expected everyone in the household to complete.

At some point, the living room and other parts of the apartment had been covered with red carpeting, but after a number of years of pattering feet wearing it down, my mother had decided to cover the red carpet with new brown carpet. Ever practical and economically minded, my mother thought, *Why waste money by paying for padding?* and she had the new carpet installed directly over the old carpet instead of ripping it up. As a result, there were patches of red carpet tufting out from under the brown at the edges, like the fur of some imagined forest animal.

Each room had old-fashioned steam radiators that would hiss on in the winters and clank loudly at night; that is, if they were working. Inevitably, the radiators would either fail to work completely, leaving us ice cold and shivering in the winter, or they would be whistling hot and leaking water all over the floors—there was no happy medium. My mother always warned us not to touch the radiators but of course I did, and burned my hands once or twice. I knew not to complain to my mother, though—a world of pain would await me if I let her know that I'd ignored her warning. In summertime, we had fans that I swear blew hot air throughout the apartment, doing nothing to alleviate the boiling-point conditions. Glifford and I would talk into the fans to distort our voices until my mother got sick of hearing our vibrating, robot voices and told us to cut it out, Glifford and me snapping to attention for our mother but conspiratorially sneaking mirthful glances and making silly faces at each other when she had her back turned.

There were bars in front of all our windows, which I would peek out of when I was too young to go outside unaccompanied by my mother, calling down to kids in the yard below, hoping they'd acknowledge me with a wave. Sometimes, when my mother wasn't looking, I'd crumple up food I didn't like— often slimy okra that my mother loved to cook—into a napkin and run to the window to dispose of it by dropping it hurriedly into the yard below, before casually walking away. In summer, with the windows cracked for circulation, I would watch the neighbors below set up camp around a huge pit, a few of them carrying over a whole, huge, trussed-up pig to barbecue for pernil. Others would come bearing plastic containers with yellow rice and beans, potato salad, and cake. They would hold cans of beer dripping condensation that came from seemingly bottomless Styrofoam coolers, people hauling bags of ice to keep their cervezas cool. Everyone sweating and swearing and singing, bumping music filtering up to my window, along with the fragrance of graying charcoal and cooked meat. These were the smells and sounds of summertime, and if I close my eyes, I can transport myself back easily. Of course, we were never allowed to join the neighbors in their raucous merrymaking, but I'd pretend to be a part of their good times, wondering what the tang of their adobo-spiced pork actually tasted like, not able to have the privilege of cutting the top of my mouth on an overly toasted bun filled with tender meat until years later. I would also hold pretend conversations with the people far down below, opining on whatever it was my young mind imagined that the folks on the ground were discussing. It was almost like I was there with them. Almost.

Lining the windowsills of the living room were plants of every stripe, their leaves happily dappled by the sun in spring and summer and reaching hungrily for light in the harsh city winters. It was perhaps another rare showing of nostalgia by my mother for the lush greenery of her youth. She would rarely talk about Haiti unless prodded, and many times, not even then— she saw no point in looking back, only in looking ahead at the success that was surely to come knocking on the padlocked door at any moment.

In fact, my mother took Glifford and me to Haiti only once, when I was five and he was six. I remember very little, only disjointed, blurry memories. I recall that the colors across the island were intensified, that the houses were bright, happy shades, and that the flowers on the roads were so pretty, nothing like the cheap, artificially dyed blooms we would see at the bodegas in the Bronx. Mango trees heavy with fruit were everywhere, and the water off the island was the bluest blue I'd ever seen.

Apparently, everyone in the family wanted to see the "New Yorkers," as they called us, and my mother dressed my brother in a solemn suit and me in a lacy, ribbon-trimmed dress, showing us off proudly like ponies. Because I was so light-skinned as a child, my relatives praised me for my beauty, and I ate it up, dancing and repeating the two words of Creole—*bonjou* and *orevwa*—that they taught me, delighting in the attention, which I rarely received at home. My brother, always an introvert, stayed silent beside me, and our relatives took little notice of him, which was indicative of how most people treated Glifford, who moved too quietly through life.

Apart from this trip, years later, my mother returned to Haiti once more to see her mother who, at the time, was dying. She returned with another painting of Haiti to hang on her wall. When I visited her at her home to hear about the trip, she showed me her painting . . . and her handiwork.

The painting had clearly been tampered with, as if an angry five-year-old had furiously used black permanent marker on it, bearing down and marking out big chunks of the painting. I stared at my mother in confusion and gestured in the direction of the painting.

"Mommy, uh, what happened here?" I asked.

She squinted over at the painting, then looked back at me and calmly replied in a matter-of-fact tone, "Oh, I fixed it."

"But what was wrong with it? Wasn't it expensive? Why would you mark it up like that? It's brand-new!"

She sighed, as if the answer were obvious and I was wasting her time by asking silly questions. Mommy explained that she had marked out the Haitian people in the painting who looked, to her eye, "poor." She only wanted prosperity reflected; she didn't want to think of Haiti as less than in any way because that would mean that *she* was less than. Even if it meant defacing a painting or rewriting her personal history, she would do what it would take to present as successfully as possible. Even if it meant only having a few changes of clothing, her kids would have *name brand*. Even if it meant only going to a restaurant once or twice a year, it would be a *fancy* restaurant. Even if she lived in the projects like her neighbors, she was still *better* than everyone else there. Was living life in that way exhausting? I do think that she burned a lot of energy concerned with appearance as much as she was. I also think it was a way of survival for her, and part of how she kept herself going. But with this mindset she also taught me to never give up; she passed on this perseverance to me, and I am grateful for that.

Glifford and I shared a room with bunk beds. Because he was the oldest, he always got to choose first, so he got the top bunk, which was obviously the far cooler option. I had to settle for bottom bunk.

Our bedroom was spartan, to say the least. There was nothing much else in it apart from the bunk beds and a dresser that we shared. We had very little clothing, so it was easy to fit everything into one dresser. Our clearance Mickey Mouse sheets gave the beds a cozy feel, though.

When we got a little older, Glifford bought a boom box and played music constantly. When he got on the subject of music, his usual reserve melted away and he would become animated, patiently explaining to me the virtues of artists like Biz Markie, Big Daddy Kane and the Juice Crew, Run DMC, and Boogie Down Productions. Rap was for *us*, it was something that Black people could proudly own—it was *our* music. We would lie in our bunk beds and his whispered rapping would put me to sleep. In the mornings, he had always retreated back into himself, and it was anyone's guess as to what was going through his head—was he thinking about music during these silences, or something troublesome?

I couldn't rely on the comfort of going to bed, as the darkness welcomed the cockroaches, which were ever present in our apartment even during the day, though they'd grow bolder at night. They'd scuttle around the room in the dark, and sometimes I'd wake up in horror to find them on me. I'd swat them away in my sleep, but there was no real escape. One morning I woke up with parts of a roach *in my mouth*. The antennae were pasted to my bottom lip. I still shudder to think where the rest of it went. And I couldn't tell my mother about it, either—I knew if I did, she would smirk and say it was my fault because I kept my mouth hanging open all the time; perhaps she'd make a lunge at me to press my lips together herself. So I stayed silent and did what I had to—I slept facedown, trying to cover my face, even in the stifling, hot summers, or I would cover my mouth with my hand as I nodded off to sleep, hoping that would be enough of a fortress to keep the roaches out. It's not an exaggeration to say I was tired for years, traumatized and scared by this particularly disturbing facet of project living. It felt like I was never alone and couldn't have even a minute to myself—even if my family wasn't around, the roaches were a constant fixture. They were my roommates just as much as my brother was, and I could never escape them.

My mother's bedroom—and my father's, but he was almost

never around so I assigned ownership of the room to my mother in his absence—was similarly modest, with a bed, a dresser, and a vanity. One of the few luxuries to be seen in the room were the exotic-looking perfume bottles and tinctures that she scattered around her vanity. Sometimes, I'd hover by her door, watching her putting cold cream on her face and applying other mysterious potions to her hands and décolletage. She never invited me in, though, and I never asked to join her.

Later, after my baby brother Philip was born in 1984, my mother put his crib right next to her bed. Philip was always her favorite, and she doled out all of her affection to him, even if it meant she came up short for Glifford and me. But then she was never worried about me, as she thought I was the smartest out of the three of us and could make it in the world by myself. She constantly fretted about quiet and withdrawn Glifford, who never did well in school. She felt that out of the three of us, Glifford would have the hardest time in the world, which is also why she encouraged him to go to college, thinking that higher education could protect him from the streets.

Saturday mornings were a gift she handed out to all three of us. Saturdays were for WWF (now WWE) on TV. My mom had gotten us a giant satellite dish that blocked our view outside—no more could I watch kids riding their bikes on the streets below, but that was okay because now we had cable and I could distract myself with shows. She warned us not to tell anyone because technically we were stealing, but seriously, I think me telling my classmates was the least of our worries when this huge-ass NASA-sized satellite dish was sticking outside our window, its big white dome broadcasting to anyone who could see it that we weren't paying customers. We would pile into the living room and turn on the TV excitedly, ready to watch our favorite wrestling stars duke it out against one another, wearing WWF-themed shirts my mom had found on deep discount for us. She would relax, her shoulders sinking, her mouth pulling into a soft smile, as we cheered on Junkyard Dog, Andre the Giant, George "the Animal" Steele, Jimmy "Superfly" Snuka, Macho Man Randy Savage, Hulk Hogan, and the guy you loved to hate, Roddy "Rowdy" Piper. We loved watching these spandex-clad giants slamming into one another, their theatrical roles of good guy versus villain predetermined, obviously, but we felt freedom in choosing who to root for, and we were able to pull ourselves temporarily from the dreariness of reality by watching mostly white men rolling around, yanking arms and legs, dancing a twisted ballet with each other. Glifford and I pantomimed moves on the red-brown patchwork carpet, careful not to knock anything over to avoid our mother's wrath.

With Philip far too young to play with us, Glifford and I were each other's partners in mischief. My mother had found us a Nintendo on sale somewhere, and Glifford and I would park ourselves in front of the TV, fighting over whose turn it was to play Super Mario Brothers, punching each other in excitement when we reached a new level or came into contact with Bowser. When we weren't playing on the Nintendo, we were watching *Teenage Mutant Ninja Turtles*, *Transformers*, or *The Smurfs*. And if we weren't zonked out on TV, we were usually playing small, harmless pranks on our mother, excited by the high stakes given the outsized reaction she would have if we were caught. One of our favorites was to take turns creeping up on Mommy and looking up her skirt, then racing away before we were detected, smothering our laughter into our hands.

Every so often our mother allowed us a special sugar cereal on Saturdays. This long predated the outcry for parents to not feed their children sugar, but my mother was still strict and usually only allowed us Corn Flakes or Rice Krispies without any added sugar on top. On these occasions, we'd feel like royalty, toasting each other with Frosted Flakes or my all-time favorite, Cap'n Crunch, slurping up the cereal milk and licking our bowls when my mother wasn't looking.

These small comforts were just about all we had and we didn't take them for granted. One Saturday morning when I was eight, I poured out my Cap'n Crunch—slowly, to check that no roaches had secreted themselves in the box. To my immense delight, a plastic-wrapped sticker fell into my bowl. It was the Cap'n himself come to surprise me. I didn't get a birthday present that year because there was no money for presents, so the sticker felt like a recognition of me as a small but real presence in the world. I stuck the Cap'n to my bunk bed so I could always look at him as I was falling asleep and waking up. Having so little, that Cap'n sticker was everything to me. When I saw him smiling at me, I knew I was special and that my days ahead would mean something. Of course they would—the Cap'n had ordained it.

Chapter 4

Lucille Murray Day Care Center was one of the first places outside our apartment that I had been allowed inside of. The center stared across at the projects, a similarly somber building of brick, no cheery crayon drawings or gluey macaroni projects taped to the windows. Still, it was my home away from home for ten years, first when I was in preschool then when I was dumped into its after-school program while my parents hustled to provide for us. Well, hold on, scratch that—when *Oline* hustled to provide for us. Like I said, Fab hustled only to provide for himself.

Now, it is undeniable that Fab was prone to constant exaggeration, telling tall tales to puff himself up, spewing out nonexistent accomplishments, putting himself in the middle of danger only to inevitably come out the hero, but in this particular story, he didn't lie. At least, his scars told the truth. One late night, the kind in which steam rises up from the manhole covers and the brake lights of the car in front of you blur red and everything feels like a dream, Fab was stopped at a light, on the lookout for a tired partygoer ready to go home, tired himself. As Fab tells it, two men stopped him while the cab was idling and held him up at gunpoint. Apparently, what he gave them wasn't enough—I could see him lying and trying to hide his earnings from them—or maybe they didn't want a witness to their crime because they coldly shot him in the face before streaking off into the night.

Blood dripping down his neck, Fab calmly drove himself to a nearby hospital's emergency room where the ER doctors, most likely unsurprised by sights like this, dug the bullet out of his cheek, plinked it into a nearby bowl, bandaged his face up, and sent him back out into the night. Fab had survived with miraculously little harm done to him, like a roach that has been flattened but manages to resurrect itself and march forward, undeterred. Whether the robbers were random thieves or part of a larger racket—the city was notorious at the time for gangs that smuggled heroin onto the streets and caused havoc— didn't much matter to Fab. His head was so twisted that he convinced himself that my mother had hired the men to shoot him.

He had apparently gotten word to my mother that he had been shot, so she told us Fab would be coming home with a bandage on his face—nothing more than that. When he did stagger through the door, it was terrifying to see him bandaged and bloody.

While we waited for him to come home, Oline had a frantic, worried look in her eyes, which surprised me, even as young as I was. She could give me a belt whipping, could watch me cry without a look of concern passing over her face—in fact, it was often satisfaction that crossed her features, as she figured she had successfully taught me a lesson. But this? This had her plain scared.

When Fab finally made it home, I tried to jump into his arms—he could walk, that was a good sign!—but my mother swatted me away. *Sendy, get down!*

Fab's usual crisp, collared shirt was untucked; he looked disheveled and ragged. What I thought at first were gravy stains splattered across his shirt were in reality dried blood. But it was his face that made me recoil.

It reminded me of when Glifford and I would hold contests for who could hold their breath the longest, puffing our cheeks out cartoonishly. He was *that* swollen. I longed to pat his cheek, which was swathed in a chunky bandage, to tell him that he would be OK, but I held back. Our household was not one in which anyone ever gave comfort to someone else when hurt. I always kept my pain to myself and didn't complain, which is why I didn't even know how to reach out to Fab to let him know he had my sympathy. Besides, Poppy, as I called him then, could stand. He seemed fine enough—he wouldn't want me to make a fuss about him.

When I asked Oline what happened, she only told me that "bad guys" tried to rob Poppy for his money, and when he didn't give it to them, they shot him in the face. She drilled it into me that if someone ever approached me with a weapon that I shouldn't fight back, that if I did, a fate like my father's would await me.

Over the next few days, I studied Fab and his wound. He cleaned it every day, peeling the bandage slowly from his face, green pus staining the bandage, wincing as he dabbed his wound with a reddish-brown solution, fingers feeling gingerly around the wound.

As terrible an injury as this was, this didn't stop Fab from continuing to hit the streets to make money. He returned to work right away, he and my mother buying a gun for protection at night. My mother approved of the weapon, telling us that this was how we would stay safe. That said, the gun was always kept locked in Fab's glove box in his car.

Their arguments intensified after the shooting, Fab going so far as to accuse my mother of hiring the goons to kill him. My mother would laugh in his face, waving him away with her hand. She, in turn, thought it was very possible that Fab had gotten his own ass shot to set her up for attempted murder. Dysfunctional? You bet. It was all I knew, though, so parents accusing each other of murder plots was entirely normal to me. I even began to suspect that my mother *did* have something to do with the shooting. In my young eyes, it was clear to me that Fab had wronged my mother and my mother had decided to do something about it. I could relate—Glifford made me so furious sometimes that I wanted to hurt him bad. My mother had simply taken the next step. I was actually proud of my mother for not letting my father bully her! I hoped that this "lesson" would be enough to get Fab to treat her better. And maybe, just maybe, this would also be a lesson to Glifford in case down the road he got any ideas to mess with me.

After he was shot in the face, Fab would eventually stop driving the taxi, hopping from one murky moneymaking scheme to the next, happy to fleece others and even, as with the insurance policy he took out on my mother, happy to fleece his own wife. He'd disappear for weeks at a time and we didn't know where he was, whether he'd succumbed to the violence of the city or had simply walked out on us—both seemed equally possible. Turns out Fab had begun faking passports and helping Haitians come to the United States—for a steep price, of course, certainly not due to any charity he felt in his heart toward his fellow countrymen. His new "career" had him shuttling back and forth to Haiti with regularity, though we had no idea at the time. He ran his shadow work for years, and it wasn't until we'd heard that he'd almost gotten Oline's father, our grandfather, sent to jail, because he'd dropped his name in connection with his fudged passports to the wrong person, that we learned what he had been up to. Can't say we were at all surprised.

The bastard was resourceful, though, and many of his endeavors were creative. (What would he have done—what *could* he

have done—if he hadn't been raised in such traumatic circumstances? Was he a product of nature, a sociopath born into this
world, or nurture, his malevolence forming as a result of his
harsh upbringing, wrapped in poverty and tied in a bow made
of suffering? Guess we'll never know, but I can say with certainty that regardless of how it got there, that steely glint in his
eye never left him.)

My "favorite" of his machinations, if you could ever say that,
was his gas station swindle. Back in the seventies, gas stations
in the city still had attendants who would fill up your gas tank
for you and squeegee your windows with deft, efficient strokes.
Fab had the brilliant idea to corrupt the attendants at the gas
station closest to Patterson. He'd have them pump people's gas
as normal but charge inflated fares to drivers. The attendants
would pocket the change, with the drivers and the owners of
the station none the wiser for years. Without having to lift a
finger, Fab took a cut of the attendants' illicit earnings once a
week. A small-time gangster with big-time aspirations, if you
ever saw one.

The common, desperate-throated refrain we would hear
ringing out in our apartment when Fab graced us with his presence at home was, "Don't you want to provide for your children?
These are *your* children!" along with some choice Creole curses.
Oline went red-faced and apoplectic when Fab would treat
himself to Calvin Klein jeans and T-shirts, polos, and French
cologne, but buy Glifford and me, and later Philip, the cheapest
possible items, if Oline made the mistake of tasking him with
shopping for us.

Anyone who lived in the Bronx knew of Alexander's, a department store on bustling Third Avenue, with its glary lighting and
scuffed walls. Think of a Filene's Basement but worse. It had certainly seen better days and would eventually go bankrupt, shut-
tering all eleven of its stores in 1992. But it was still going strong

when we were kids, peddling its discount wares, the perfect place for Fab to save a few bucks for himself. Before my mother learned better, Fab would stroll into the apartment with shopping bags full of designer swag for himself and then a telltale Alexander's bag, with the shittiest clothing for us, all of which would fall apart after only a few wears. He even tried to get us to wear "tabletop" sneakers, which was completely unacceptable to Oline. Everyone knew that the poorest kids wore tabletops, discount, no-brand Velcro sneakers bound with elastic and heaped on a table in the back of the shoe section. Well, that was Fab for you.

Once Oline wised up and learned not to let my father run errands of any kind, that is, if she wanted them done right, she did the shopping herself. She bought us name-brand clothes from Macy's when she could—we didn't have much clothing at all, but what we did have was nice. She made sure of that. She refused to let the outside world know how poor we actually were because we were Haitian—we were better than everyone else, even if the neighbors knew we were all in the same boat. She wouldn't even let us *look at* them, instructing us to look straight ahead when passing people.

Equipped with a few outfits that my teachers saw on repeat again and again, I was trundled off to the day care center. Say what you will of public education, especially in the projects, but those teachers had me learning my alphabet and how to read before I hit first grade.

Lucille Murray played host only to Black and Latinx kids, and the majority of the teachers there were also Black or Latinx. It was at Lucille Murray that I learned what love tasted like: The Black ladies who cooked lunch for us served up soul food dishes, and it felt like they had put pieces of their hearts into these meals. They made us macaroni and cheese, greens with ham bone, tender chicken, creamed corn, biscuits, serving them family-style straight from giant aluminum pots. The pleasure centers in my brain lit up like a Christmas tree with these new flavors, salty, fried, fatty, rich, smooth, silky. It was the best food I'd ever tasted. Without formally registering it, I somehow knew, even as a five-year-old, that immense care had gone into these time-honored recipes. Knotty-knuckled hands had rolled out doughs, pounded meat, and stirred stews to offer us nourishment not only to survive but with hope to, one day, thrive, so that we could cross the borders of "low-income" and "subsidized" and be welcomed into the middle class with an imaginary ticker tape parade heralding our arrival out of poverty, the inner city, and all those other smudged words that marked us as clearly as our discount clothing.

Even though the building and nothing inside it was fancy, the center did its best to stimulate us and open our eyes to the world. We went on field trips—to the Bronx Zoo, to Central Park, to Chinatown to sample dumplings and duck (my mother forked over two crinkled dollars for me to be able to go on the trip with the other kids. It's a measly sum now, but back then it was a lot, and it was a considerable sign of her love to offer it, however silently that love manifested). The day care center director, Mrs. Beverly Brown, was one of the few people in my childhood to tell me that I was smart. She talked to children like they were human beings capable of intelligent thought, which was, back then, not entirely common, at least not from what I saw. Respect children? No, children were to be silent and respect adults. Mrs. Brown had an entire rainbow of Reeboks to match whatever she wore—orange Reeboks to go with a loud orange dress; purple Reeboks to match a purple sweatsuit; green Reeboks with a green skirt. She was *cool*. She bought Michael Jackson's *Thriller* album and we danced to it with joy before we knew what it meant to be self-conscious.

Mrs. Brown taught me how to do a split. She often wore African-inspired garb and taught me and the other kids African dance. And she encouraged us all to participate in the Colgate runs.

Colgate—the toothpaste brand—sponsored, and continues to sponsor, national track tournaments, with winners receiving scholarships for schooling. Anyone could enter, but many were low-income city kids like me. Mrs. Brown and the other center adults encouraged us to enter the Colgate runs, and had us training as if we were preparing for the Olympics. They'd have us running laps around the small park nestled in between buildings at Patterson, circle after circle, and we would pump our little legs as hard as we could, sweat dripping off our brows and down our noses, our salty mouths gasping for air, stitches in our sides, our hearts beating out a fierce staccato rhythm like the drumbeat in Mrs. Brown's music. The teachers would clap in time to the pounding our feet made on the concrete, would yell at us to go faster, go, go, go, keep going, don't stop, you're not weak, you're made of iron, you can do this. They pitted us against each other, not meanly, in competition with one another only in service to the greater goal of victory, shared whether one kid won a race or many because that win by one was a win by all. They timed us carefully with cheap stopwatches, urging us to beat our best times. I was one of the fastest at the center, flying on the pavement, hoping to make my mom proud, trying to demonstrate to her that all the effort she put into bettering our family wasn't going to waste, that I had been listening intently when she told me I could do anything. I won several races over the years, and my mom would come out to watch, would smile and say, "You're so fast, Sendy!" and I knew briefly what it felt like to be warmed by an outward showing of her affection. I even participated in the Junior Olympics, winning gold for the one-hundred-yard dash, silver for shotput, and bronze for a relay race. I was so proud of my victories, cherishing my ribbons for years. Sadly, the last year I competed in the Colgate runs, when I was eleven or so, I fell in the middle of the race, bruising myself badly but injuring my pride more, and I stopped competing after that. I only wanted to be a winner. I had to move on to the next challenge.

Leaving the center for first grade, I still continued to go to Lucille Murray for its after-school program until I was around ten, when it became too embarrassing to admit that I still went to the center with all of the babies.

The night before I was to begin first grade at St. Jerome Elementary School, my uniform pressed and ready for me to slip into the next morning, my mother sat me down on our slipcovered couch and told me that she was paying tuition for school so I needed to do my best and be a good girl. I could tell she was serious, maybe more serious about this than she'd been about anything else in a long time, at least when it came to me. I nodded gravely back at her—we had come to an understanding. I knew I'd do my best because failing my mother was not an option. She took our schooling seriously—she forked over a hundred dollars a month for Glifford and me to attend parochial school, the two of us walking to school each morning while Oline worked. Some months were easier than others for her to find the cash to pay for school, but she always did it.

"I will always pay for your school first before I pay to live in this apartment," she would tell Glifford and me, her mouth pursed. Because sometimes it had to be one or the other during tight months, and she'd have to scrape the hundred dollars out of our rent payment. I always knew it was a bad month when I received a dreaded slip from the school office informing us that we would be suspended if our tuition wasn't paid at once. After all, what were the Catholics running, a charity?!

St. Jerome Elementary School was connected to St. Jerome's Church, a Roman Catholic baroque revival–style church built in the late 1800s on Alexander Avenue. The school had actually been built before the church, in 1871, and staffed for years by an order of Ursuline nuns. The Ursulines were one of the first orders dedicated to educating girls, specifically in Christian doctrine— quite revolutionary for the time in Brescia, Italy, where the order was founded in 1535.

The nuns were no longer in charge of the school; instead, a quirky cast of characters taught there. The principal loved to creep out students, telling us on repeat that we should eat exotic animals like alligator and snake because they were so filled with nutrients, and besides, we should be adventurous eaters and "open our palates" to possibility. Maybe her intentions were good, but her stories of eating scaly creatures uneasily put me in mind of getting lost in dark swamps and stranded in dry deserts, mythical places I'd never been and didn't think I ever wanted to visit, not even if it would broaden my palate.

Mrs. Menard was my first-grade teacher, one of the first white people I'd interacted with on a regular basis at six years of age, and she looked like she was straight out of *Mad Men*. She wore cat-eye glasses and came to school every day with her white hair fastidiously combed and sculpted into a beehive, long out of fashion by then.

Mrs. Noble was my second-grade teacher, and she was a light-skinned Black woman who wore her long hair in a fashionable knot. I never ached for my teachers' hugs—my parents never showed us any kind of physical affection, ever, so I didn't know to miss it—but I did want recognition for my stellar grades because it meant getting to do the fun tasks that our teachers would hand out like candy, chores like clapping the eraser boards outside or, better yet, washing the blackboards with long, soapy strokes, watching chalky math equations and spellings disappear in the wake of the sponge, gleaming black blankness replacing that day's learning in preparation for the next. I always earned top marks yet I was never chosen for these proud, self-important little errands. Instead, Mrs. Noble almost always predictably chose Lisa, a Latinx girl, for these tasks, despite the fact that her grades weren't as good as mine. I wasn't surprised because I'd already learned from a very young age that life isn't fair, that the deck can be stacked against you for no good reason at all, that chance can dictate your fate despite your best efforts, even when you bet your bottom dollar.

Maybe it also had something to do with Lisa's impeccable neatness. As much as my mother tried to hide our poverty, there were certain facets of project living that she couldn't mask, and maybe that, too, weighed against me. For example, I always had to be careful about opening my textbooks, cracking them open slowly to make sure a half-dead roach wouldn't dart out, its existence revealing that I lived somewhere that the roaches found desirable. In other words, the projects. I desperately didn't want the other kids to think I was dirty. But it was also hard when you're young and your mother makes heavy silence, or, alternatively, yelling, her main methods of communication. She rarely talked to Glifford and me, and she failed to teach us the fundamentals of cleanliness, probably assuming that we understood by her example that we needed to present as impenetrable a front as possible to the harsh, outside world.

One day I was eating lunch, sitting next to a classmate named Steven. He was a short, pudgy kid with curly hair, and he had a single mom. Nothing remarkable about him either way, but his words are forever seared into my brain. He looked over at me while I ate my sandwich and scrunched up his nose.

"You smell a little," he said to me. My face heated up immediately.

"What? What do you mean?" I asked him. He shrugged and grimaced.

"Yeah, something just *smells* on you."

I was mortified. The only kind of response I knew how to give was a defensive one.

"Oh, yeah? You're probably smelling your upper lip," I taunted him back, but I was embarrassed beyond belief.

I only had one uniform skirt to wear five days a week, whereas the other girls in school usually had at least a few. Sometimes I missed my mother's once-weekly laundry days, and if I did, that meant I had to wear my one skirt for an entire additional week. Looking back, I'm sure I stank.

As soon as I got home that day, I stripped off my skirt and hand-washed it in the sink. Black water swirled down the sink's drain, and it took me several washes before the water ran clear. I made sure never to miss laundry day after that.

But more than roaches or single skirts, I felt the world's unfairness even more when the book fair came to school every year. I was always an avid reader, escaping in my mind from the projects to far-off destinations on the page. As soon as those blurry, Sanskrit-like symbols magically turned into letters, words, and sentences for me, I dove into books one after the other—it beat sitting in the apartment doing nothing, waiting for my parents to come home from their hustles. The first time my mother took me to the neighborhood library, I felt like I had come to a house of worship. There was so much more salvation to be found here than at mass that my mother dragged me to every Sunday—the musty smell of old paperbacks my incense, the hush across the building a silent prayer.

I started with classics—reading about cats in hats and green eggs and ham and redheaded girls getting into mischief. I ravenously devoured Beverly Cleary, riding with Ralph S. Mouse on his motorcycle, sympathizing with Ramona's hot embarrassment in the lunchroom when she unknowingly cracked a raw egg on her head and felt the quivery wetness slide off her scalp and down the planes of her freckled face, the yolk intermingled with her tears. I quickly moved on at far too young an age to Judy Blume, then bodice rippers, then Jackie Collins, particularly her Santangelo series, reading anything and everything. It was exciting to read about sex, drugs, and crime families, and I felt like I knew much more than my peers about the real world. I couldn't sit without a book in my hand, and if I didn't have one, I'd hungrily absorb whatever was around me—cereal boxes, grocery store advertisements, store signs.

Running your hands over the cool spines of books is a unique pleasure that all book lovers indulge in. As a kid, I would do this at the library and take my allotted number of copies home with me each week (sneaking more than I was allowed to take in my bag), but these books, with their color-coded stickers affixed to spines, sometimes encased in protective plastic like our living room couch, didn't belong to me. I desperately wanted to have a neatly ordered row of books to call my own, to pick up and read and reread whenever I felt like it. The two-week-loaned copies from the library, as precious as they were, just weren't doing it for me. I wanted to see my name in my own books, displayed proudly in the spiky, serial killer lettering young kids have.

One week, when I was in third grade, the book fair descended on the school, and kids were infected with the thrill that comes from getting new stuff. Weeks before, our teacher Mrs. Rodriguez had handed out the thin-sheeted order forms to everyone to mark what they wanted, a veritable bounty of books, calendars, crayons, bookmarks, and pencils available for purchase. Everyone, including me, pored over the order sheet with laser-like focus. Tick, tick, tick. (I didn't have anything against Mrs. Rodriguez, but her daughter was in the same class and was a complete snob; her unearned sense of entitlement came from having her mother as the teacher. She lorded it over us by making a show of calling her mother "Mom" in front of all of us. Having your mom at school in any capacity was strangely pride-inducing, and Mrs. Rodriguez's daughter took full advantage. It didn't hurt, either, that she was delicately pretty.)

Book fair time was like Christmas, or at least what I thought Christmas was like, since we didn't get many presents at any time of the year. When orders came in, the teacher would call students up to her desk one by one, handing them an elasticked bundle, their names proudly scrawled on a piece of paper that detailed everything from their order. Kids would trade things from their orders and the teacher would give everyone time to revel in their new purchases.

But I never got to tick any of the boxes on the order sheet. My mother wouldn't allow me to buy books when I could get the same books at the library—she couldn't understand the preciousness that I felt sure would be bestowed if I actually had my own copies, even if they were identical to the library's. And Fab would never finance such an extravagance—after all, he brought home giant tubs of bargain-basement ice cream and buckets of KFC every so often. He'd give me sticks of Big Red, and would even supply me with a quarter here and there for combing his hair and plucking out his grays. How could he improve on that?! (He would even go so far as to tell the police officers, when they came to break up his and Oline's latest fight, that he *couldn't* be a bad father because he provided KFC to his children—at the time, at least in the circles Fab was running in, KFC was thought of as a high-quality meal.)

But I was tired of putting on a show, pretending to be happy for my classmates when they got their slick new paperbacks and pencil toppers while I sat at my desk burning with shame, the teacher never once calling me to pick up my own bundle. Why couldn't *I* have new books?

I made a terrible choice. Or rather, I made a choice that many kids would have made, but perhaps only a few would have suffered the consequences that I did: I craftily forged my mother's signature on the order sheet and handed over five dollars to my teacher, which I'd quietly stolen from my father's Calvin Klein jeans that hung from a hook in our bathroom. Bad. Because of course my parents immediately discovered the theft, probably only a few hours after I'd done it, and it likely only took a short amount of time for my mother to determine that between Gliff and Sendy, I was the one who was the thief. I knew I was a goner when the school secretary knocked on the classroom door that same day and breezed in, beckoning me to follow her to her office. I felt like a prisoner walking to the guillotine. The secretary handed me her phone and I heard my mother on the line. I was so scared that my hearing hollowed out and I couldn't catch everything she said, but the tone of her voice was clear: They knew I'd taken the money. I'd better bring it back. I was in deep shit.

Focusing on my remaining classes was pointless—I sat sweating at my desk for the rest of the afternoon, furiously racking my brain for a solution, trying like Houdini to escape from an impossible situation.

When I got home, I faced my mother's relentless interrogation. Knowing punishment would be fierce, I lied and said that I hadn't taken any money, had no idea what she was talking about, but that I'd look for it. I magically "found" the five dollars I'd had to embarrassingly take back from my teacher under the laundry basket and brought it back, hoping against hope that this sin would be forgiven. But Oline's God was a stern one, and apparently He wasn't in the mood to forgive. Neither was she.

That evening radically shifted the dynamics of our household forever after. My brother and I both learned how cruel my father (and yes, my mother) could be. And I do believe my father enjoyed what he did next because he was insidious about it—coming home, feeding me dinner, acting almost solicitously toward me, at least as much as he was capable of. I could barely breathe, as I didn't want to do a single thing that would disrupt the current calm flowing through the house. But it was the calm before the storm because after dinner, when I thought I'd miraculously avoided punishment, my mother called me to the living room. She and my father were waiting for me.

"You know that stealing is wrong, and we must make sure you never do this again." She looked over at my father, who was twisting a belt in his hands in some sort of sick anticipation. I could almost feel the electric sparks flying off him, but it was too hard to look at him directly. I swallowed hard and stared at my mother.

"We must take this evil out of you, Sendy," she explained, crossing herself piously. I didn't even try to reason with her—I knew that if I did, whatever punishment was going to be meted out would only be increased.

"Lie on the floor," she instructed me.

"Put your hands behind your back."

I did as I was told, craning my neck around to try to see what it was they were doing, my anxious breath moistening the thick carpet. I clenched my teeth hard so as not to cry—doing this for years would actually make me grind my teeth, a problem I still have today. I heard the distinct sound of metal touching metal but my brain wasn't making the connection—that didn't sound like a belt buckle.

I then felt the cold bite of the metal around my wrists, tight, gnawing at me. I realized that my mother had just hand-cuffed me.

In the next few seconds I had time to vaguely think, "Huh, I didn't know they had handcuffs. Wonder where they got them," before the thought was knocked out of me. My brain, my body, my spirit only knew pain, as my father hit me across my back as hard as he possibly could, while my mother held my trembling, cuffed body to the floor so I couldn't move. Of course I had been belted before—both my parents believed that they were instilling discipline into us through corporal punishment, and I'd received my fair share, but this was different. Inhuman noises came out of me—I didn't even know that I was the one making them. Fab continued to lash the belt mercilessly across my body, growing angrier and angrier by the second because he wanted me to stay silent while taking punishment, but I couldn't stop the screams from wrenching out of me, and so he put even more power into his strokes. I could feel my skin splitting. I lost control of my bladder, peeing all over myself. Explosions burst across my eyelids, as I gasped and screamed wordlessly in agony. I thought I might die before I had no more thoughts.

Finally, it was over. Glifford, who'd been forced to watch, so that he, too, could understand the evils of stealing, helped me slowly off the floor and to my feet, leading me to the bathroom. I looked in the mirror and saw a tear-stained, snotted face staring back. I gingerly lifted my shirt, which was an enormously painful act because my blood made it stick to my back. A kaleidoscope of colors was already forming on my ribboned skin. I looked back at myself in the mirror again, defiant, and I knew then that I had lost something, invisible as it was. I now know it was a part of my innocence. I could never get my childlike trust in my parents back. And I would now be forever wary of men after what had transpired at the hands of Fab.

While I would eventually forgive my mother, years later, I would never forgive my father. No more would I be happy to see him at our door, no more would I pluck his gray hairs out for him. No longer did I think he was cool with his Calvin Kleins and his swagger and the gold fillings that he flashed at people with his charming grin. He beat an eleven-year-old senseless.

I could barely move—every step I took was painful, but it was at that point that my parents shuffled us out the door to take us to an arcade. They needed to show us that they were good parents, that this violence was for our own good, that you needed to take your punishment and cry silently (if you didn't, the whipping would be prolonged). I should have been in bed recuperating, but instead I played *Pac-Man*. I vowed not to let them see me enjoying myself—they didn't deserve that. I ignored Glifford's overtures though I could tell he felt bad for me—I didn't know how to receive comfort from anyone. Philip, now around four, was still too young to sense that something was terribly wrong—he was happily overwhelmed by the smell of popcorn in the air and the bleeping of the games that beckoned him as he strained to break away from our mother's hand. I felt something inside me harden as I watched Fab leaning against a pinball machine, that ever-present smirk on his face, his eyes lit up by the flashing lights around him.

When I went back to school on Monday—I wasn't allowed to miss class even if I was sick—I made what I thought was a smart chess move. I told my teacher what had happened. After all, I saw signs plastered all over the building stating that students should speak up if they were being hit, that there were resources available to help them. My teacher listened to me with a grave look on her face, taking care not to interrupt as I recounted the brutal beating.

"You know, Cin, there are places where children can go that are safe and fun, and you wouldn't have to worry about anything . . . like that," she said, seemingly unable to mention the incident itself.

She described a warm, happy place where kids never had to deal with their parents if they didn't want to, where there were good snacks and lots of activities to do. Being in a house full of kids didn't sound bad to me, I mused. My teacher told me she would give me a pamphlet with more information on this kids home, Covenant House, if I wanted it. I paused as she rooted around in a desk drawer.

"No," I blurted out. She stopped searching and looked up at me quizzically.

"I-I'm okay," I said. My teacher gave me a long look before shutting the drawer and folding her hands on the top of her desk.

"If you change your mind, Cin, I hope you'll let me know. You're not alone, all right?" She gave me a wan smile. She had likely had this conversation with many children before me.

I nodded quickly and backed out of the classroom. I was too scared to actually go through with something like this. Still, the conversation had gotten my mind turning, and I thought about how I could use this information to my advantage.

When I got home, I grabbed a pencil and paper and set to work.

"*Dear Mommy,*" I scrawled. I explained in my letter that if she didn't want me then I could go to another home where they would take good care of me. If she didn't love me, I thought, she should just let me go.

I finished my letter, satisfied, and waited for my mother to return home. When I heard her key in the door, I readied myself.

She walked in, looking tired, and headed straight for her bedroom.

"Mommy," I called out. It was now or never.

She stopped, giving me a "what now?" look.

I smiled and ran over to her.

"This is for you," I said, shoving the letter into her hand.

She sighed, years of exhaustion in her exhale.

"Give me a minute, Sendy," she said, and walked into her room, closing the door behind her, the letter still in her hand.

I waited patiently. One silent minute went by, then two, then three.

And then, *boom.* My mother wrenched her door open and

it banged violently into the wall. She marched toward me, a strange look of fury and panic in her eyes.

"What is this?" she screamed at me, waving the letter in my face.

I looked at her coolly, not saying anything in response.

Her eyes bugged out of her head and she grabbed my shoulders, shaking me hard.

"If you ever, *ever*, tell anyone about what goes on in this family, I *will* give you up!" she shouted, her face inches from mine. "And if I give you up, where you go will be *so* much worse than you can even imagine!"

I stayed mute, locked in her gaze until she broke her stare. She walked away, saying nothing else.

I smiled to myself. *Success.*

See, I knew that I had done something bad—I had stolen from my parents. That was wrong. But what was worse was the punishment inflicted on me. That was not okay, and I needed my mother to know that I knew it was wrong. It was clear that Mommy was deeply shaken by my letter, and I wanted her to be. I had put her on notice.

I wouldn't even try with Fab. It didn't matter. He reveled in the beating—he didn't care about anything except enriching himself and inflicting pain on others. He enjoyed each stroke of my lashing.

But ultimately, I knew that Oline was a victim, too. And as wrong as she was to let the beating go so far, I somehow understood that she was just trying to help me grow up right, to not sink into one of the many terrible endings that could come from living in the projects.

We needed to get out of this hellhole. We needed to get away from my father.

A couple years later, in the middle of the night, my mother would make that happen.

Chapter 5

WHAT DOES IT SAY ABOUT YOUR LIFE—ABOUT you—when you have to move homes and all of your worldly possessions are stuffed haphazardly into garbage bags, the same things that are used to discard everything that people deem unworthy of keeping in their lives?

This thought occurred to me years later, but back then, I wordlessly packed up all my clothing and the few other items I owned. My mother and brothers were doing the same with their own black garbage bags and one battered blue suitcase that held all of our family's important documents. We were moving in the dead of the night. It was finally happening.

For years now, my mother had vowed to get us out of the projects, but she said it so often and nothing ever seemed to change that I thought it was just wishful thinking on her part. I shouldn't have underestimated her.

A year or so before we actually moved, my mother took me aside and pulled out a burgundy savings book surreptitiously; back then they were called passbooks because they looked like passports. She told me that if anything ever happened to her, that my father was absolutely not to find out about this secret savings account of hers. Even though she still didn't trust banks, she had been forced to open one to hide money from my father,

who saw that her hustle had picked up and was always corner-
ing her, demanding money. She told me that the account was
for the house that she was going to buy us one day. I still didn't
believe her.

But Oline wanted to get out badly. So did I. Things had gone
from terrible, to even more terrible. The neighborhood was getting even more dangerous and my father was becoming absolutely unbearable.

One afternoon, I was in my after-school care program eating
a snack, juice box in hand, when my mother burst into the center, wild-eyed and disheveled.

"Sendy!" she yelled hoarsely, looking frantically for me. As
soon as she spotted me, she ran over to me and grabbed me. I
slung my backpack over my shoulder and awaited the worst. I'd
gone snooping in my parents' things earlier, and I figured they'd
found out. A whupping was probably on its way.

But no, no punishment came. My mother led me outside to
a chaotic swirl of noise and flashing lights, police officers, and
fire trucks. Apparently, there had been a huge gas leak and the
bodega and building next to our own apartment building had
exploded in a spectacular fiery conflagration. She was terrified
that I'd been in the bodega buying candy, and was supremely
relieved, of course, that I was alive, but still she didn't hug me.
That just didn't happen in our family.

That night Manhattan Borough President David Dinkins,
who would later become the first Black mayor of New York City,
made the rounds in the neighborhood. TV cameras followed
him and we all went outside to witness the spectacle. My dad
was making the rounds, too. He swaggered over to Dinkins,
shaking his hand, as if they were two compatriots in arms. He
hammed it up in front of the cameras, looking solemn, describ-
ing how he had been desperately searching for his children as

soon as he heard the explosion (not true), and that more funding needed to be put into the neighborhood's infrastructure so
that tragedies like this wouldn't happen again.

These fifteen seconds of fame—he got his picture in the
paper, too—gave him the genius idea to "campaign" for a leader-
ship position in the community. Which position, exactly, he
was running for always remained opaque. He sauntered around
the neighborhood, crowing about the improvements he would
make when he was elected, and he collected donations, telling
people that if David Dinkins could become borough president,
why couldn't *he* be a voice for them? Just wait, and he would get
more money injected into local businesses and would make the
streets safe. Fab to the rescue.

My mother knew what he was up to—the only business Fab
was funding here was his own. She got increasingly anxious about
the people my father was soliciting from—some were shady
groups who would be very unhappy to find out that the donations they were offering were going straight into Fab's pocket.

Fab's ego, too, had also been alarmingly inflated by his brush
with the cameras, and this made him even more difficult to be
around, which we didn't think was possible. More often than
not, when he did manage to find his way home, he returned
stinking to high heaven of cheap booze, which resulted in more
fights between him and Oline. Late arrival home, yelling, slapping, crying, rinse, repeat.

One day I walked into our bathroom to find a couple of little
square packets sitting on top of the toilet. Puzzled, I grabbed
them and brought them over to my mother, asking her what
they were. I'd never seen them around the house before—what
did these little flattened squares hold? Candy?

My mother took one look at the squares in my palm and
grabbed me by my shoulders, shaking me violently.

"Where did you get these from? Tell me right now, Sendy!"

Shit. These things were dangerous. I pointed in the direction of the bathroom and told her I'd found them there and asked her again what they were. She didn't tell me that they were condoms—she just gave me a beating for the discovery. One of the reasons why I learned to so often keep my mouth shut.

Things between the two got so bad that my mother began to use our baby brother, Phil, as a human shield between her and Fab in their bed. Poor Phil wasn't able to prevent their worst fight, though. One night, Fab came back, stained and sauced. He pulled my mother out of bed and dragged her roughly into the living room, screaming profanities at her for seemingly no reason. I quickly grabbed Phil and locked him in my and Glifford's bedroom so he wouldn't have to witness the abuse. Through the thin walls we could hear my mother crying and yelling, and my father beating her without stopping. Then things quieted down a bit and I only heard my mother's sobs interspersed with an occasional grunt from Fab. He likely sexually assaulted her but my mother never shared anything further about that nightmare scene with us. After a while, all of the noises ceased and my mother weakly called out for us to stay locked in the room. We didn't emerge until the next day. I can't remember my mother smiling for a long time after that. She was able to kick Fab out following that altercation, but like the disgusting, persistent roach that he was, he always managed to find a way back in, sweet-talking her, reminding her of the good times they used to have, that they could still have if she would only let him back in, joking, all goodness and light until he had gotten his way and then he was right back to being the alcoholic asshole we all knew so well. Classic abuser tactic. I always hoped, each time my mother kicked Fab out, that he would leave and not return. It would take years, though, before she was rid of him for good.

It's not like this was unique to us—violence could be heard in the other apartments, too, shouting matches and stinging slaps ringing out into the stairwell, and it definitely wasn't from the TV sets that were also left blaring in a halfhearted attempt to drown out the shouted arguments. Drug trades and shootings were increasing around the neighborhood, needles littering the sidewalks, and even sometimes a shell casing would crunch underfoot. My mother became even more paranoid about us going outside in an attempt to shield us from our bleak reality. I'd sneak outside anyway and hang out in front of the building with the other kids, sitting on the stoop, listening to music, or watching boys play slap box with each other (slap box was a risky game that involved two kids, usually teenage boys, slapping each other progressively harder. It always started out as a game, but if you went too long or too hard, or you surprised someone with a slap when too many people were around to watch, it could turn into a real fight, accompanied by serious punches or even knives). I was always ready to bolt inside at my mother's approach, beating her up the stairs and trying to steady my breathing so she wouldn't know what was up. Even the other adults in the building were in on it—maybe they thought Oline was stuck up and they wanted to go behind her back—she didn't make it a secret that she thought she was better than everyone else in the projects and would never deign to interact with them. Or maybe they just thought I should be allowed to be a kid and not be stuck indoors. They'd always warn me if they saw my mother approaching with a "Hurry, your mom's coming!"

Even when Monica, a seven-year-old girl in the building, was brutally raped by her mother's boyfriend, the talk of the complex for weeks, it still didn't click for me. I thought my mom was just being mean and strict. I didn't see how hard she was trying to hold the seams of our lives together.

But that was her style. She never shared what was crossing her mind and didn't let us in on her plans.

Which is how I found myself, one March afternoon after school, with my mother unceremoniously handing me an oversize black garbage bag and telling me to pack everything quickly because we were moving. That night. Chop chop.

I didn't have a chance to tell anyone I was leaving—my teachers didn't know, my friends didn't know, I didn't know!

"Why didn't you tell anyone, Mommy?" I asked. She looked at me before giving a terse response.

"Because nobody needs to know our business, Sendy. Just pack your clothes."

And that was that.

She was so worried about people in the building finding out where we were moving to that she left all our furniture behind so nobody would see us moving. She had secretly gone out and bought a house and furnished it fully, too, without us knowing.

At the time, I was astonished by the fact that my mother had actually gone and done what she had sworn she would do, getting us out of the PJs and into a house, but I never should have doubted her steely resolve. And in retrospect, it makes sense. Our rent at Patterson was around sixty-five bucks a month and Oline was notoriously frugal, ingeniously repurposing our belongings for other uses once they'd become too worn out to serve their initial function. While she did spend on items of quality when she could, she also thrifted and penny-pinched and went without for years so that she could eventually afford a down payment.

So nobody would see, we quickly packed all of our trash bags and the one suitcase into my mom's white work van that she used to haul her street merchandise, and with that, we were off, the projects fading fast behind us in the rearview mirror.

My brothers and I had no idea where we were going—the dark streets quickly became strange and new. My mother kept silent in the driver's seat and didn't clue us in on our destination. It was an adventure.

We may as well have been driving to the other side of the world—our new neighborhood was completely unrecognizable from Patterson. There were no people milling around on street corners, no yelling, no music blasting, no high-rises looming over everyone. We pulled into a driveway and got out, the *thunk* of the van doors closing thunderously loud in this new silence. I wasn't used to such quiet—it was eerie, almost dystopian. What was everyone doing? They couldn't *all* be asleep right now, could they? Were they watching our arrival from behind their curtains?

My mother led us inside and showed us around, but nothing stuck with me on that first tour—we were all wiped. I did see that she'd already provided everything we needed in each room—sheets and blankets and pillows were already on the beds. She guided me to my bed and I passed out immediately into the dreamless sleep of the exhausted.

The next morning, I was ready to explore the house and our new neighborhood of East Elmhurst, Queens. I popped out of bed and wandered outside. I didn't even have to sneak out! Before my mother left for her hustle that morning, she had told me I could go outside if I wanted to but that I had to find a school to enroll in in the next day or so. I was thirteen years old and she had made it my responsibility to find my own school to attend (she had already found a school for Philip, and Glifford continued to go to his Catholic school).

This newfound freedom was intoxicating. Everything around me seemed foreign—across the street in what looked to my eye like a yellow mini-mansion, two white boys were getting into a car. They saw me and waved. I was too shocked to wave back—

I'd only seen white children on shows like *Punky Brewster* and *Little House on the Prairie*—it was like these kids had crawled out of our TV set.

I was also mesmerized by the fact that we had our very own yard with real green grass in it. It was enclosed by a gate and a fence around our house so I knew I couldn't be wrong—it had to be ours.

I slowly walked around the block and took in all of the new sights and sounds. I saw a couple of kids riding their bikes in their front yard. The boy had dark hair and bronze-colored skin while the girl, who watched me slowly approach, had bright blue eyes and light brown hair. I greeted them and asked them if they knew of any schools I could attend because as a thirteen-year-old in pre-Internet days, what else was I supposed to do?

The girl shrugged and called her older sister out to help. Her sister had darker skin and jet-black curly hair.

"Wait, that's your sister?" I asked the blue-eyed girl. She laughed and said yes and pointed to the boy—"and that's my brother!"

I was incredulous. They couldn't be fully related to one another.

"And you all have the same father?" They gave me a strange look and confirmed that they indeed shared a father.

I was used to knowing kids in families who had different parents from one another. My mind couldn't quite grasp that these kids all looked so different but shared a dad.

The curly haired girl, Catalina, invited me into their house, and when I walked in, the first thing I noticed was the smell. It smelled so clean, so inviting, so homey. Apparently, their mother had just done laundry.

I saw fluffy sheets on a clothesline hanging in their basement—I wanted to bury my face in them and rub myself all over the sheets so I could smell that good, too.

"Why does your clothing smell like this?" I asked.

I could tell Catalina thought I was being weird—*why is she showing so much interest in laundry?*

"It's Tide—doesn't everyone use Tide?" Catalina asked me. I stayed silent, not wanting to disagree.

Later that night, I would ask my mom to buy Tide and she would shut me down, scoffing.

"There's no reason to buy that stuff, Sendy—it's too expensive. What we use is fine."

She always bought the cheap, blue-and-white powdered detergent that I suppose got our clothes clean, but that didn't bring with it an immediate sense of security like Catalina's laundry did. A hug from Catalina enveloped me immediately into a cloud of clean scent that felt like love. I always felt safe and cared for in Catalina's house, and later, whenever she let me borrow a piece of her clothing, I would stick my nose in it so I could breathe in that comforting scent. My addiction got so strong that I'd sometimes head into the cleaning aisle of a store and open a Tide bottle to sniff it.

We ventured into her room, which was girly and pink and had a giant bed in its center. I didn't understand why her bed was so . . . big. I only had a twin-sized bed.

"Oh, that's because my sister and I share a bed," she explained. I was even further mystified.

"But that's so . . . close . . . in one bed. Wouldn't you be touching?"

She shrugged. "I guess sometimes . . . so?"

My family and I never touched each other—if I accidentally happened to touch, say, my mother or one of my brothers, it sent a shock wave through my system and I would quickly draw back as if I had been singed. The thought of familial affection to such a level where two sisters could sleep in one bed comfortably flat out confused me.

But then again, their whole lifestyle did. These sisters had invited me into their house without a second thought and when Catalina saw me admiring her Sweet Valley High books on the bookshelf in her bedroom, she said I could have them because she had already finished reading them. What kind of game was she playing at here, exactly?! What was the catch?

Her mother didn't question me when she saw me, choosing to minister to several bubbling pots at the stove instead—only when I headed for the door to leave did she ask me what I was doing, why I wasn't eating with the family. She made me pull up a chair and she filled a plate with chicken, plantains, rice, and beans and ordered me simply to "Eat! Eat!"

I paused, torn. My mother didn't like us to eat other people's food—she didn't want us owing anything to anyone else, to be in their debt. But it smelled *so* good. My mouth immediately filled with saliva, I was so hungry.

Catalina just smiled at me and shrugged. "Guess you're eating with us now! She likes to feed the neighborhood."

Deciding to approach those kids on their bikes all those years ago was one of the single best decisions of my life. Catalina and her sister Kenya became my sisters—they taught me not to recoil from an embrace, they showed me what true friendship and acceptance looked like, all while never asking for anything in return. I didn't know what a "normal" family was or how one operated—that it was acceptable to show affection to one another, even encouraged. I saw that it was okay to laugh together, loudly, without fear of getting yelled at and told to be quiet. I stayed for so many dinners and was never told to leave; I shared in all the triumphs and sorrows their family went through over the decades. Without objection from my mother—I was staying out of trouble, after all—I attended birthday parties, quinceañeras, funerals, weddings, baptisms, graduations, communions, christenings, and everything in between.

I went from having a couple of aunts and cousins I didn't know to having dozens of aunts, uncles, cousins, and grandparents. I learned what a home and a family truly could be. And it smelled like Tide.

❧

In time, after the newness of Queens had started to wear off and I'd become a bit more accustomed to our surroundings, my eyes adjusted. I saw that, even though we had our own driveway and fenced-in yard like the other houses, ours needed a bit more love, at least when it came to curb appeal. While the other houses on the block looked well maintained, it was obvious that the previous owners of our house had not taken care of it and had let it fall into disrepair. Our house was a one-story ranch, and I grew to think that it was hideous. It was a muddy dark green color that clearly needed a fresh coat of paint. The windows were sad and old—the frames sagged and there were cracks in the glass. We were forever holding our breath, hoping that the cracks wouldn't multiply, as if we were standing on a frozen pond beginning to thaw. The gate to get into our yard was rusty and always broken, and it was strangely short—it only came up a bit past my knees. But my mother did her best to spruce things up outside, planting flowers in the front yard, hacking back the overgrown bushes with a machete that she used for almost everything, and, eventually, replacing the windows.

Inside, the house was nicely decorated; after all, my mother had bought all new furniture, but it was always dark—there weren't many windows, and the ones at the front of the house were always at least partially covered by a dirty green-and-white striped awning that prevented the sun from getting in. My mother never liked turning lights on in the house, so it always felt oppressive. Our living room had new plastic-encased furniture—this time the couch was green—and there was new dining room furniture, along with a new TV, but I never felt like watching TV anymore because it was just so damn dark. Fortunately, my room was bright, as was the kitchen, which is where we usually clustered.

My bedroom, my mother's bedroom, and my brothers' shared bedroom were all located toward the back of the house, along with the bathroom, with the kitchen, living room, and dining room in front.

At first, I was overjoyed to see that there were no roaches in our house—I could finally get a good night's sleep! But once we started unpacking our clothes, the roaches made their presence known, flashing across the floor and up the walls. They had stowed away in our garbage bags, and they were soon scuttling around, tormenting me like before. It took a long time before we successfully got rid of them, and I was terrified that someone would come to our house and see a roach—then they'd know that we had come from the projects and were poor, even though we were living in this nice neighborhood like them.

To try to be like the other kids in the neighborhood, Glifford and I hung posters we got from magazines on our walls. Glifford would always buy the rap mag *The Source*, and I switched between various teen rags. We papered our walls with Run DMC, LL Cool J, Madonna, New Edition, and Cyndi Lauper, along with the occasional WWF wrestler like The Hulk or Junkyard Dog or Jimmy Snuka. In a rare outward showing of brotherly concern, Glifford would solemnly lecture me about the importance of staying true to our Bronx roots even though we lived in Queens, and to never, *never* move to Brooklyn—the ultimate betrayal.

In Queens, I began to see the outlines of a different kind of life taking shape, one where I could be free to walk around without being in danger or hooked by drugs, where I could get a job, wouldn't necessarily be consigned to getting pregnant and staying on food stamps in the projects as so many of the kids I knew in Patterson were doing starting in seventh or eighth grade.

In addition to the roaches, one of the vestiges of our old life that was still present in this new one was . . . Fab. At some point after the move, he and my mother signed a shaky peace treaty and he moved in with us. But this time, it was on my mother's terms. Fab was not the owner of the house—my mother was, and if Fab wanted to live with us, he needed to abide by her rules. This meant that he had to contribute rent and he was only allowed to live in the basement, which had its own bathroom, and, more importantly, had a lock on the door opening to the first floor. He could get out of the basement through a separate entrance, but if he wanted to join us in the house, he needed to knock like any other visitor, which was fine with me—he wasn't a member of our family, as far as I was concerned.

Sometimes, if my mother was feeling generous and up for cooking, we'd play pretend as a family and he would join us at the dinner table, dumping okra and cow's tongue on his plate as if he did this every night with us.

But there were plenty of times where Fab would knock on our door and we wouldn't answer him, telling him later that, oops, we hadn't heard him knocking. He knew he had a good thing going here so he couldn't complain—and he mostly didn't.

✧

While Glifford still went to Catholic school, I finished out my last couple of months of eighth grade at my middle school, P.S. 145 Joseph Pulitzer, and then I started high school at Queens Vocational Technical, a public school that I had located and registered for all on my own by asking various adults around the neighborhood. This was the first school in which I'd ever interacted with white kids—Patterson didn't have white families living there, and my previous schools only had Black and Latinx kids attending.

Probably not surprising, then, that I encountered the first act of racism against me as soon as I bumped into some white kids, though at first I didn't even recognize it as such because I didn't know what racism was at the time. I was unfortunate enough to have homeroom with a kid named Bryce. He was huge, both stocky and tall, built like a football player. He had red, curly hair and skin so pale that it looked translucent, dotted all over with freckles, like a toddler had gone wild with a marker on his face. His eyelashes were faint, but you could see the flutter of their motion when he blinked. A classic comic book villain, he had a sidekick named Michael, who would accompany him everywhere he went, parroting whatever he said. On my very first day at school, Bryce asked me why my lips were so huge, and he and Michael both stretched their top lips upward with their thumbs and forefingers to demonstrate how big they thought my lips were. I rolled my eyes and responded in classic Cin fashion with, "My lips aren't big, yours are just too thin." They would do this until the end of the school year, but it rolled off me, as I didn't even fully comprehend as a thirteen-year-old that this was overt racism. Hell, there was a lot I didn't know at the time, and I said ignorant things, too. This was the first time I had gone to school with kids outside of Black and Latinx identities, and this included some Asian kids. I still cringe to think how I tried to become friends with an Asian kid in my class, asking him if he could teach me how to make beef fried rice and chicken wings—all the Chinese restaurants around Patterson served chicken wings. Yikes.

As a Haitian immigrant who felt she was better than everyone else, my mother had internalized societal prejudices that she openly shared with Glifford, Phil, and me, which certainly didn't help me in my new environment. While Oline would never have used the word "feminist," she believed that she—and I—could do anything that men could, if we set our minds to it.

She was unaware of the concept of intergenerational poverty and trauma, waving away the challenges that kept her neighbors in Patterson stuck in the projects for generations. Frankly, neither did I until years later, when I was able to unlearn her teachings.

She started working on me from birth. To improve my posture, she would make me square my shoulders and pace around the living room with a book on my head. One morning, as she watched me march back and forth across the room, she made noises of displeasure.

"You don't have a butt," she told me, shaking her head, as if she were a doctor having to give a patient a terminal diagnosis.

Where is this going? I thought. *Of course I have a butt—I sit on that shit every day!*

"Your butt is flat," she said, with heavy disappointment. "And there's nothing I can do about it."

She sighed.

"But at least I fixed your nose."

Book still on head, I reached up to delicately touch my nose. What did she do to it?

She explained matter-of-factly, "When you were a baby, your nose was huge. Your nostrils flared so badly. But I fixed the problem."

She told me that when I was an infant, she had massaged my nose every day in an attempt to reshape it. Apparently, she felt that her efforts had paid off and that my nose was slimmer and smaller after her daily ministrations. That's some Eurocentric beauty ideal shit right there, if I ever heard of any.

And it didn't stop there. Oline made me go to the hair salon every week to get my hair done. She was enormously proud of the fact that we both had straighter, finer hair, and she wanted the world to know it. Every Saturday for years, she would send me off to the salon to get my hair done. The ladies in the salon would ignore me and do adult customers' hair for hours before getting to me, so I resigned myself to listening to them speak in Spanish, waiting patiently for my turn. The one time I asked my mother for Jheri curls, which would translate to less upkeep and time in the salon for me, she adamantly refused, bewildered as to why I would want curly hair. Jheri curls were only for nappy-headed kids with coarser hair, and did I want to be known as a "Nap"? Only "people with the worst kind of Black hair" got Jheri curls, she told me. I didn't tell her I'd seen kids with Jheri curls getting teased at school, getting insults like "follow the drip" thrown in their faces. That was the end of that conversation.

Oline urged me to find friends who went to private school because if they went to private school, that meant that they weren't street urchins and their parents clearly cared enough about them to make that kind of investment. She wanted me to marry someone of Indian descent because that meant that they would be smart and have "good" hair. She warned me that if I married a Black man and had kids with "bad" hair, she wouldn't take them to the playground.

The texture of my hypothetical future children's hair was the last thing on my mind, and who said I was going to get married and have kids, anyway? But these casual comments that Oline dropped here and there still wormed their way insidiously into my brain and I internalized these beliefs. It took a lot of unlearning for me to understand that racism among Black people can exist and that it's a product of white supremacy, that Oline believing that Haitians were inherently better than African Americans was a prime example of this concept in action. Being from the Caribbean, she also didn't understand the specific and enormous baggage that came with being Black in America.

This superiority complex applied to white folks, too. Oline

wasn't impressed or intimidated by the white Americans she came into contact with; she felt that all they had was the color of their skin to define them.

As for me, I am proud of being Haitian—we Haitians are a resilient and resourceful people, with a rich culture and history. I'm proud of our land, our food, our art. I would never want to be anything else but Haitian. But I am also an American and I take pride in that fact as well.

Oline's warnings followed me into high school at Queens Vocational Technical, but I wasn't interested in romantic endeavors—I was much more concerned about my growing lunch ticket business and how I could buy my way to financial freedom. My mind was always churning, assessing situations for profit. Any chance I saw an occasion to make money, I'd take it—ethics be damned if I needed to lie in order to do so.

I'd spot these opportunities like rare game in the wild and confidently take my shot. One day, Qi Liu, a kid in my class, happened to tell me that he found a beautiful gold bracelet glinting on the floor of the school's main hallway. That chump picked it up and promptly and honorably turned it in to Principal Serber. I couldn't believe that Qi would hand in such treasure like it was nothing. But whatever—his loss, my gain.

Feigning mild curiosity, I asked Qi what the bracelet looked like. He described it at length for me and then I went on my merry way, patiently readying myself for a windfall. I waited a week—I figured if the rightful owner hadn't picked it up by then, the bracelet was fair game.

After a week had gone by without a claim on the bracelet, I marched my flat, honorless ass to Serber's office and knocked gently on the door. I put on my most winning smile and explained that I had lost a gold bracelet last week but had only just realized it was missing, and that my mother would be furious if I didn't get it back.

Serber raised an eyebrow and studied me.

"Okay, describe the bracelet," he said.

Armed with Qi's intel, I regurgitated his description of the bracelet, down to the small red ruby in its center.

Serber looked at me for a moment longer, then pulled open a drawer and rifled through it.

"You're lucky that someone honest turned this in, Cin," he said. I nodded emphatically, holding my breath. He dangled the bracelet in front of me and dropped it into my outstretched hand. My little jewelry heist had actually worked. As soon as the last bell rang, I burst from the school's double doors and made a detour to the Diamond District with a friend, selling the bracelet for a tidy two hundred dollars. Not bad.

After pulling stunts like this, my mind would seize upon Fab. He always used his wiles to his own advantage only, charming and swindling wherever he went. He would pull gold fillings out of people's mouths if he thought he could get away with it. Was I any better than him?

Now that Fab had been relegated to the basement, we at least didn't have to see him as much and be directly exposed to his dark abuse. But that didn't mean that we avoided the effects of his trickery, which became abundantly clear to us one spring day my sophomore year. We never could figure out which of his many varied scams put us in serious danger—perhaps it was the Haitian passport swindle, who knows—but if that day had transpired any differently, I might not be around to share this story.

On that afternoon, I got back from school and nobody was home. My mother was at her hustle, Phil was at after-school care, and Glifford—now an aspiring rapper—was busy with an internship at *The Source*, where he hoped to make industry connections to lift his future rap career off the ground. I still have one of his rhymes forever imprinted in my brain:

I'm quiet, swift, slick and so damn legit
And like that I flow on a smooth tip
I kick a rhyme smoother than any brother can
I'm labeled #1 cause I'm a supreme Black man
I'm on top and I rise above all
Ta stand in my path they soon shall fall

I loved days like this when I could have the place to myself—when Fab or my mother was around, there was an unwelcome heaviness that permeated the air. I'd learned to take in the stillness, enjoying the drowsy drone of a lawn mower in the distance, feeling the coolness of the living room's hardwood floors on my bare feet. I'd grab a library book and lie on my bed, and the silence would be broken only by the turning of a page.

That's why I was able to hear the noise so clearly. It was a cough, but I didn't know it at the time. A cough wouldn't have fit into my afternoon ritual, so I didn't register it as such. We had gotten a dog by then—Phil had pleaded with my mother for one, and she had finally relented, unable to say no to her baby. I just thought the noise was from the dog, that my mother had stuck him in the basement to safeguard against any accidents he might have without us being home to monitor him. Without a second thought, I swung open the basement door, but no dog bounded up the steps.

"Rusky, come here, boy," I called out into the darkness. There was a single bulb dangling from the ceiling at the top of the stairs, but for some reason that day I decided not to yank on its chain to turn it on. It was a good thing I didn't.

Slightly puzzled, I closed the door, thinking vaguely that it had been a rat. We'd recently had one raid my mother's small garden; maybe it had found its way inside. Mentally shrugging, I made my way to the kitchen to get some Sprite for my read. But when I opened the fridge, it was gone. I knew an unopened bottle had been there this morning. Huh. I padded off to my room to read a bit of Danielle Steel, but I couldn't get the missing Sprite out of my head. Nobody had been home since this morning, and dammit, I really wanted my soda! It didn't make sense, but I was past trying to logic this one out, so I went to a nearby store for more Sprite, patting myself on the back for my charitable contribution to the fridge.

By the time I returned, my mother had gotten home. She looked shaken.

"We've been robbed," she informed me. I was confused—I'd been gone only a few minutes. When did robbers have time to break in, take our stuff, and escape without detection?

Turns out they didn't escape notice. Our neighbor Nina told us later that she'd seen me leave for the store, and only a minute or two later, a pair of men left the house as well. She'd just thought they were friends of ours.

They'd taken the few valuables we had in the house, including my mother's beloved boom box and her gun that she kept for protection. In return, they'd left a threatening note, something about Fab and collecting debts with lives. That was what did it. That is what convinced my mother to get rid of Fab for good. Apparently, the tipping point was threatening her with goons who lurked in basements with guns while her daughter was home. If it was the last thing she did, she would find a way to disentangle all our lives from Fab's.

Oh, and they took the Sprite.

❧

As I learned from Patterson, though, roaches are extremely hard to exterminate. You think you've finally gotten rid of them for good only to suddenly see one on the wall, taunting you with its waving antennae after you figured you were in the clear.

I think Oline knew that she'd need to do something drastic

to root out Fab. He hadn't even felt any guilt regarding the robbery—in fact, he was mad at *me* for somehow not stopping the robbers!

While she was plotting, Fab's brother Gesner came to visit from Haiti, taking up temporary residence in the basement with Fab. Oline had already made up her mind that Fab had to go, but Gesner's presence sped up the process further—she hated him and didn't try to hide it. And while he was only supposed to stay for a few weeks, Gesner ended up staying for months, Fab likely charging him rent and paying him very little for whatever work he had enlisted him to help with.

Because he was my father's brother, my family and I thought that he, too, was a freeloader, coasting off my mother's good graces, not knowing that he had outstayed his welcome as soon as he'd arrived. He hadn't learned English and he stuck close to Fab, which likely increased our distaste for him. We kept our distance, and I purposely avoided interacting with him whenever I could. His presence in the household only made this strange upstairs-downstairs living situation more tense.

But it went deeper than that. My mother forbade Gesner from coming upstairs unless she had given her explicit consent and Fab was with him. Gesner was not allowed to use our dishes and he was not allowed to use our bathroom. My mother furiously cleaned anything that Gesner may have touched on the rare occasion that he did come upstairs. If she wasn't home, my mother put me on watch, making sure to have me bark at Gesner, forcing him back into the basement if he tried to creep upstairs. My mother entrusted me with this task, and I took it seriously. I was in a constant state of anxiety, worried that Gesner would somehow escape my notice and touch something.

My mother told us that Gesner had HIV.

Our family knew almost nothing about AIDS and HIV when Gesner came to stay with us. At this time, in the early 1990s, there was still a great deal of public debate, confusion, and misinformation about how the disease spread and who its carriers were, and heavy stigma was applied to anyone with HIV or AIDS. It was only a few years before, in 1989, that the public was scandalized when, in a now famous visit, Diana, Princess of Wales, toured Harlem Hospital and invited physical contact with patients, cradling babies and hugging a young, pajama-clad boy with HIV. He was one of many children in foster care who couldn't find homes because of prejudice against the disease.

My mother likely was also sensitive on the topic because Americans often associated Haiti with AIDS, stereotyping so many Haitians as having the disease when that simply wasn't true. Per an article in the *New Yorker* by fellow Haitian American writer Edwidge Danticat, this dangerous misattribution sprang up in the early 1980s because "the CDC named four groups at high risk for the disease: intravenous drug users, homosexuals, hemophiliacs, and Haitians. Haitians were the only ones solely identified by nationality" because early on in public reporting of AIDS, a group of about twenty Haitians arrived at a Miami hospital and were found to have the disease, which the media then ran with, spreading this misinformation like wildfire.

My personal knowledge of HIV and AIDS was virtually nonexistent. Prior to Gesner, my closest association to the disease came from reading about Ryan White, the thirteen-year-old who had gained national attention when he was diagnosed with AIDS from a blood transfusion and then wasn't allowed to go back to school. He had recently died when Gesner came to stay with us, and we all thought that close contact with Gesner might result in transmission of the disease, that we could be infected with it if we weren't careful.

I could sense a murky wrongness clinging to any mention of the disease. Shame was sharply attached to it, I could see, but I didn't know why. I only knew that my mother seemed to hate Gesner for it, implied that he'd done something very wrong to contract it. Gesner, emaciated, graying, unsmiling, seemed to match his diagnosis.

I understand now that my mother wanted to protect us, but in doing so, she, like so many people in that time, denied Gesner his humanity when he likely needed it the most. He might have been a trickster, selfish and self-absorbed, like my father, but we never actually found out because we didn't try to talk to him, to shake his hand, to give him a hug or even a smile. He stayed in our dank basement, hidden away, emerging into the light only to run an errand for my father or, according to my mother, to receive treatment for his disease. After a few dragging months with us, he went to Canada to stay with his sister Yative, and I didn't hear anything more about him for a long time. A cousin later told me that he'd been caught trying to get back into the United States using fake papers that my dad had supplied him, and he was deported back to Haiti, where he stayed put until he died. Odd thing, though—my cousin said that my father told her family that Gesner had diabetes, not HIV. She said that her mother, my aunt, never wanted to talk about Gesner. Apparently, the shame lived on in our family long after Gesner was gone and buried.

Chapter 6

I HAD BEEN CALLED TO THE PRINCIPAL'S OFFICE AGAIN. Mr. Serber and I were on familiar terms by now, and not necessarily for the better. In case it hasn't dawned on you yet, I was a bit of a shit in high school.

While I was smart and theoretically *could* have aced my classes, they bored me and I had trouble focusing, words on the blackboard blurring as my eyes crossed and I struggled to stay awake. I vastly preferred to spend my time playing on the school's crappy softball team or working at the part-time job I'd managed to secure at an eyeglass store in the mall. My grades declined steadily over four years. Instead of turning in assignments, I focused on figuring out how I could cheat my way into good grades. And with graduation coming up, I needed to pull off something spectacular for Ms. Leung's computer class. This was long enough ago that we weren't born with a cell phone and laptop in our hands, and we had to be taught things like typing and how to use programs like Microsoft Word.

I really shouldn't have taken advantage of Ms. Leung because she was cool. Her class was my first two periods and I was always running late in the morning. But she knew that most of us were going through shit elsewhere in our lives, so she allowed us to make up any assignments that we had missed or failed. At this point, I was about ten projects behind. I should have taken time off work or softball to finish my assignments, but that wasn't my style. Instead, I eyeballed our class grade sheet, which was readily available at the front of the classroom on a bulletin board. I knew Ms. Leung wasn't the sort to keep laser focus on who had turned in what so I figured I could fill in my missing assignment grades on the sheet as long as I wasn't obvious about it. A couple of times a week, I'd casually stroll up to the sheet when Ms. Leung was out of the classroom and add a seventy or a ninety on it, making sure to mimic her handwriting as closely as possible. I was a good forger, and I knew not to attempt an eighty because Ms. Leung's eights were hard to craft with precision. So seventy or ninety it was.

Ali was my downfall. Ali, who had told me about the stock market and who faithfully bought my lunch tickets whenever I could find him. The bastard saw what I had been up to, and instead of ratting me out, he started writing in his own grades on the sheet, too. I had a good thing going, but Ali just couldn't be cool about it. He marked big loopy eights on the sheet, and they stuck out horribly. I had a bad feeling that things were going to come crashing down. But they didn't, at least not in that moment. It was when other kids, emboldened by Ali's obviousness, joined in on the plot that Ms. Leung caught on. We had flown too close to the sun. One morning Ms. Leung briskly walked in while we were sitting in front of our chunky, ash-colored computers and demanded that we all turn in our assignments on our floppy disks. Shit. I cast around in my mind for some wild excuse I could throw at her, but I was now a whopping twenty assignments behind—I was screwed, and I knew it. I got a big, fat "F" in that class and was exposed as the mastermind behind the cheating scandal.

It was for shit like this that I thought I was being called to the principal's office. I figured Mr. Serber wanted to get his own time in to yell at me about something or other. Or that he had found out that the bracelet I'd tricked him into giving me wasn't actually mine. I walked down the hallway to his office, pasting a smile on my face.

"You rang?" I asked him, the picture of innocence and light.

He pointed at his phone. "Your mom is on the line, Cin."

I groaned. This was even worse than getting reamed out by Serber. If my mother was calling the school, she must be furious about something I had done. I racked my brain, but I truly couldn't think of anything that would have incurred her wrath so severely that she felt the need to pull me out of class to talk to her. I braced myself for the worst and lifted the phone to my ear, cringing at the inevitable shrieking that was surely to come.

"Sendy, it's our house. It's burned down," she delivered to me in a matter-of-fact tone.

It's funny where your mind travels to first when you are given life-changing news like that. Everything slowed down around me. I wondered fuzzily if the Halloween candy I had stashed in my closet would be safe or if it had melted in the fire, a rainbow swirl of molten goo. And then everything suddenly sped forward and the realization that I didn't have a home anymore crashed into me. Were our belongings gone? Where would we live? Was our dog, Rusky, in the house when it burned down? Had he been waiting for one of us to save him, barking in vain, then choked silent by the smoke? Would we have to walk through the rubble to find his little charred body? Dramatic, I know. But my mother's clipped voice over the phone didn't leave me much to go on.

It was decided that my softball coach, Mr. Reichek, would give me a ride home. Windows manually cranked down in his beat-up sedan, he made small talk with me in an effort to get my mind off the worst-case scenarios. We talked shop about the team, and I confessed to him that I hated my calves. They were big and muscular and I got teased about them all the time, so much so that I always tried to hide them by wearing culottes, which stopped right above my ankles. In fact, the weekend before, a stranger had walked up to me and called me Popeye Legs, sneering that I walked like a boxer. Reichek gave me a quick sideways glance to see if I was serious and awkwardly assured me that other athletes would kill for my calves and that I would appreciate them someday. It was cold comfort for a teenage girl who felt that her calves were the size of Christmas hams.

But that all fell away when we pulled up to my house, which was, to my relief, still standing. But everything was chaos, a frenzy of action. Fire trucks were parked haphazardly up and down the street. Firemen clomped in and out of the house, snaking their hoses back to their trucks. I saw my mother standing in the driveway with her arms crossed against her chest, looking impassive despite the catastrophe that had engulfed us. I ran up to her, looking around wildly for Rusky because I didn't see him in the yard, but there he was, safely ensconced in my mom's car, his scruffy face peering out the front window. He looked perfectly content. At least one of us was.

A couple of hours later, the firemen let us walk through the house to survey the damage. I was devastated—even though the fire had started in the basement, the smoke and water damage had still made it up the stairs and ruined parts of the first floor. Everything was sopping wet from the hoses and our shoes squelched across the carpet, which was stained dark from the moisture. It reminded me of blood, not freshly drawn from a new wound, but rusty and crusted from an old Band-Aid. There was no way we could continue living here.

I broke off from my mother and walked into my bedroom, listening to the intermittent dripping of our waterlogged belongings. My closet door was open and I could see only a few old shirts that were hanging limply from hangers. I didn't pause to think about where my clothes had gone; I was still in a deep state of shock. I did manage to locate my candy, though, which hadn't melted, but a fireman told me not to eat it, as it could be poisoned from the smoke and soot of the fire. I took it with me anyway, a comforting artifact of my life before it had literally gone up in flames.

Soon after, Red Cross representatives appeared at the scene and said they would help us relocate to a hotel while the home insurance claim was sorted out. We jumped at the chance to stay in a nice hotel and were put up in a swanky Marriott near LaGuardia Airport, which was not too far from our now former home.

My mother had miraculously managed to save our family photo albums and important documents, along with garbage bags full of my clothes and Philip's. They didn't even smell like smoke. And what about Rusky, who was always left in the house when we were at work and school? My mother explained that Rusky had thrown up the morning of the fire and, taking pity on him, she decided to bring him with her on her morning errands.

Which would have made sense to me if my mother were less precious about her car. She had just bought a brand-new Nissan Stanza and she was ready to pounce on us if we even looked at the car in the wrong way. She wouldn't even let Phil or me walk the dog down the driveway when the car was parked, because she was afraid Rusky would jump up and scratch the finish. Phil and I would jokingly come up with crazy, pigs-will-fly scenarios that would be likelier than my mom letting Rusky in her car. So you can see why this story coming from the woman who wanted to name our pet "Dog" didn't ring true to me.

The firemen reported that the fire had started in the basement on the couch where we threw all our dirty laundry in lieu of a hamper. Strange—I knew I hadn't yet done my laundry that week, but the clothes that I had thrown on the couch were in the garbage bag that my mother had handed over to me.

Oline had been even more stressed than usual of late. She hadn't realized that a house would require so much upkeep, and that our battered house had a litany of things wrong with it. Her mortgage payments were steep, and she had, as a last resort, pulled my brother out of Catholic school to save money. She'd even come to me once, asking to borrow money to pay the mortgage that month.

My father, who was supposed to pay her rent for his basement lodging, had stopped, offering some feeble excuse while refusing to move out. His sweet-talking and reminiscing about the good days no longer worked on her. She desperately wanted him gone but, due to generous renters' laws in New York, she'd have to go through the courts if she wanted him gone for good, and that would be expensive.

I'm not saying my mother started the fire, but . . . she started the fire. Not that she ever admitted it to us, but looking back, it's clear that she did. If you're still skeptical, here's something that might sway you: years later, I learned that in the days before the fire, she had stored some of our furniture in a friend's garage. Yeah.

I don't think my mother actually knew what she was up against when she decided to engage in some lighthearted arson. I think she thought that her insurance company would see that her house was damaged by fire and would write her a check, simple as that, case closed. Obviously real life doesn't work that way, and the investigation was ruled as "suspicious," which meant that it dragged on for months.

In the meantime, my mother, Phil, and I stayed at the Marriott gratis. Phil and I had our own room, which connected to my mother's by a door on both sides of our rooms, but that meant that she was out of sight. We could jump on the beds if we wanted to, and we could watch whichever TV show we wanted. We both had our own sinks in the bathroom, and the steaming shower always produced hot water, fast, without sputtering rust. The sheets were soft and the comforters were thick, and the swag valances for the windows were in the same burgundy paisley pattern as the comforters. We could even order room service, which my mother said the insurance would pay for, so we tried out the entire menu, always ordering more than we needed to, sampling things that we'd never had before, like shrimp cocktail, eggs Benedict, and chicken cordon bleu. Steak and eggs was our go-to for breakfast, arriving hot, hidden under silver-domed plate covers, accompanied by fancily cut sliced strawberries that we never ate.

But even luxury can get boring if it's a constant. Phil and I started grousing at each other, annoyed to be stuck in the same room together all the time. Jumping on the bed lost its appeal. We got bored of steak and eggs. There was no stove for my mother to cook on, of course, and she missed her Haitian standbys. Even though I hated when my mother would drag us to the chicken seller where she would pick out a chicken soon to have its neck wrung, and serve it to us a few hours after we'd last seen it clucking, I missed her cooking, too. I would even settle for staring at the creepy, glassy-eyed goat heads she'd bring home if it meant that she could make one of my favorite dishes, tassot cabrit, fried goat.

Luckily, just around the time that Phil and I were ready to strangle each other, the investigation concluded in our favor and my mother got her payout. Having learned her lesson with the Elmhurst house, Mommy decided we would take up residence in an apartment again—this time in Briarwood, Queens, which was about a twenty-minute drive away. We could still go to our respective schools and see our friends, which was a relief. Things were looking up for Oline and her little family.

There was a slight hitch amid all these positive developments, though. That unpleasant business with my computer class cheating had come back to haunt me—the school told me that even though I was allowed to walk with my class at graduation, I wasn't allowed to graduate because I would be required to take the computer class again. It was some floppy-disk fuckery, and I simply couldn't have it. How would I ever be able to look my mother in the eye and tell her I had failed my senior year?

In despair, I went to the guidance counselor's office to plead my case. It looked like a lot of others had the same idea, as there was a long line snaking out her door, students there to complain or to sign up for summer school or night school. When it was finally my turn, I sat down and faced the counselor. I was surprised to feel hot tears pricking my eyes. She looked back at me and said as kindly as possible, "Cin, you've managed to scrape by these past four years, but you know that Ms. Leung failed you for her class." I nodded mutely.

She continued, more softly, "And I know you know why." I hung my head, fighting the urge to start bawling uncontrollably in front of her.

"But—" she continued. I raised my eyes. "But" was good!

"But I have discussed this issue with Mr. Serber, and we think it's in your best interest to let you graduate with your class. We just don't think it makes sense for you to stay," she finished, smiling at me.

"So off you go," she said, and I rocketed out of my seat before she could change her mind.

I couldn't believe my luck. Maybe they needed to up their graduation rate, or maybe they were just tired of me and my antics. It didn't matter—I was out of here!

On graduation day, I fiddled with my cap's tassel and prepared to enter the gymnasium with my mom, Glifford, Phil, Catalina, and Kenya for the ceremony.

Suddenly, and unwelcomely, Fab suddenly appeared out of the blue, all smiles and goodwill. We hadn't seen the man in months—he had disappeared shortly before the fire. We figured he was in Haiti, selling fake papers that might get a desperate soul into the United States—or not. Either way, we believed we were rid of him once and for all, and his appearance at my school was unwelcome. I wasn't sure how he had even known that today was the day—he must have called the school. In case you think Fab had finally seen the error of his ways and decided to step up as a father, I'm going to stop you right there. Fab always had an ulterior motive, and his daughter's graduation was no exception.

He put his arm around my mother's shoulders, which she shrugged off immediately, so he grabbed Phil and me and strode confidently into the auditorium, making loud noises about how proud he was of his family. What a charade.

While I waited for my turn to be called to walk onstage, I tried to ignore my father, which wasn't hard, as he was ignoring all of us—he didn't wish me congratulations, didn't ask us how we were after the fire. I sneaked a glance at him and noticed a button on his flashy suit jacket that called out, "ASK ME HOW TO LOSE WEIGHT!" He had swiveled to talk to the people behind us about his new business venture, which sounded an awful lot like a pyramid scheme. He clearly had come looking for fresh meat.

When my name was called, I walked down the aisle and onto the stage where I had a clear view of everyone in the auditorium. I waved to my mom, Glifford, and Phil and then watched in horror as Fab passed out pamphlets to the family sitting next to us. He hadn't even realized that my name had been called—he was trying to pass pamphlets to the whole row! I was mortified and pissed off. Dude shows up to my graduation hawking some weight-loss program and telling my friends' parents that they're fat and need to lose weight? Good God.

After the ceremony, everyone milled around and my dad continued to sleaze. I'm surprised he didn't find a way to set up a folding table for his pamphlets. As my teachers walked up to me to congratulate me, Fab rejoined our group so that he could show off as Mr. Dad. He squeezed my shoulder, laughing with them about something, which I knew was my cue to smile and not move. My teachers lapped it all up like cream—in a few short moments they'd already fallen for his charms. I doubt they'd be laughing if they knew that Fab couldn't even tell them how old I was.

They finally drifted away, one of them looking back over her shoulder to eye my dad approvingly, and Mr. Serber walked over. Would he rat me out? I had never told my mom that I was in danger of being held back. I waited for the hammer to fall. But he just said, "You must be so proud of Cin!" I looked up at him in surprise. He just winked at me and said, "Enjoy your summer, Cin, and be your best," before walking off to greet a happier family.

Chapter 7

COLLEGE WASN'T IN THE CARDS FOR ME. WHILE I had no doubt that I was smart enough to get by in college, there was just no money for me to go, and I wasn't about to take out loans. Oline had burned all her savings to send Glifford to college upstate, buying him a dark blue Chevy Beretta so he could drive down to visit us on weekends. Besides, she had shown me that with enough hustling, I could still be successful and make something of myself in this world. Her faith in a better life was intrinsically tied to New York City, where anyone could achieve their dreams if they just tried hard enough. And I was already here, wasn't I?

I had a good thing going, too, working at a corporate store of Cohen's Fashion Optical, where I had begun selling contacts to passersby at just fifteen, and by eighteen I'd worked my way up to become one of the franchise's top salespeople in the area. Not too shabby for a teenager from Patterson Projects.

I'd stumbled onto the job because of Catalina. She had fast become my best friend and we were always getting into shit together for better or worse. I was a constant fixture at her house and was always grabbing an extra plate to eat as much as I could there. Catalina's dad owned a couple of stores on the Lower East Side, a bodega and a butcher shop that he'd given the family name, the Santos Bodega. A sweet gesture, but I always thought it was kind of funny that the family was memorialized with animal parts. While always clean, the air there was permeated with the iron tang of blood, and whole hogs were hung from the ceiling by chains. Hams and sausages, too, were strung up like party balloons as if for a meaty, macabre celebration. And if you stooped to look into the store's gleaming glass cases, something would inevitably stare back at you. On weekends, the shop was always at its busiest. *Abuelas*, husbands, or children sent on errands by their mothers would come in, the tinkle of the store bell announcing their arrival, to retrieve whatever would be on their plates that night. They'd pull a paper ticket from the take-a-number dispenser and greet their neighbors loudly, shouting out their orders in Spanish for one of the butchers who always started out dressed crisply in white, accessorized by a paper hat and an apron that would be bloodied by the end of the day. They'd watch as the butcher would grind "hamburg meat" or truss up a whole pig or wrap up chickens tidily in brown paper before they would head out with their neatly wrapped parcels bound for cramped kitchens.

This was the respectable side of the business. The shop always served as a meeting place for an odd assortment who came in and out, with workers leaving the store out the back entrance flush with cash, and maybe some lunch meat for a snack.

We all had a vague inkling that Catalina's dad was supplementing the family's income through other means beyond pork and beef but it didn't faze anyone—you did what you had to to make it, even if those efforts were not always aboveboard.

Catalina's dad was soft-spoken and nice, totally unlike Fab, always asking how I was doing, never bothered by my almost constant presence in his house. Unfortunately, both he and Fab were infected with machismo, though I never told her that—I never talked to her about Fab or the abuse he heaped on our family. Catalina's dad, Dominican and Catholic, never hit her and never yelled at her, but he was still able to make her feel small. Though he had no qualms with a woman working, he believed that a woman was meant to take care of family needs first. That included his girls catering to men. In fact, Catalina and Kenya would need to take off his shoes and socks when he arrived home. Catalina's brother was constantly spoiled, forever getting the latest video games and sneakers, their mother coddling him, picking up his plate for seconds as soon as he put his fork down. On Christmas, Catalina and Kenya got far fewer gifts while their brother made out like a bandit, all because he was male.

Catalina dutifully quashed many of the dreams that she had for herself in service to her family's expectations. Her only small transgressions were staying out late at the club with me, sneaking back into her home quietly so as not to wake her family. On these nights I'd stay over at Catalina's, sleeping in and waking up to the smell of her mother cooking breakfast. Always hungry, I'd pad downstairs and grab a plate, Catalina's mother loading me up with dishes that make my mouth water to this day: fried salami and eggs, dripping with grease; seasoned, smashed plantains called *mangu*, boiled yuca topped with red onion and garlic.

"So, I heard something around two a.m., or so—that wouldn't have happened to be you girls, would it?" Catalina's mother would ask me, plying me with food.

"Oh, yeah, that was us," I would say, gulping down some fresh-squeezed orange juice that Catalina's mother had.

After several bribed breakfasts in which Catalina's mother peppered me with questions, Catalina pulled me aside, realizing that while she slept, her mother was interrogating me. She needed to do damage control before I confessed everything!

"Cin, you can't tell my parents anything!" she hissed at me. "I'll get in trouble!"

Fab being so incredibly disconnected from his children's lives, it simply hadn't occurred to me that Catalina's parents, her father in particular, would care what we were doing and at what time we returned home. Mind you, this kind of overreaching from Catalina's parents continued for years, even when we were nineteen and twenty. Catalina always chafed for her freedom, never quite managing to get it. A few years later, she would move from her parents' home to a new home complete with controlling husband, who ended up being worse than her parents.

When we were teenagers, Catalina helped out her dad by taking orders and answering the phone on Sundays when the shop was the most crowded. In return he would pay her an entire forty bucks a day. As a result, Catalina was always loaded and her spending money was forever burning a hot hole in her pocket.

This is how I found myself in a mall for the very first time in my life at fifteen, tagging along with Catalina as she tried on platforms at Nine West and frowningly assessed herself in the mirror at Contempo Casuals in the Queens Center Mall. Even though I had some disposable income from my lunch ticket business, I was pretty good about saving it except to serve my sugar fix, handing over scrounged coins and crumpled dollars for Boston Baked Beans, Now & Laters, or Chicco sticks at the bodega. I rarely joined in with Catalina on her buying sprees at the mall, content to watch her buy whatever flimsy top or tight skirt she had in mind for wearing out that particular weekend.

A rare exception to this rule was the starter jacket I bought at the Colosseum in Jamaica—I gladly ponied up for what was, at the time, the coolest piece of fashion in 1990s Queens. All the trendy kids wore them, and mine was a Syracuse University jacket, dark blue with orange. Starter jackets were so coveted that unruly teens would terrorize the subway trains and steal these prized possessions off kids' backs. I was never robbed but I always kept a close eye out when I was wearing mine, wary that someone would demand I hand it over.

One lazy afternoon while Catalina and I were strolling around the mall, I heard someone call out to us. I looked over to see a girl stationed in front of an eyewear store. She waved us over and asked whether I wanted to try out colored contacts for free. Colored contacts were all the hype back then, especially for Black girls who were tired of their brown eyes and wanted a shade more "exciting" (read: more white), like green or blue. I was perfectly content with my brown eyes so I demurred, but I did see something I wanted. I knew I was likable and persuasive when I wanted to be, and I didn't give a shit if people turned me down; I'd faced much worse than a stranger telling me "no." I knew I could do better than this girl who hadn't swayed me or Catalina even a bit on the contacts. I could do this job easy. That poor girl must have regretted her decision to try to reel me in because I applied for a job on the spot, and I was quickly approved; maybe the store owners thought that I could get Black folks in for colored contacts and then the eyewear salespeople could take over and get people to pay real money for sunglasses, who knows. The reason didn't matter to me.

Back then, you only needed to be fourteen to get working papers, and I was fifteen, so it felt nice to be making an honest living again. My evenings and weekends were soon taken over by Cohen's as I sought to make as much cash as I could, and if I wasn't at school or at home, I was inevitably at the mall. My mother didn't mind, as she knew I was staying out of trouble, and it might also have been a relief to her that she could fall back on me to borrow money for her mortgage or, later, the rent, which she did once or twice, though she always paid me back as soon as she had the money to do so. Even though I would never have admitted it out loud, I craved her approval and it made me happy to lend her the money, to show her that I was industrious and I was succeeding, actively participating in her American dream. She never said anything beyond a gruff "thank you," though, and I didn't know how to ask her for the validation I so desperately sought from her.

Shopping malls are facing extinction these days as people rely increasingly on online retailers, like Bezos's behemoth, Amazon. The convenience of clicking and having a package arrive neatly on your doorstep with whatever you'd decided you needed in your life the day before *is* hard to beat. You see articles online titled "SEE WHAT HAPPENED TO THIS ABANDONED MALL," with photos revealing a Sears with ghostly mannequins in terrifying shadow or cracked atriums in which plants have taken root, nature slowly but surely reclaiming what man so carelessly abandoned.

Gen Xers often recall malls of the eighties and nineties with warm nostalgia. There was a certain guaranteed familiarity and security attached to the mall—you always knew what you were getting when you entered that air-conditioned sanctuary of comfortable capitalism. Malls were tied up in our collective identity then, much like *Family Matters*, acid-washed jeans, and *The Firm*–era Tom Cruise (not to mention the Gulf War, Princess Di's death, and the Rwandan genocide).

This is the energy that you have to tap into when thinking about my years working at the Queens Center Mall. Everyone went there—white, Black, Latinx, a mélange of Queens residents, all ready to spend their hard-won paychecks on retail goods. All the buses and trains conveniently led to the mall, located in Elmhurst, and I could easily get there from our house, and later, after that burned down, our apartment.

The mall was always brightly lit, signage blazing into the darkest corners of the parking garage where people would drop

off their boxy sedans and minivans, Aerostars, Trans Ams, and
Celicas reigning supreme in that day, before heading into the
mall.

Upon entering from the parking garage, you'd find yourself
deposited into the food court. As soon as you walked in through
the food court entrance, you'd be greeted by the slightly nauseating smell of old grease, thanks to the Arthur Treacher's Fish
and Chips, which was headquartered there. Mixed into the fish
smell was the more alluring scent of hot pretzel, which you
could score at Auntie Anne's, the clear winner there being the
cinnamon-sugar pretzel that would get your hands deliciously
dirty. There was also a McDonald's, a Sbarro, and an Asian
fusion place that in later years would offer little bites of General
Tso's chicken on toothpicks in the hopes of luring customers
away from the food court's other offerings.

There were, of course, the other requisite retailers scattered
throughout the mall's three floors: a Gap, which was usually the
most crowded; a KB Toy Store, a Victoria's Secret, a Bang Bang,
an Aldo, an Aéropostale, a Macy's, a JCPenney, a Claire's, a Bath
& Body Works, and the aforementioned Contempo Casuals,
Nine West, and, of course, Cohen's Fashion Optical.

It wasn't the swankiest mall by far—if you wanted premium
stores, you'd need to drive into Long Island to Roosevelt Field
Mall (nobody I knew ever thought to go into Manhattan), and
once there, you could shop at places like The Limited, Charles
David, and Armani Exchange. But Queens Center Mall was
busy enough, as convenient as it was for Elmhurst and its surrounding enclaves. And Cohen's Optical, next to the food court
on the second floor, was prime real estate.

This was my home away from home for the next three or
so years, and while the customers may have shifted, most of
us who worked at the mall stayed there, our names and faces
imprinted on each other. There was Ralph, the burly Black secu-

rity guard, who was always patrolling the halls. He went out with a Latinx girl who worked at the mall, and they had a serious relationship. The guy who ran the kiosks that were sprinkled across the mall sold hand lotion and assorted light-up toys and tchotchkes, and he was mysteriously ageless—he could have been thirty or sixty for all I knew. The food court workers were mostly young people who would serve me my crispy fillet and for dessert, my cinnamon-sugar pretzel with a friendly nod and a "hey."

I was always running late to work but my bosses didn't seem to mind, as I was so good at my job. I would work a couple of days a week after school and then at least one shift on the weekends, often being entrusted to the late shift starting when I was just a sophomore in high school.

I began at the store's entrance, passing out flyers and holding demonstrations for those I could convince to try colored contacts, urging people to sit in my chair so I could interview them and show them what they would look like with different-colored eyes using what was, back then, cutting-edge graphics software on a computer. Within only a few months, my bosses had taken notice of my skills and promoted me to the sales floor where I was the youngest by far—everyone else on the floor was in their twenties to fifties. I wasn't at all intimidated, though; I was energized by the challenge, and I would set sky-high sales goals for myself, only to raise them when I'd beaten my own targets. The single rule I gave myself was that I wouldn't offer anyone a special deal. Nobody was getting a discount off me. They'd buy from me at full price so I could reap the rewards.

While the mall itself wasn't flashy, Cohen's sold high-end brands—Cartier, Gaultier, Gucci, Valentino, Burberry. Think of a designer brand and we most likely had it. As a result, theft was high in our store. The bottoms of our glass cases could be pushed out to show customers frames, and if we weren't watching like hawks, these "customers" could slip a frame or four into their pockets and amble out without buying anything. I could always spot a real customer from a fake one, which also made me a better salesperson—I never wasted my time on a mark unless I knew I could get them to shell out. My natural abilities, especially as someone who was still a teenager, didn't win me any friends in the store, but I didn't mind. I'd sell a customer sunglasses and then, in the same visit, get them to upgrade their prescription *and* buy contacts, the latter of which was definitely not in my department—I was supposed to refer them over to the contacts salespeople. Better me than them was how I looked at it.

And I was making very good money, enough for me to be promoted to other stores that wanted my skills. By this point, right before I hit eighteen, I had saved enough money to get the hell out of Dodge and rent my own room in Bayside, Queens. This was a relief, I suspected, to both my mother and me. We had been fighting more, as I chafed for independence, to get out from under her thumb, away from her heavy moods. I waited until she came home from work; then I broke it to her as she assembled ingredients for dinner, each efficient movement she made I'd seen a thousand times before.

"Mommy, I'm leaving. I found a place of my own," I said.

She finished chopping her onion, her back to me. She put down her knife and turned around, giving me a long look, staring at me down the bridge of her nose.

"Okay," she said finally.

"Okay?"

"Okay."

She knew she couldn't hold me back, and while I knew she might have wanted us all together, she wasn't worried about whether I could take care of myself. She knew I'd be fine.

With my salary, I also bought myself a car to take me to the various Cohen's across Queens and Long Island.

One store on Long Island was a non-franchised Cohen's, which meant that I'd get paid more—base salary plus increased commission and bonuses—plus they'd pay for my gas to and from work. The owners were seemingly nice enough—Burt and Carol Wheeler had a few businesses, including this Cohen's, but something struck me as just a bit off. The store was huge, but often empty. Sometimes, I wondered if the store was a front for something illegal. Carol was an optometrist and always dressed professionally, but her long, lank hair looked dry and brittle, and she always had dried blood crusted around her cuticles from picking at them. She was someone who could only be described as "faded"—it was as if you could see through her when she was standing right in front of you. She was very quiet and rarely spoke to me except for the times when I might fall asleep standing up because business was slow. She'd shake me awake and I'd startle to attention, but then she'd evaporate to the back of the store, emerging only to wake me up again if needed.

On the flip side, Burt was charismatic and extremely good-looking, much younger in appearance than Carol; he put me in mind a little bit of JFK Jr. He had thick, dark hair and intensely icy blue eyes that you could feel yourself falling into if you weren't careful. He liked to wear tight Levi's and work boots and, in winter, trendy ski jackets. He was always joking around with customers and staff, but still, I didn't trust him—he gave off a creeper vibe that I just couldn't shake. It was only after one of my coworkers at a different Cohen's filled me in that I knew I'd been right all along, even if I didn't know why. Burt was a registered sex offender—he'd been caught masturbating in front of a school bus filled with children. By the way, did I mention he had twin toddlers?

This was horrifying, and I wanted to get away from the store as soon as possible, even though I was making up to a thousand dollars a week at that store. I didn't care—I didn't want to be around a pedophile if I didn't have to be. I dropped the store from my rotation and subbed in a Cohen's in Hicksville on Long Island.

⤖

I don't know about you, but it's easy for me to pinpoint certain times in my life that I knew would change me forever. Believe if you want to or not, but the hand that came for me in my crib when I was a toddler settled something heavy and ominous on me for years to come. My parents handcuffing and whipping me until my back was shredded was another turning point in my life. And one seemingly quiet day at the Hicksville Cohen's Optical offered a surprising moment that propelled me forward into a new life.

I had just turned nineteen, had escaped from the deviant Burt Wheeler, and was newly installed at the Hicksville store. This mall was nothing special—it, perhaps, was slightly nicer than Queens Center Mall, but not by much. Still, I could land big sales because I knew how to get people to stack their purchases. I'd sell them glasses, sure, but then I'd get them to upgrade their lenses to scratch guard (bonus!), anti-glare (bonus!), and high index (bonus!), sign them up for a credit card (bonus!), and get them to purchase the most expensive insurance (bonus!). Then I'd scoop the contacts girls and sell their contacts out from under them. No mercy.

It was a perfectly nondescript Monday and I was trying, again, in vain, not to fall asleep on my feet—a habit that had followed me to this store. Catalina and I had gone out the night before to party even though it was a Sunday, and I was exhausted. The pervasive buzzing of the store's bright lights also wasn't helping the headache that was ravaging me. Still, I straightened up when I saw a customer walk in. It was pouring that day, from one of those storms that dumps rain from the skies to the point that you don't remember what dry feels like and you've resigned yourself to having damp, steaming socks for the rest of your life. It was that kind of storm.

The woman was pasty white and slightly chunky; to protect from the weather, she had on a tan, trench-style raincoat, the kind with floppy, oversize lapels and a drooping belt. She wore her hair in a frizzy ponytail, her big, curly bangs mussed beyond repair from the rain. Her oversize, cheap-looking glasses were fogged and she seemed very out of sorts, wringing moisture from her clothes and looking around helplessly like a fawn in the woods, lost without its mother. I had a live one, folks.

In my years of working at various Cohen's stores, I'd learned that you should never judge anyone by their appearance. I treated everyone exactly the same, with respect, because you never knew, someone seemingly flashy could end up being miserly and someone looking unremarkable could easily spend thousands. So I certainly wasn't going to assume this disheveled, out-of-sorts woman was a lost cause. Besides, I really did enjoy what I did: I took pride in finding the best pair of lenses and frames for each individual I encountered, no matter their budget. After all, having a pair of glasses on your face every single day shapes your identity and how you're perceived by others. I wanted everyone who worked with me to walk out of the store feeling amazing. If they did, there would be a good chance that that customer would come back or would refer someone to me.

I walked over and solicitously asked the woman if she needed any assistance. Turns out she was in the market for a new pair of glasses. Her current frames were incredibly dated, and her lenses were thick, making her eyes look owlish. She desperately needed an overhaul, and I was up for the task. That day I sold her multiple pairs of glasses that she dropped some serious dollars on, which was a very nice, tidy sale for me. I figured I was on a roll, so I entreated her to sign up for the interest-free Cohen's credit card, which would net me a quick ten-dollar bonus if her application was approved. I always attempted this with customers so that they would feel able to breathe a bit easier and spend more. She seemed to be under my spell, this Shannon, let's call her, and when offered the card application, she meekly took it and began filling it out submissively. Of course, I never walked away when customers were filling out their applications—I didn't want them to begin feeling hesitant about sharing intimate details about their financial history. So I'd make small talk with them while slyly pulling out some expensive frames and placing them gently atop the glass case for them to notice the first time their eyes strayed from the application. By the time they left the store, not only had I made them feel like a million bucks, but I also had them thinking they'd made a new friend. I wasn't good at what I did, I was great; more than great, in fact. In my years of working in the eyewear business, I only had a single, solitary return—a wife had spied how much her husband had spent on the frames that I had sold him that day so she marched him back to the store to return them. By the time I was done with her, not only did Hubs keep his original purchase but Wifey had bought her own pair, far outspending him!

I could see Shannon was adding a lot of zeros to the income box on the application. I glanced down and saw that she had estimated that she made ten thousand dollars a month. I looked up and surveyed Shannon with fresh eyes. What did *she* do to make this kind of money, exactly? I couldn't wait for her to finish her application to find out—I had to know right now. I interrupted whatever it was that she was saying to ask and was dumbfounded by her response. She looked up at me over the rim of her thick glasses, which were sliding down the bridge of her nose.

"Oh, I'm a stockbroker. I work on Wall Street," she told me, pushing her glasses back into place with her pointer finger, the universal sign for geek, before turning back to finish the application.

I knew very well that I shouldn't judge people by their appearances, but hold the phone. Haggard, tired, messy Shannon was a stockbroker? I knew very little about stockbrokers—even though I never forgot the conversation I'd had with Ali and still very much had designs to someday get in on the stock market, I didn't think that someone like *this* could actually be a real, live stockbroker, making trades, yelling at assistants to fetch them coffee—whatever it was that my young mind believed stockbrokers to do. I thought that all stockbrokers were, first, men, and second, white men. Slickly attired, hair meticulously coiffed, ten-thousand-dollar-suit-wearing men who looked and sounded like Gordon Gekko in *Wall Street*, who had car phones and knew how to play squash and held Ivy League degrees and were married to people with ridiculous nicknames like Bitsy or Missy or Betts.

Not . . . Shannon.

My brain put these seemingly mismatched puzzle pieces together, things slowly clicking into place in my mind. If *Shannon* of all people could be a stockbroker . . . why, then, couldn't I?

Chapter 8

I T'S LONG GONE NOW, JUST A MEMORY PULSING IN MY head, but back in 1996, the Treinta Treinta Club at 30-30 Northern Boulevard in Queens was bumping. And it was a large part of why I kept falling asleep at work. Catalina loved to drag me to the club and dance the night away, she returning to her home sweaty and satisfied, me to mine exhausted and rumpled, shortly before the pink sun broke across the skyline on us. I was ambivalent about the scene—the shadowy bodies pressed up against one another, the tinny trumpet ringing constantly in my ears, the intermittent flashes of light illuminating the crowded dance floor, revealing swinging skirts and nimble feet stepping to salsa and bachata. It didn't do it for me, but Catalina's entreaties for company always worked on me. Not that she needed me—everyone loved Catalina, and it's not an exaggeration to say that when she walked into a room, people would break out into wide grins just to see her arrived to them. Back then she had a beautiful, wild mass of long, curly hair haloing her face and falling down her back. She wore thick mascara and ringed her warm brown eyes in black smudgy eyeliner, and men—and women—would do a double take to get another look at Catalina when she walked by. But the attention never went to her head—she truly was nice to everyone. *Santa*

Catalina, I would think to myself, when I'd see her taking time to talk to the *viejitas*, the stooped old ladies in the neighborhood, and the awkward wallflowers at the club who couldn't gather quite enough courage to ask her to dance.

Treinta Treinta required us to dress up to gain entrance. For Catalina, that meant tight skirts and even tighter, low-cut shirts that revealed a dangerous dip of curve and skin. It wasn't out of the question for Catalina's breasts to make an accidental appearance at the club, to which Catalina would simply adjust herself and laugh it off. As for me, I'd wear dresses, mostly from Ann Taylor—one of my bosses at Cohen's had insisted that I buy nicer clothes for work so one day she took me to Great Neck's Miracle Mile mall to stock up, as the pants and blouses that I'd been wearing weren't cutting it.

A performer that Catalina adored was going to be at Treinta Treinta that night so I cut off Catalina's pleas to join her with a resigned yes and we got ready together at her house. My own place wasn't really a viable option: I had moved into a sort of boardinghouse that let rooms cheaply in exchange for rent payment once a week. I'd lucked out and found a room in Bay Terrace, an exclusive neighborhood of Bayside, Queens, filled with quiet families who lived in well-kept, multistory homes on the water. It was a largely white, sleepy, affluent neighborhood that didn't see much crime or action of any kind. I found the room through one of my coworkers, Marge, whose mother had owned the house for years, having bought it for chump change decades before. I roomed with Marge in her spare bedroom for a few months before she, having gone through my stuff one day and found wads of cash—my life savings—informed me matter-of-factly that it looked like I had enough disposable income to move downstairs into my own room. So I did.

Marge's mother, a *yia yia* named Helen, was an elderly Greek woman who was very clearly dealing with a serious case of

PTSD, though we didn't have the language to identify it as such back then. Many years before, Helen had been violently raped in her home. After the ordeal, she picked herself up and limped outside where she would recount to me later that she saw a white rose on her doorstep, which she interpreted as a threat of death if she reported the rape. Helen was forever marked by the violation. She took to her home with her Shih Tzus and rarely left, terrified that the shadowy intruder would return to finish what he started, even decades after it had happened.

Helen was lovely—she considered me her best friend after her dogs—and she cooked Greek delicacies for me, ordering me in a firm, grandmotherly fashion to eat her spanakopita and dolmadakia and baklava, which I did with pleasure. We were close, and I was honored that she shared her history with me. But poor Helen's trauma kept her forever shuttered in her house, and as a result, the house reflected her habits. The walls of the house were stained a sooty gray from years of Helen's anxious chain-smoking—she was never found without a shaky cigarette between her gnarled fingers. Because of this, everything I owned smelled like stale smoke, and I was constantly worried that people would smell my clothing at work and I'd be penalized in some way.

My bedroom was tiny—it had a daybed and a cheap prefab dresser that I'd bought at IKEA, and not much else. I left my bedroom window cracked even in the winter to get some much-needed ventilation, choked from the smoke as I was, and I constantly battled with Helen's children over it, as they felt I was wasting precious dollars in heating. I was lucky enough to have my own bathroom, but the one time my toilet broke I had to use Helen's bathroom for a couple of days. I was horrified to discover dozens upon dozens of stubbed-out cigarettes littering the bathroom—in the soap dish, on top of the toilet, everywhere— all of them crooked, waterlogged reminders of Helen's pain. I was relieved when my toilet was fixed and I didn't have to visit her bathroom anymore—I didn't want to imagine Helen putting out the embered remains of a cigarette into her soap, surveying the invisible scars on her withered body in the bathtub.

Because she rarely left the house, Helen did not walk her Shih Tzus, which meant that the dogs pissed and shat all over the floors. Helen wasn't up for cleaning, so the urine would sink into the carpet and the little piles of shit would add to the sharp stink of filth in the house. Maybe now you can see how I was able to afford to live in such a nice neighborhood.

About a year after I moved in with Helen, a fire ravaged the house next door. There was damage done to Helen's house, and off we were to a hotel for a bit; this scene seemed all too familiar, the irony. Helen was able to get brand-new floors and finishing for the house. It could have been a fresh start, perhaps, but the new-old house soon fell back into its grimy state, as Helen couldn't change her habits with her trauma that ran deep.

Treinta Treinta was on Northern Boulevard by the Queensboro Bridge, so it wasn't a far trek for us to get from Catalina's house to the club in my car, a nice white Acura Legend that my mom had scored cheaply for me at an auction. Unfortunately, the transmission went kaput soon after we bought it, and my mother took the former owner to small claims court and won, but not before he had hidden a dead rat under the hood of the car. It was summertime and the smell was foul—even worse than eau de Casa Yia Yia—and it lingered long after we'd extricated the rat. I was the only one in my friend circle to have a car, though, so we used it anyway, breathing out of our mouths and driving with the windows all the way down for weeks.

The line to get into Treinta Treinta snaked around the block, but we never had difficulty getting in, the price of entrance being the flash of a smile from Catalina. The bouncer glanced over at us and immediately let us in, not bothering to check

our IDs. We were underage so we didn't often drink there—
the energy in the club was usually enough of an intoxicant for
us, though occasionally we'd sneak sips of Malibu Rum from a
shared flask before entering the club.

Catalina and I pushed through the crowd to the dance floor
and I let Catalina do her thing while I bobbed along in time to
the music, some brassy, fast number that had everyone dancing
in seemingly perfect rhythm with one another.

After a while, Catalina, sweaty with exertion, went to the
bathroom and came back with a strange message for me.

"Cin! Guess who I ran into!" she yelled at me above the din
of the music. She didn't wait for a response.

"I bumped into Alex outside of the bathroom! He looks
great!" she shouted. "And he wants to talk to you! Something
about business," she yelled, grinning at me before making her
way back to the dance floor. I raised an eyebrow. Catalina was
so loving that she trusted everyone, including our mutual
friend Alex.

Even though I liked the guy well enough, I was on my
guard—Alex was a fast talker, and he often was found sharing
schemes and telling tall tales to anyone who would listen. He
had a twin, JP, who would weave his own stories together with
Alex's, to make them all the more believable. Having grown up
with Fab, I knew a player when I saw one and took anything
Alex or JP said with a mountain of salt.

Still, I was curious to know why Alex was looking for me specifically. I spotted Alex and wandered over to him, where he was
in the midst of regaling a small audience with one of his stories.
When he saw me, he broke into a grin and gave his admirers the
universal "be right back" sign and ambled over to me.

I looked Alex up and down, a bit mystified. He was dressed
in a sharp suit, admittedly expensive-looking, but out of place
for the club, which was sweltering—everyone else was in short

sleeves. Frankly, he looked ridiculous in a suit and tie. Who was he trying to impress?

Me, apparently. When I posed the obvious question to him—*Why the hell are you wearing a formal suit in a club?*—he told me that the suit was exactly the reason why he was looking for me. Huh.

Alex gave a self-satisfied smile and I could see he was winding himself up for another tale.

"Cin, this suit is from my broker, Abel. He had it made for me—it cost him a couple thousand. I'm working for an investment firm down on Wall Street."

The mention of "Wall Street" piqued my interest. Only a few days before I had made my vow that I would become a stockbroker on Wall Street. Was Alex—fork-tongued Alex—my way in? I was skeptical. Still, I took the bait, knowing full well that he would give me an earful.

"Okay, Alex, but why wear a suit to a club? You can't dance in that."

Alex gave me another smile and an "aha" face.

"Cin, that's it, exactly! I'm not going to be dancing tonight. I'm going to be conducting business."

I cocked an eyebrow and gestured for him to continue, which he did excitedly.

"I'm working with brokers. They're making hundreds of thousands of dollars *a month*. I know you, Cin. You know how to sell. This could be *you*."

I scoffed. That was Monopoly money. Nobody made that much in a month. I was making almost $50,000 a year at Cohen's, and I was doing just fine, more than fine. Fifty K a year in 1996? I was living well.

"My broker is dressing me for the part. He's setting me up for success, Cin. And I want you to have that, too. I have an in. Come *on*."

This sounded like pyramid scheme bullshit to me, and Alex could see I was suspicious. He motioned for Mateo to walk over. Mateo was Catalina's ex, and I knew him to be a good guy.

Mateo stepped over to us and nodded along with Alex as he waxed on. Apparently Mateo was working with Alex at this brokerage firm on Wall Street, too. It was starting to sound a tad more believable. If Mateo was doing this, there had to be some sort of merit to it.

"Cin, you could be making millions down the road, I swear. It's easy work, it really is. You just have to take an exam to become a stockbroker. I know you can do it. This could change your life."

He was selling me hard on this. I didn't fully trust him—he had to be getting something in return to be putting in this much effort on me. Still. Was the universe giving me a sign? I'd just encountered Shannon a few days before and ever since, the thought that I, too, could become a stockbroker, *should* if Shannon could, had wormed its way into my brain, the thought rising again and again in my mind, stubbornly sticking, not going away.

"I can get you an interview at my company, Cin. Come on."

What did I have to lose? If it didn't pan out, so what? At least I had tried.

I gave Alex another long look, just to make him sweat a bit more than he already was. Then I slowly nodded at him, told him yes, I was in. He slapped my back and high-fived Mateo, looking gleeful.

It was a Saturday night. The following week, Alex already connected me for my interview.

Chapter 9

A PAIR OF NARROWED, UNBLINKING EYES STARED ME down, willing me to look away. I stared back—I knew that game, I wasn't going to lose.

I was looking at Brad Ambrosi, head recruiter for cold callers at VTR Capital, which was an offshoot firm of Stratton Oakmont, of *Wolf of Wall Street* infamy. We were in his glass box of an office, all chrome and black leather, and he hadn't said anything to me yet. A cheap intimidation tactic, I figured. I had time, I could wait him out. I stared around his office, my gaze settling on a signed football in a glass case, which was probably worth a good chunk of change.

Right after my somewhat impulsive decision to say yes to Alex, he had promptly followed through and connected me to this Brad guy. Or rather, his secretary, who, on the phone, sounded like she'd had this kind of conversation a million times. She recited what I needed to know in a mechanical, rushed jumble, her words holding on to each other for dear life as they flew out of her mouth. I envisioned her sitting at her neatly arranged desk, her hair permed and teased to dizzying heights, snapping her gum in annoyance whenever someone who wasn't Brad asked her to do something. I could feel her eye roll through the phone line. Whatever—I didn't care about her attitude—I wasn't going to be interviewing with her. She stayed on the phone with me long enough to deliver only what I needed to know before promptly hanging up, her receiver making that garbled crunching sound of being placed back into its cradle. The secretary had told me to report to 17 Battery Place, seventeenth floor, on Monday morning. I appreciated that little bit of tidy symmetry. For some reason, it felt like a sign that things would go well for me. Not that I needed signs—whenever I set out to do something, I was confident it would work out for me. This wasn't purely arrogance on my part, though if I'm being honest, there was some of that baked into my personality. It was largely that I knew I could achieve whatever I put my mind to, thanks to years of my mother drumming into me that anything was possible in America, that women could do anything that men could, and better. I loved proving that over and over again.

When Monday morning rolled around I was up earlier than I needed to be, excited to get going. I had been given an opportunity people would kill for, and I wanted to beat the morning traffic. I wasn't nervous—I knew I had this in the bag. In the two weeks since Alex had booked me for the interview with VTR Capital, I had already notified my bosses at Cohen's that I was going to work on Wall Street, that my days of selling eyewear were over. They just smirked at me and said I'd be back on the floor in no time; they weren't worried at all about losing one of their top salespeople. In fact, most of my friends and family who had heard about my impending interview felt the same way. I was only nineteen and had most likely been sold bullshit by some enterprising huckster on a dance floor—what the hell did I know?

I dressed quickly, choosing a serious-looking navy blue skirt suit and a blouse neatly tucked in with my collar partially up, which I felt would broadcast "She's a professional," before jumping into my car and zipping over to Battery Park in record time.

I had never been to Battery Park before, hadn't been to many neighborhoods in Manhattan, my life being firmly cemented in Queens, with excursions outside the borough made mostly to visit other Cohen's branches. Battery Park was located at the southern tip of Manhattan, Wall Street just a few steps north. Tall buildings crowded the streets, blocking out the sky almost entirely depending on where you stood. Broadway cut through all the way down to the water, where you could catch the Staten Island Ferry and see Lady Liberty tirelessly holding her torch. Nowadays, the Battery Park neighborhood is clean and manicured, with acres of sanitized park surrounding the water, families picnicking, couples holding hands, impromptu Frisbee sessions popping up. But back in the nineties, the neighborhood hadn't yet been revitalized to welcome the hordes of tourists it hosts today. The streets were grimier, sootier, its sidewalks mostly holding Wall Streeters, who, from the air, I imagined, looked like a swarm of horseflies, one collective body, a single swell of people attired in dark suits and ties, rushing to get to the trading floor, or, after work, to escape to a bar or a strip club. At night, the neighborhood was desolate, tumbleweeds of litter rolling in the streets, buildings darkened, sewer grates smoking, coffee carts locked and chained, awaiting their red-rim-eyed, caffeine-starved customers who would arrive the next morning demanding coffee and bagels. Only in recent years has the scene really picked up, with restaurants and bars popping up to cater to young professionals cashing in on FiDi rent deals and families dragging foot-sore children to see the sights and pay for overpriced artisanal whatever at Brookfield Place.

I found a parking spot on the street near 17 Battery Place almost immediately and eased the Acura expertly into the tight spot. I have always had good parking luck. While others might circle endlessly in the parking garage, searching in vain for a spot that wasn't miles away from their destination, delighted then furious to see a motorcycle hiding in what they thought had been an empty spot, I have always been able to laser in on those prized parking spaces. I can also magic a spot seemingly out of thin air, parallel parking in a space that shouldn't fit a Volkswagen Beetle, let alone my boxy car. I've parked in front of hydrants and in no-parking zones and have always escaped tickets. My friends always joked that I must have enacted some sort of vodou to have my luck. Maybe I did, maybe I didn't.

I had this in the bag! I smiled at myself in the rearview mirror, smoothing a few unruly hairs back into place, before locking the car and ignoring the parking meter. I walked the short distance from my parking spot to 17 Battery Place and craned my neck to look up at the building. It towered over me with more floors than I could count, a few architectural flourishes up its sides, with large windowed archways on the ground floor. I wasn't at all intimidated by its imposing stature and took my time, despite the fact that I was more than ten minutes late, entering the dark, sepulchered lobby, riding one of the gold-doored elevators up. I didn't need to rush—it would be the company's privilege to have me.

The elevator dinged and its doors opened to reveal a clean, nondescript hallway. I followed a sign for "VTR CAPITAL" and opened one of the double glass-paned doors, finding myself in a quiet, plush front office. The carpet was green like money, the furniture richly polished. The room radiated wealth, which was helpful for VTR—the company did its best to take it all from you. A receptionist at a big mahogany desk barely looked up at me and pointed me toward another room behind her without interrupting the call she was on. Okay.

I walked into the room and surveyed what was before me. The room was far less luxe than the waiting area I'd just exited— windowless and gray carpeted, with only a couple of chairs scattered around haphazardly. Harsh fluorescent lighting, the kind you often find in large offices, buzzed overhead. Despite the lack of sitting space, the room was full of people—all of whom were young guys, either Black or Latinx, and all of them looked like green motherfuckers. Most hugged the perimeter of the room, backs against the walls, arms folded or hanging listlessly by their sides. The room felt strangely heavy and lifeless. Nobody spoke to or even looked at one another. I didn't like the energy in here and didn't want to be near these chumps so I stood at the front of the room, waiting for my name to be called.

Despite the crowd of people assembled in this weird antechamber, I had no doubt that I would be hired. Alex had told me that he had assured Brad I was a top-notch salesperson and that Brad would like me. Turns out, Alex had good reason to try to get me hired. In addition to being a cold caller, Alex (Mateo, too) was a recruiter for VTR, sweeping up whoever he could bring to the firm, getting paid a referral fee if someone he brought in was hired as a cold caller. Cold callers were at the very bottom of the Wall Street food chain, ringing up strangers in the hopes of interesting them enough to do business with the firm. At that point, if the caller successfully netted an interested customer, the caller would hand that lead over to their broker, who did the "real" work of trading with the client. To supplement his cold caller income, Alex trawled wherever he could, malls, dance floors, wherever young men, almost always of color, congregated, hoping to harvest them for VTR so that he could reap the rewards. VTR also put ads out in the newspapers and went to high school fairs, always on the hunt for fresh meat to bring back to the company, as turnover was incredibly high. I suppose Alex thought I was one of the guys or that I was tough and could handle the, to put it mildly, challenging environment that VTR cultivated. Or maybe he just wanted to up his numbers that month. Whatever the reason, here I was, the only female in a sea of men. I didn't mind at all; in fact, I was more than ready to show VTR what I was capable of.

I didn't have to wait long. Some assistant read my name off a piece of paper, stumbling over "Fabré," like most do, pronouncing it "*Fay-ber,*" instead of the correct "*Fah-bray.*" She led me down a short hallway to Brad's office, where Brad, head recruiter of VTR, was awaiting me. Silently, he motioned to a chair. I sat down.

Here we go, I thought, excited.

But Brad clearly wasn't having fun. His hands crossed over his chest, he glared at me, refusing to say anything. His snarl reminded me a bit of Sylvester Stallone's from the Rocky franchise. I wasn't about to break, though. I stared back. I was fascinated by his hands—though small, they were the thickest, meatiest hands I'd ever seen on a person, which was comical because Brad didn't look to be a large man. His hands looked like they would be good for choking someone out or for throwing a heavy punch. While I waited for Brad to speak, I glanced over at his window. He had an amazing view looking out on the park and, past that, the water. I envisioned myself in Brad's place, leaning back in the leather chair, my feet up on the desk, speaking importantly to someone on the phone, twirling a pen idly, waving an assistant away because couldn't they see I was too busy with this important call?

I left my reverie because it looked like Brad was warming up to say something. Finally.

"Who sent you here?" he barked.

"Alex Navarro," I calmly replied. He stared back at me as if there was more for me to say and I was wasting his time while he waited for me to say it.

"Alex said that I could be a broker selling stocks and make quite a bit of money here," I told him.

He kept staring back at me vacantly with dead eyes. I was starting to get tired of his routine.

"What do you know about the stock market?" he asked me accusingly. He stood up from his giant leather chair, which looked far too big for him, and paced around me, sizing me up. He couldn't have been more than five-foot-five but his angry mafioso impression was strong.

"Not much," I replied calmly. "But I'm good at selling, so just tell me what to do."

He didn't seem to like that answer.

"Your job is to make five hundred calls a day and get eight to ten qualified leads that you will give to your broker," he yelled at me.

Clearly, Brad hadn't had his morning fix, whatever that consisted of—coke, women, alcohol. Whatever it was, he sorely needed it because he radiated displeasure, tension rising in waves off his body. My annoyance deepened, and I wondered why Alex had decided to waste my time like this.

Brad suddenly bent down to my chair and whispered in my ear, "You think you can handle that?"

This was getting dramatic. Was he enjoying this? I think he was, sociopathic asshole.

"Yeah, I like the phone, I can do that."

He grimaced.

"We only want people who are hungry—who are prepared to eat, sleep, and shit this business!"

Brad started pacing and looked ready to knock me out with one of those meaty fists if I said one wrong word. Damn, this was intense. Was I signing up for a cold-calling gig or a UFC fight?

"I need people who are going to get on the phone and not put it down. I want to see calluses on your hands from dialing and gripping that phone. The phone should be glued to your ear! Smile and dial, smile and dial!"

He looked unhinged as he repeated this mantra. I wasn't fazed, though—I'd been through much worse. Some short white guy doing his best mafia boss impression was not going to throw me off. I just needed to know if this was ultimately worth my time.

"I can do that," I responded coolly. "But," I continued, "when can I get my books to study?" For good measure I added a sneer to match the one that slashed across his face.

I thought he'd like this question, see that I was driven to succeed, that we could reach a detente. Nope. He waited to answer me, staring at me some more, apparently disgusted with what he saw before him.

"No one gives you your books here—you fucking earn them!" he shouted, flecks of spit flying from his mouth.

Apparently, there was to be no talk of books at VTR Capital until your third month—if you even lasted that long. Once you'd paid your dues as a cold caller, you could "get your books," meaning that you could be put up for sponsorship by your firm to study for the Series 7, which enabled you to trade securities—stocks, bonds, mutual funds, options, and the like. In other words, once your firm made the decision to sponsor you and you passed your Series 7, you could become a broker. If I could make it past Brad, I knew I could get myself there.

He stopped pacing, turned, and looked at me.

"You'll work twelve hours a day, five days a week, and you'll get two hundred and fifty dollars a week."

Wait a minute. I thought I'd misheard him. That was pennies compared to what I was making now. I almost laughed out loud. That was absurd. Fuck this place. I cursed Alex in my head.

Brad must have sensed a shift in me because he changed tack.

"Follow me," he said, not waiting for my response. He led me down a narrow, fluorescent-lit hallway, secretaries and under-lings scattering in his wake as he marched forward with me in tow.

I could hear our destination before we got there, a low roar that grew as we got closer.

Brad flung open a double set of doors and led me into a giant boardroom. There were at least a hundred and fifty peo-ple crammed into the room. It was controlled chaos, constant motion and chatter. This was the Pit, with brokers on one side, cold callers on the other.

Men talking, ripping up index cards, writing furiously on whiteboards. Phones ringing and, in fact, phones sometimes hurtling through the air, as I saw one guy get frustrated and rip his phone off his desk.

As soon as someone slammed down their phone, they picked up another index card and kept going. It was all so fast. It was deliriously intoxicating.

There were no women and no people of color on the brokers' side. I was ready to be the first.

A switch inside me flipped immediately. I was in.

"When can I start?"

Chapter 10

BRAD AMBROSI'S SOUR BREATH ON MY FACE WAS THE best gift I'd ever received. I knew that all I needed was one opportunity and I would ride it into the sunset. When leaving his office, I told him that I needed to give my boss at Cohen's my two-week notice, which he begrudgingly accepted before sitting back down at his desk and forgetting about me, picking up his phone to no doubt yell at someone else. I floated back to my car and returned to Queens, triumphant. One successful interview and I felt like I'd already conquered Wall Street. That sweaty motherfucker Alex wasn't so bad after all.

Later that night sleep evaded me. I tossed and turned in my little twin bed, too electrified with the knowledge that my life was about to arrow upward in ways that I couldn't even begin to fathom. Scenes from the day played out on my ceiling, and I watched as a participant instead of as a player, noting details I'd missed earlier—the sun breaking from behind the clouds right as I stepped into the building; the little newsstand in the lobby, selling candy and papers; the receptionist's warm cloud of sweet perfume that I inhaled as I swept past her; the glassed management offices lining the left-hand side of the hallway to the Pit. I saw myself entering the Pit and was struck again by how the brokers' side was such a boring white canvas. I boldly painted myself into the middle of it, vibrant among the otherwise drab, uniform brushstrokes. Let me be the dark horse, I thought. Just let them try to underestimate me. Sleep came then, and I drifted off with a smile on my lips.

The next morning, I was still on a jittery high, unable to get the blood-pumping energy of VTR out of me. I fingered the business card Brad had given me before I walked out of his office. Heavy, creamy card stock, in the company's signature colors of green, gold, and black. I made up my mind—I couldn't wait. I called Brad and let him know that I would see him Monday morning bright and early. It would have been smarter to sock away as much money as I could in my final two weeks at Cohen's before starting at VTR—two hundred and fifty dollars a week was so little to live off—but it now felt that every day I waited to begin was a day that I was wasting. Each day at VTR would mean I was one day closer to getting my books, to passing my Series 7 exam, to becoming a bona fide broker and making the big bucks. I wanted to be so much more than just a salesperson behind a counter at a mall, entreating people to sign up for a store credit card so I could get a ten-dollar bonus here or there. I yearned for the respect automatically accorded to someone with the title "broker," to be able to invest in the stock market for myself, to not be weighed down with debt for years if I tried to pursue higher education. This would be my schooling, among fast-talking financiers, swindlers, and wannabes who would crash and burn. But I wouldn't. I was ready to learn furiously and make it.

I told my boss and my coworkers at Cohen's that I was ratcheting down my hours—I'd still work there on the weekends to make up for my lost income—but they were completely mystified. Why would I give up a comfortable salary, a comfortable job? They just didn't get it. But they were adults, saddled with children, some with mortgages, others with costly vices that they needed to finance. I was nineteen and could do anything in the world. I could afford to reset if need be.

My mother, of course, was supportive. As she had long drilled into me, she felt that the United States, particularly New York City, afforded anyone who sweated and bled effort with opportunity, and she approved of my working hard and making money because it was the American way. Catalina, Kenya, her sister, and of course, Alex and Mateo, were all thrilled for me. And, really, how hard could this job be? I was the best that Cohen's had, and if all those white boys at VTR could do this, I knew I could, no problem.

Monday morning, I woke while it was still dark and I carefully put on the clothes I'd laid out the night before—billowy, pleated yellow silk pants with a white body suit, a heavy blazer, and heels. I had no idea what Wall Street women actually wore, but I'd seen the ties and Rolexes that the men at VTR were wearing, and I wanted to dress the part. At least, what I thought the part required. Outside of VTR, at some other larger firms, like Goldman Sachs, women weren't even allowed to wear pants, only skirts. But I knew even before my first day that this role would require me to be one of the boys. I was ready for it. I wore my hair down, straight and neat, and came to work early, which, in this world, was only on time.

As I stepped out of the elevator, I walked past the empty receptionist desk—it was too early for the receptionist to have arrived—and I almost collided with Brad Ambrosi, who gave me only the slightest of nods as he barreled past me, his small body a bullet bound for some unlucky target. That was the best I was ever going to get out of him. I then walked into a conference room and was offered coffee by a friendly Human Resources staff member who led me, and all the other newly hired cold callers, through a detailed orientation. She then paused to allow us to ask questions before handing out bagels and letting us know that she was always available to discuss any problems we might have at the firm.

Just kidding—of course that didn't fucking happen. There was no Human Resources department to speak of at VTR—no manuals about company policy, no liaisons to go to with any complaints. Not that I, or anyone else who wanted to keep their job, would ever complain, however egregious the inciting event—if you complained, you'd be told to go home for the day, and it would be anyone's guess if you were allowed back. If you were a female and you complained, you'd be given that special label afforded particularly to women, you know the one—"difficult"—and you would likely never be able to ascend the ranks.

The closest I got to any kind of welcome as I found my way to my desk was merely a sympathetic smile from Matilda, one of the head sales assistants who the brokers relied on heavily for administrative support. It was a quick flash and then it was gone as she looked back down at a stack of papers, brokers already crowded around her, barraging her with questions, pawing at her with requests.

What was made very clear from the first minute was this: As a cold caller, you would not be given sick days, you would not be given time off, and you certainly would not get overtime if you worked past your usual twelve-hour days. If you were even one minute late to your desk, you would either be sent home for the day without pay, or, perhaps even crueler, you would be allowed to stay and work, but if you didn't get an arbitrarily high number of leads that day then you might not get paid despite your time on the clock. Oh, and you definitely wouldn't be getting a lunch break. Adrenaline and fear alone would fuel you.

The Pit was laid out in practical fashion: Upon entering, there was a pod where all the sales assistants sat, within close reach of the brokers who were just beyond them. The brokers all sat at desks on the left side of the cavernous boardroom in neatly ordered rows, each row spanning four or five brokers. On the other side of the room were the cold callers, who also sat at desks in corresponding rows. Your broker would sit in the same row as you so that they could easily access you—to hurl abuse, to offer advice or a very rare compliment, or to run over and co-opt a whale that you had beautifully landed (a whale being a new client who wants to invest and who has a minimum of a million dollars invested in the market already). On the left-hand wall of the room where the brokers sat, there was a bank of special phones that could connect the brokers directly to their cold callers so that they could listen in to the caller. The phones had mile-long cords so that the broker could walk close to their cold caller and whisper lines to them if they needed help landing the lead. On the right wall, the only advantage the callers had was a wall of windows with a beautiful view of the park, though we certainly didn't have time to gaze reflectively out the windows; we were too busy callousing our hands with dials and trying to survive another day. A seven-figure view wasted.

At the head of the room there were no TVs blaring CNBC or CNN, like you might see in modern offices now. There was only a dot analog board that tickered out the state of NASDAQ and the Dow, and any other markets we should be paying attention to; green if something was up, red if something was down. I remember looking up from my desk a million times a day, my gaze focused only on the red of the board. There was no art or even a potted plant to adorn the boardroom. The walls were off-white and the carpet was standard-issue gray—clean but abundantly plain, no distractions to take your mind off the work at hand.

Brokers and cold callers all had the same desks—standard-issue office furniture, accessorized with a black swivel chair.

The desk had one drawer to hold pens and a notepad, and one filing cabinet to lock your leads in—leads were valuable, and you didn't want to be the chump leaving your leads out carelessly for someone else to steal. Apart from your phone, your lead cards, and pen and paper, you were strictly forbidden from keeping anything else on top of your desk. That is, except for the *Robb Report*.

What is the *Robb Report*, you ask? If you haven't heard of it, don't feel too bad. This magazine targets the ultra-wealthy, the one percenters who either did some shady things in business, were born rich, or were extremely lucky. Their target reader usually has an eight-figure net worth *easy*. Per its company profile—try not to roll your eyes too far back into your head: "It is the brand the most successful people rely on to discover the ideas, opinions, products, and experiences that will matter most to them. Robb Report is synonymous with affluence, luxury, and the best of the best. Robb Report: Luxury Without Compromise."

If you flip through the magazine's glossy pages, you'll spot capitalistic ideals of perfection throughout: airbrushed models on yachts, listings of vintage wines with price tags in the five figures, socialite reports that would put *Vanity Fair* to shame. Headlines from the *Report* include gems like "How to Spec Your Jet," "What to Collect Next: Expert Insights on the Latest Luxury Investments," and "Investment Cigars."

Which is exactly why VTR's brokers shoved the magazine into cold callers' hands and encouraged us to pick something out from the magazine that we couldn't afford and tape the page to our desks as a reminder of all that could be possible if we just worked hard enough. If we stuck with their program, they would assuredly sponsor us and we could all become brokers so that we could then buy that villa, that car, have those women or those men, achieve that perfect, and perfectly bought, life. The only thing standing in your way is you, we were told.

Some people stuck two or even three pages from the magazine on their desks. One caller cut out a picture of a woman in a bikini on a yacht as his dream object, a tidy sum-up of how the men of VTR viewed women and their roles.

It would be a great story if I told you that I rejected the shiny allure of materialism, but I didn't. I freely admit that I gave up my soul for this green dream of things, of want, of more. I taped a cutout of a Mercedes to my desk and stared at it each time I dialed, motivated by my hunger to have what the brokers had, to have what they *were*. I wanted the cars, the houses in the Hamptons, the Gucci and the Versace. Most of all, I wanted a permanent front-row seat to see my beloved Yankees. Don't get me wrong—I loved my fellow bleacher creatures—we were in it together, a tight-knit family in the nosebleeds, cheering with each other until we'd seared our lungs from screaming on our team. But I was tired of the hard seats and the sun's relentless rays and the mile-long walk to the bathroom. I wanted to be a VIP, escorted to a padded seat, assigned someone to take my food and drink order. I wanted to be close enough to the field to see the beads of sweat on the players' foreheads drip into their eyes, see them spit on the ground before making a play. I wanted to reach over the fence to grab a ball with ease if it came my way. Most of all, if our archenemies, the Boston Red Sox, visited, I wanted their players to hear me heckling them mercilessly.

This nod to our desires was how they trained us callers—they fed us just enough hope for us to continue on, but not enough for us ultimately to be successful and to rise to their level.

Here's how it worked.

More than ninety percent of the cold callers hired by VTR were Black or Latinx, all from marginalized communities. When I first set up shop at VTR, I'd look at the cold callers' side of the room and be filled with pride—so many talented people here using their skills to get ahead. There were even three women in my section. One was a Black woman named Fran McNeil whose calls I'd sometimes listen in on in between dials. She was never aggressive but she was firm, and she flirted over the phone if she thought it could help—it often did. I was so excited for us. I couldn't wait for my Pit crew to overtake the brokers' side of the room one day. I was confident beyond the shadow of a doubt that once we all passed our Series 7 exams, we'd be doing rings around these brokers, smoking their numbers. But as time passed, I grew more confused and then miffed—with so many talented cold callers on our side, how had none of them moved on to the other side? Why was every single broker still so alarmingly white and male?

When I asked around, I was given a medley of responses ranging from "Oh, they haven't gotten their books yet" to "He's not ready yet" to "She hasn't had time to study." Some callers had been waiting six months or more for their books, but their brokers refused to sponsor them, which was the only path forward to getting your books, passing the exam, and becoming a broker. The minimum amount of time before you could get your books, as Brad Ambrosi had shared with me, was three months, so this was clearly a roadblock. Meanwhile, incoming employees with connections—that is, white guys—were somehow able to skip the line, get their books, and become brokers, high-fiving their fellow bros on the way up. A number of callers sensed the inequality present and even changed their names on the phone to try not to tip off investors as to their identities. They would choose Jewish last names because they saw how investors—for better or worse—perked up when they got a call from someone with a "Jewish-sounding" name. So Jesus Castillo became Jacob Feinberg. Alex Navarro became Alex Newman, just like Newman from *Seinfeld*. And it often worked; at least, it worked a lot better than their own last names they'd been forced to discard.

Some of the partners and brokers whose licenses in certain states had been suspended *might* make an exception with the occasional gullible Latinx or Black caller, supplying that person their books so that they could get licensed. Why? Not so that they could trade on their own, but so that the white brokers could make these people of color their account openers to register trades in their names. The brokers would close trades with clients on unrecorded lines, then pass off the client to their opener, who they made sure to get on a recorded line. In this way, the brokers could continue to steal money and make bad trades in the states in which they were suspended, and if anyone got in trouble, they could point to their opener who had *officially* made the sale, having them take the fall for their dirty deeds.

If I had been a little more cynical when I started, I would have likely seen that VTR was taking a chance on me because they took a chance on everyone like me, and that chance wasn't much of one. Nobody was supposed to graduate from their program. Anyone coming in cold, with real knowledge of Wall Street, with a college degree? They were never hired as callers. It was young kids of color who filled the caller positions because they were *only* supposed to feed the brokers with leads. They were supposed to labor tirelessly, day after day, collecting leads, passing them on for paydays that they would never see, before being ground down by the system, quitting, and being replaced with someone else who looked like them. We were disposable, and anyone with a connection to a broker or a partner at VTR flew through the program at a speed that my fellow cold callers simply could never catch up to.

I grew to understand all this after only a short while working at VTR. I knew they thought I wouldn't make it. But I'm not one to shy away from a challenge. I narrowed my eyes at the bastards, smiled, and thought, *Fuck it, I'll show them.*

Like I said, don't underestimate me.

Chapter 11

COLD CALLERS WERE NOT ALLOWED TO INITIATE conversations with their brokers. We weren't even allowed to stray to the brokers' side of the room. It was so segregated an environment that even outside the boardroom, brokers walked on the left side of the hallway and cold callers and assistants on the right. This was never a mandated rule, of course, but we all still, somehow, wordlessly knew that we could not cross over that invisible line dividing the left and right sides of the hallway. We cold callers were to stay on the other side of the tracks.

It wasn't just Brad Ambrosi who set out to make the cold callers feel like shit. Outside of the eternal promise of the program, all callers were made to feel inferior, had it hammered into them that they were lowly dialers, good for punching numbers into a phone and uttering words from a script, nothing more. Verbal—and sometimes physical—abuse was hurled at us, and if we couldn't handle it? Well, you knew where the door was.

In my first week at the boiler room, I lost a bit of the swagger I had gained from being the top dog at Cohen's. I'd never had to actually *work* at a hustle before. It all came naturally to me. This? I'd need to buckle down and actually practice—leads wouldn't roll in just because I wanted them to.

How we—and everyone else on Wall Street—got our leads was simple enough. Our brokers paid for leads from Dun & Bradstreet, a business insights company that harvested and sold information about companies to whoever wanted it. D&B had been around since 1841, offering various services to businesses, but the leads used to call investor targets had been a strategy employed on Wall Street for at least a decade, if not more, by the time I found myself at VTR in the nineties. At the time, a deck consisting of around one hundred leads would cost a broker forty bucks. The broker would pay for the leads himself and hand them over to his caller to use.

At VTR, our brokers narrowed the criteria of the leads based on who they thought would be most likely to invest, doing their best to filter out, as they called them, "non-qualified" investors, the small fish in the sea not worth their time. VTR's lead cards always included the name of the business, the name of the owner of the business, and the estimated annual revenue of the business, which had to be at least one million dollars a year to merit a dial. In the thousands of leads I called over my time at VTR, I never once saw a woman's name printed on a lead card. Obviously, there were countless women-owned businesses in the United States, but none ever popped up on my cards that I was aware of. After I logged over a thousand calls my first week, this became overwhelmingly apparent, so when my broker, a guy named Adam Sharpstein, was talking to me (he struck up the conversation, per the clear but unspoken rule that callers were not to initiate conversation), I asked why there were no women in our lead decks. The answer was depressing and infuriating. He told me that the firm's partners had made the collective decision not to work with female business owners. Why? They felt that women tended to be more cautious when investing in the market. This clearly reeked of sexism, but as I was in my first week on the job, at nineteen years old, I didn't protest. What could *I* do to change this practice? I was, after all, just doing my best to stay afloat, and I didn't want to make waves. If I did, I knew there would be negative repercussions, to put it mildly.

In my inaugural week, I quickly learned that I had to somehow find that perfect medium between quantity and quality. We cold callers were all supposed to dial realistically between 350 to 500 calls a day and cough up eight to ten leads a day. *Legitimate* leads, as in "Hello, Adam Sharpstein, I am a whale and I want to give you all of my money, thank you very much." In addition to being able to listen in on any of our calls at any time, our brokers were also able to closely monitor how many calls we made in a day. There were daily humiliation sessions held at the close of the market when we were to hand over our leads to our brokers. If we handed over "wood" leads to our brokers, watch out. "Wood" leads were leads that we embellished, or entirely made up, just to make our leads quota for the day. It was a dangerous game to play, and usually not worth it. If a broker found out that any of your leads were wood, they would march you briskly to the front of the boardroom where everyone—sales assistants to callers to account openers to brokers—would watch silently while the broker scathingly gave you a verbal lashing before ripping up the leads and throwing them like grim confetti in your face. If they were feeling particularly punitive, they'd up your quota for the following day to make up for your trash leads from the day before. Brutality and fear were the main tools the brokers thought worked best to keep us in line.

Some mornings, many brokers would come in, jittery and shaky from the breakfast coke they'd just snorted to jolt them awake, tired as they were from the previous night's raucous debauchery of drinking, strippers, and drugs. They would round up the cold callers to hype us up for our dials and scream out what was meant to be encouragement: "Do you want to be cold callers forever, making two hundred and fifty dollars a week? I just spent more than that on lunch yesterday."

They'd pace, eyes roving around for anyone who was looking too comfortable. You weren't allowed to look comfortable—if you didn't look miserable, you clearly weren't working hard enough.

"Do you guys want to sit all day making three hundred and fifty dials to continue making your broker rich? Maybe some of you guys are happy making two-fifty a week. Maybe this is the only job you could get. Maybe you like to be subservient and get our fucking shoes shined, and fetch our coffee and pick up our dry cleaning and get our cars out of the lot."

I had worked in sales—I knew they were playing mind games with us, trying to get into our heads to rattle us, to separate the weakest from the herd.

"If I wanted a slave, I can get one for a lot less than that; he will even fuck my wife if I tell him to! If that's what you want to do, then this is not the business for you so you better get the fuck out of this firm."

The brokers would go red in the face, working themselves into such a froth that you could see the spit flying from their mouths.

"You know how many people would die to have your desk? To work for our company and have an opportunity to make more money than they've ever dreamed of? We've got guys with MBA degrees calling us, dropping by our firm, lining up outside Brad's office for an interview, for a chance to get on the phone. We don't even have enough desks for these people, so we either have to expand our office or fire the nonproducing assholes—and firing you slackers is a lot easier!"

I always kept my face impassive, a blank canvas, impossible to read.

"You guys are like a cancer that's starting to spread, and we need to cut the cancer out. You know that we can't have cancer in our office."

And so on and so forth.

I was tough and I knew I could handle it, but I did have to give myself regular pep talks so that the psychological warfare wouldn't go to my head. I saw what happened when a caller couldn't take it anymore—there might be tears, a public break-down, yelling, storming out, and they would never be seen again. I vowed that I would not let the brokers' bullying ever get to me. The protective emotional shell that I'd built for myself out of the hardship and pain of my childhood came in handy during these noxious sessions.

One of the most intimidating brokers at VTR at the time, a guy named Jameson Logan, always liked to make sure he kept us on our toes by pulling theatrical stunts. Nobody ever wanted to get a wood lead because it meant profit loss, but Jameson was probably the closest to enjoying one. He seemed to take perverse pleasure in shaming his callers in front of everyone. He considered it a creative form of motivation, or that's how it was justified, at least.

Every couple of hours, Jameson would stride over to our side of the room to see how many leads we had successfully man-aged to capture for the day so far. When he was in a bad mood, he would get in a froth and antagonize the four callers assigned to him: Jesus Castillo, Mike Sanchez, Mark Hernandez, and Vinny (just Vinny).

"My guys," he would bellow. "GET UP!"

Whenever he snarled this, Jesus, Mike, Mark, and Vinny would be forced to make their cold calls on their feet for the rest of the excruciatingly long day. No sitting allowed, no putting the phone down at any time.

One day, Jesus wasn't doing as well as he would have liked on his dial count. Unfortunately, Jameson Logan decided it would be a great time to check his dial sheet. Uh-oh. Jameson wasn't impressed. Of course, we couldn't stop our own cold calls to watch what we knew would likely be a spectacular scene, but we all had one eye glued to the escalating situation with Jameson and Jesus.

Jameson walked over to a desk, grabbed a roll of masking tape, and walked back over to Jesus. He quickly wound the tape around Jesus's hand and the phone.

"There." Jameson smirked. "Now you can't put the phone down."

Jameson walked back to the brokers' side and Jesus was left, quite literally, stuck to his phone. To his credit, he took it in stride. He never showed any resentment or anger over the abuse that Jameson heaped upon him. In Jesus's eyes, this "training" was just good-hearted hazing meant to make him stronger. He actually engaged in some of it himself—once, he used his tie to wrap his phone to his mouth so he could have his hands free just to dial. I would have liked to have seen what Jesus could have achieved with the advent of hands-free dialing.

At VTR, it was ingrained in us that we would learn to go beyond ordinary to extraordinary for our brokers. It didn't matter that it robbed us of our humanity to get there.

❧

To avoid such humiliations, where do you even begin when trying to snag a lead? In the fury of the Pit, it's easy to get caught up in the stress. Ripping through so many calls per day, with the cold knowledge that you must get leads *or else*, most people can't keep a clear head and they succumb to the pressure and fold. You'll never see them again, buh-bye. But you'll barely notice because you must focus and use all your cunning to make your quota. You must feed the ravenous brokers fresh leads, throw them their bleeding red meat to snap up, tear and swallow, pitch and open, or you're gone. They have devoured you, too.

In all sales calls, your number one job is to get through the "gatekeeper." The gatekeeper is the person getting in the way of your true target, a monied white man, most likely. These gatekeepers are usually the secretaries, personal assistants, or even, depending on which number you call, the family members who pick up your call. A gatekeeper can be your friend or your foe. Usually, they're not your ally, and they will try to impede you, most likely hyperaware of what you're after, and not in the mood to forward on an unsolicited call from someone like, well, me.

I had a flair for feeling out these gatekeepers, understanding what it would take to get them to pass the phone over to their boss (or husband), and knowing the exact amount of friendliness and pushiness I needed to succeed. Then, once I was on the phone with the target, I kept it up and almost always snagged the lead.

With this in mind, let's now play a round of Get Past the Gatekeeper and Nail the Target. Johnathan is the target name on the index card; his business grosses seven figures a year.

Cin, friendly, expertly abbreviating target's name: "Hey there, is John around?"

Gatekeeper: "Who is this?"

Cin: "Oh, hi, tell him it's Cin."

Gatekeeper: "Cin *who*?"

Cin: "Cin Fabré."

Gatekeeper, suspicious: "What, exactly, is this about?"

Cin, firmer: "Ma'am, it's a personal business call."

Gatekeeper: "Does he know you?"

Cin, brightly: "Well, if you tell him it's Cin from VTR, that should ring a bell, thank you!"

Gatekeeper: "Well, *I'm* his wife and *I'm* not familiar with VTR."

Cin, closing in: "Oh, that's okay. John is familiar, and I'm returning *his* call."

Gatekeeper, defenses down: "Hmm, okay, hold on."

[Passes the phone to John]

John: "Hello?"

Cin: "Hi, John, it's Cin. I'm getting back to you from VTR Capital."

John: "VTR Capital . . . *(pause)* . . . Who?"

Cin, authoritatively: "We are a boutique investment firm on Wall Street, specializing in IPOs, private placements, secondary offerings, and occasional penny stocks."

John: "I've never heard of VTR. . . ."

Cin: "Look, John, I get it. You are used to the same type of brokers calling you with the same stock picks with the same average returns. What we do is bring you unique investment ideas that your current broker does not have access to, such as IPOs and private placements. John, when was the last time your broker got you involved in an IPO?"

John, conceding: "Well, never."

Cin: "*Exactly!* That's the reason I am calling, John, to give you an opportunity for when we do have something that makes sense, which you'll never get from your current advisers, and to make sure we are free to give you a call. Are you still at 1234 ABC Street?"

John: "Yes, I am."

Cin: "Great, this is what I will do. I will tailor a package just for you, send it out, and get back to you in the next couple of weeks once you have had a chance to review it. And if you don't like what you read, just let me know and we will part as friends. Is that fair?"

John: "Yeah, that's fair."

Cin: "John, I really don't want to waste your time, and I want to bring you something that tickles your belly, so can you tell me about a few stocks you're currently holding onto?"

John, retreating: "Uh, I'm not sure I'm comfortable giving you that information."

Cin, persuasive: "John, I understand. Again, all I want is to make sure that the only shot I have to impress you with is something that makes sense *for you*. Just name a few. Are you a blue-chip, conservative, options?"

John: "I have some Cisco, Hewlett-Packard, IBM."

Cin: "Okay. Are you open to diversifying a bit?"

John: "Yeah, it just depends on what it is."

Cin, praising: "I'm glad to hear we're speaking the same love language, John. Is it fair to say that you have at least a couple mil in the market?"

John, flattered: "Oh, not that much."

Cin: "Would you say about a mil?"

John, abashed: "Hmm, I'm not sure."

Cin, cajoling: "You and I both know you are aware to the nickel of what you have in the market, John. Just give me a ballpark. Three-quarters of a mil?"

John, appeased: "Yeah, that's fair."

Cin: "Okay, great! John, it was a pleasure talking with you, but more importantly, please look out for my package, and I or my partner Adam S. will get back to you soon. Remember the name again, it's VTR Capital!"

[*Cin hangs up without saying goodbye—the target must know she is busy and doesn't have time for pleasantries.*]

[*End Scene*]

This, my friends, is what victory looks like—to get past a gatekeeper and connect to the target, get personal finance and address information from the target, and have him agree to accept a proposal from VTR. If this script makes it look easy, it's not. A precise amount of flattery and pressure, praise and push, is needed to not get hung up on in the first five seconds of a cold call. Got it? Now just do that nine more times successfully in your twelve-hour shift, longer if you haven't hit quota. Go home, hit the bed, sleep uneasily, dreaming of faceless Grim Reapers wearing suits and choking you with their ties. Wake up in a cold sweat, grasping your neck. Time to do that shit all over again.

⌗

Most times, clients like John were few and far between. If it were easy, you wouldn't have to make three hundred, three-fifty, up to five hundred dials a day if things were in the shitter, to net ten successes. It was all a numbers game. Lacking headsets or auto-dialers, you dialed and dialed and dialed and dialed then dialed some more. When, after giving it another dial for good measure, you finally managed to get a live human being on the phone, you would jump out of your chair, sending it spinning, immediately on the alert, heart racing, blood pumping. If you were lucky enough to sit on the aisle, you might even be able to pace, which always helped somehow. Your every muscle was tensed, ready for the kill.

Having to make so many calls, my ears constantly burned, and in the first few weeks, I had too much pride to take my earrings off, as I didn't want anyone to think I was weak. Over the next year, my earlobe would painfully tear twice because of the constant phone usage. In the beginning, I could tell that my earlobe was thinning, but I didn't think much of it. That is, until one day when I had just hung up the phone and heard a little clink. I looked down—my earring was on the desk. Huh. I pocketed the earring and made my way to the bathroom, cupping my ear as discreetly as possible. Once in the bathroom, I peered into the mirror—holy shit, my earlobe ripped! It looked as if someone had taken a pair of scissors and—*snip*—neatly cut my earlobe in half. It wasn't really bleeding; I supposed there wasn't too much blood in the cartilage, but it looked absolutely terrible. I found a Band-Aid and kept it bandaged until I could get it sewn up by a doctor. He told me to cut out whatever I was doing to have caused this strange injury.

Nope, couldn't do that. I ignored his advice, continuing to call, and a few months later my earlobe ripped again. At this point, I was lucky to have an earlobe at all. I got it stitched again and pierced new holes in my ears, also helpfully switching to a headset.

The cold callers had their own styles and tricks for landing leads. Some were soft-spoken, others were loud, aggressive, passive, nonconfrontational, confrontational, or downright rude. They did whatever it took to get the job done.

Mateo, for example, employed a hard-hitting style in which he would demean the gatekeeper with heavy sarcasm.

"Why don't you go be a good girl and get on your roller skates and roll yourself down to his office to let him know I am on the phone, hmm?" he would say.

Or "Do your job and put him on the phone right now. Do it or you may not *have* a job when I tell him how rude you were to me."

He would sometimes bang the earpiece of the phone on the desk and say, "You hear that? That's opportunity knocking for your boss and he's missing it because of you! Now get him on the phone before you cost him even more money!"

I don't know how this kind of bashing proved effective, but he found a way to get his leads every single day with that approach. Without him, I never would have found my way to VTR, as Mateo was the one who recruited Alex who then brought me to the firm. Mateo was a cold caller for one of the partners at VTR, Ari. Mateo gained major cool points with Ari because he dressed so sharply, just like the brokers. This was due to the convenient fact that his dad worked in the men's shoe department at Bloomingdale's and Mateo was able to use Pop's discount, snagging suits for seventy-five percent off, while most of the other male cold callers bought their polyester suits for ninety-nine bucks in Chinatown, where shopkeepers with folded arms watched tourists from the entrances of their tiny stores, clothing displayed on racks outside, while inside, clothing hung from floor to ceiling with large orange square price tags advertising perpetual sales.

While Mateo made his leads, he didn't have the burning-hot passion for the business that I feverishly felt—he wanted to become a famous DJ and his nightly sets didn't bring in much money, so cold calling it was. His true skill at VTR, though, was in his recruiting—he recruited so many cold callers for the firm that Ari, the other partners, and even asshole Brad Ambrosi never gave him a hard time. They wouldn't even bat an eye when he would leave after lunchtime, something absolutely nobody else could do without being slaughtered. They had even, amazingly, given him his books, but he failed the Series 7 repeatedly and wasn't able to ascend to account opener without his license.

When it came to callers, the Pit was split between the hapless—who wanted to become brokers but were purposely held back—and those who were biding their time until the next big thing came along and they were out. Perhaps due to the fact that his DJing career really wasn't taking off in the way that he wanted, Mateo was perpetually dissatisfied with being a license-less cold caller, no matter the preferential treatment he received from the partners. For a brief period, he left VTR to try his luck with other, smaller firms, but he was soon back to VTR with his tail between his legs.

He told us, when he'd been allowed to return, a soldier back from war, that the smaller firms would lure you in by creating a chaotic false sense of productivity and profit, instructing the employees in advance to be on the phone looking busy whenever a new hotshot from a larger firm would show up for an interview. Mateo bounced around a few of them, attracted by the firms' empty promises that he could become a junior broker if he opened enough accounts, no license, no problem. If that sounds suspect, that's because it is, and it tricked many others as well, not just Mateo. What would happen, instead, is that you would be told to open accounts posing as the broker whose name you were pitching to the potential client. Then, when the real broker made successful trades with the account you opened on their behalf, you would be rewarded with, say, one to two thousand dollars, depending on the profit made from the trade. But it was, of course, not that simple. The broker would inevitably offer one excuse or another to you for why you repeatedly weren't getting paid, informing you that the client account you opened on his behalf didn't end up trading after all, or that he would get you that commission the following month, as commissions were paid monthly and, unfortunately, you had just missed the cutoff date. There would always be an excuse at the ready for why you weren't getting your money until, eventually, it dawned on you that your check was never coming and you'd make your departure. Another firm would then get wind that you were on the move and they would pay their cold callers or account openers a referral fee to get you in *their* doors, assuring you that they weren't at all like the previous firm you'd worked at, and the vicious cycle would be repeated ad infinitum. It would take years for the hopeful broker-to-be to get licensed or, much likelier, the person would burn out, wadding up their dreams and tossing them in the trash on the way out before leaving the business entirely. This story never changed, just the characters.

⟡

I picked up a few tricks from the other cold callers when I faced a brick wall. Inevitably, we would encounter plenty of yellers who would magnificently slam their phones down, sending the dizzy buzz of the dial tone down our ear canals. To try to avoid a hang-up with a yeller, I'd wheedle, placate, or yell back at them. I might tell them after they'd screamed that they absolutely weren't interested in talking to me, "Get interested! I'm calling from one of the leading NASDAQ firms on Wall Street." Or, "Sir, don't judge me on a thirty-second phone call. Let me get my information out to you. Then you can be the judge and jury." I'd sometimes taunt them, saying, "If you weren't interested, then you wouldn't have picked up my call." If none of those rebuttals were successful, I'd bring out the big guns and say, "I actually have nothing to offer you right now because we only make a few recommendations a year. Down the road when we have a winner and you like it, great, we can do business, but if you're not interested, you don't ever have to hear from me again, fair enough?"

If someone tinnily screeched that they were busy, I'd respond dryly with, "Yes, I know you're busy, and I'm busy, too." Or sarcastically quip, "You're the CEO of a successful company. I would hope that you're busy."

I learned that you could get a potential client to stay on the phone long enough to get your foot in the door if you asked them questions and put the burden right back on them. Sometimes, I'd disarm the person on the other end of the line by saying, "What, you're too busy to make money?"

If they groused that they already had a broker and didn't need to talk to VTR, flattery would go a long way with, "A man like you should surely have two or three brokers, not just one," or "I wouldn't waste my time calling you if you didn't," or "No one firm has a monopoly on good ideas." But my favorite was, "I want you to keep your local guys—they're good for the small stuff."

If they said that they weren't currently in the market, I'd slyly hit them back with, "My data tells me that you have traded in the last six months, so we need to talk." Or, with velvet in my voice, "Come on, a guy like you *always* has his hands in the market."

And if they challenged me, well, I was ready for it. I could hear doubt in their voice when they'd tell me, "I've never heard of your firm," and I was always ready to quickly hit back with, "Well, pick up the *Wall Street Journal* then," or, "Fine, just take a look at my track record," or, "I'll be happy to send my credentials to you," or, "I'm well aware you get these calls all the time, and I'm prepared to separate myself from the pack right now."

Some of these lines might sound cheesy, but let me tell you, when you were good—and I was good—they very often worked. The potential client would halt to think about what I'd just said, and I'd take advantage of that ever-so-slight pause to proceed with my pitch.

Regardless of whether my lines worked, I always knew how to judge the guy on the other end of the phone and would at least know what to say next. There was only one time as a caller that I was truly stumped when a potential client asked me a question that I, in fact, had not even once thought to ask myself.

"What does VTR stand for?"

Shit. I had no idea! So I cobbled together an answer and said in one breath, "Oh-it's-an-acronym-now-if-you-could-please-confirm-your-full-name-and-address-that-would-be-great-what-is-it?" That's what you had to do—you could never admit ignorance, which was simply another flavor of weakness, a bitter pill dissolving on your tongue. You always had to think on your feet and lob back with a question, back swing powerfully into their court. After that call, I asked first the other callers then the brokers what "VTR" stood for. Nobody could answer! Not one person could tell me what it stood for, so I simply shrugged my shoulders and moved on, content enough to tell people that it was an acronym before hurrying to my prepared follow-up question.

Chapter 12

VTR CAPITAL WAS AN OFFSHOOT OF STRATTON Oakmont, the infamous firm that coked-up—and all the other "ups" that you could ever dream of—Jordan Belfort started. Before he spectacularly ran it into the ground with his stock chopping, he made his debut killing with shoe brand Steve Madden's IPO under Stratton. And just like that, Jordan bloodily carved out a niche for himself on Wall Street, however isolated he was from the other, more legitimate companies there, etching his initials crudely in concrete for all to remember. He raked in hundreds of millions of dollars that people and companies alike entrusted him with, setting a precedent for the industry with his chop shopping, that is, fraudulent sales phone tactics, that many others, including VTR, tried to mirror.

When things started getting sticky with the SEC at Stratton, a number of Stratton's most powerful brokers under Jordan decamped and started their own firms. VTR was one of these expat companies. The partners at VTR—Ari, Levi, Greg, and Gene—employed and taught their juniors the same shady strategies that got Jordan and Stratton shuttered; namely, those nail-biting, high-pressured sales calls, and OTC trading. OTC, or over-the-counter, trading, is not in and of itself illegal. In fact, many reputable companies, like Hertz, as well as foreign subsidiaries of behemoths like Nestlé and Bayer, are OTC traded. OTC trading simply means that trades are made directly between a broker and an investor. These trades, most commonly consisting of stocks or shares of a company, are not completed on a standard market exchange, like the NYSE (New York Stock Exchange) or NASDAQ. Companies that might not meet the more stringent requirements of a standard market exchange, or those that can't raise enough capital to be traded on these markets, might trade OTC. Some might trade OTC in order to raise said capital and transition to one of the standard market exchanges. So what, exactly, were the benefits of not trading on an exchange and going directly to the buyer? The obvious upside for us was that there were far fewer regulations guiding—and restricting—these trades. Companies that traded via OTC weren't required to publicly disclose as much about their financials, and it was well known that OTC trades were far more volatile. Investors would—or at least *should*—have known that they were speculating, and if they lost big, that certainly wasn't on us. With this in mind, many of us just made shit up because we weren't being watched as closely as, say, brokers trading on the NYSE. It was only when we really went over the top swindling investors who would then make noise that the SEC would begin sniffing around, and even then, it might only issue a gentle slap on the wrist. Jordan got a lot of slaps on the wrist before the SEC shut him down for good.

OTC trading was how we most often pitched ourselves to clients—we'd tell them that we had a niche product for them that their regular brokers didn't know about, and that if they stuck with us, they could make a fortune with the valuable secrets that we had hidden up our sleeves.

If VTR sounds like a small boutique firm, you're not too far off the mark. It wasn't, say, a Merrill Lynch or a JPMorgan or a Goldman Sachs—they never had to stoop to net a client—investors came to them with money burning in their pockets.

VTR was a fraction of the size of one of these titans, but given the Stratton association, tarnished as the name was, we were able to get people's attention. Still, even with over a hundred people at the firm, which was quite sizable for a chop shop, it often felt like a small operation, complete with characters straight from Central Casting.

The president of VTR was one Edward J. McCune, but nobody had ever seen him—some people didn't even believe he existed. Some thought he was an invisible head who put his name on company documents, perhaps even unknowingly, a chump the partners could hide behind to avoid prosecution for their murky dealings.

Of the partners, Greg was clearly the overlord of VTR. He looked like a juicehead, hulkingly large, with strawberry blond hair and mottled, pale skin. He always looked as if he were slightly too big for his suit, his shirt buttons straining, at risk of pinging off into the air like tiny missiles. Greg rarely spoke, and if you were called into his office, it was either for something very good or something very bad. He was in charge of monitoring the brokers, and even though he rarely left his office to speak to them, you could still feel his presence radiating through the thin gaps of his window blinds.

Levi had been one of the most successful brokers at Stratton before starting VTR with the other partners. He was tall, with deep-set brown eyes. I wouldn't have called him attractive but there was something magnetic about him. When he directed his smile at you, it felt like he had gifted you something precious and rare that you didn't want to share with anyone else. When Levi was in a good mood, he would sometimes make his way to the Pit to show us cold callers how it was done, offering tips that I eagerly ate up. Other times, he would retreat to his office, close his door, and turn his lights off. When we saw the lights in his office extinguished, we knew not to bother him.

Ari was the rabble-rouser of the bunch. Technically, he couldn't trade at VTR because he was in the midst of an SEC investigation, an unwanted parting gift from his time at Biltmore, another chop shop. Ari was the epitome of a Wall Street wolf (even though he couldn't actually trade). Having no other real duties at VTR, he was the de facto general manager, publicist, and cheerleader of the company. He positively reeked of money, driving a rare split-windshield Corvette, strolling around in designer suits, leaving a faint trail of expensive cologne in his wake. Ari was our motivational speaker, responsible for rallying us and reminding us that if we just tried hard enough, we could have what he had—everyone wanted to be an Ari. When he felt we were behind on dials, he'd jump onto someone's desk in his Ferragamo loafers and work us up into a froth until we were all out of our seats, cheering and trying to snag the one-hundred-dollar bills that he was raining upon us. Seriously—this shit actually happened.

Ari was also the self-appointed strip club ambassador. He'd take brokers and clients alike out to Scores and Tens, ensuring that they would have a good time, grinning lewdly with all the smug entitlement that you'd imagine a suited guy in a strip club ordering bottle service would possess. VIP room only, of course. Before going to the club, Ari and the other top brokers would play mind control games with their cold callers, instructing them to run to Citibank to withdraw ten or twenty thousand dollars in cash for them to spend at the club. Their callers weren't invited, of course; they were only money messengers. Still, this was enough for many, holding twenty g's in cash, even if it was only for a few minutes from bank to brokerage, before relinquishing those perfectly crisp, unworn bills to their brokers. The cold callers would temporarily feel drunk with power, holding that much money, and they'd be reminded of why they were allowing themselves to be treated like dog shit in exchange for two hundred fifty bucks a week. It was so they could eventually play in the big leagues like their brokers. Fetching the money was a double reminder because the brokers would purposely have the callers see exactly how much money was sitting in their accounts, tantalizing them with all that material wealth.

Ari took the mind control games even further by making one of his cold callers, a guy named JP, get his shoes shined for him every Monday at the downstairs lobby stand. You're thinking, *Okay, that's not that bad.* But Ari hated creases in his Ferragamos and the only way to keep them shaped was by, well, having feet in them while they were being shined. So he made JP put his shoes on, march downstairs, and get them shined for him. He would then have to take the elevator back up, take the shoes off, and hand them back to Ari. How degrading is that? Poor JP tried to pass off the shoes as his own in front of the shoe shine man by dressing up in his best suit on Mondays to match those eight-hundred-dollar loafers. We all laughed about it back then, but looking back now, it makes me sad to think about.

Gene was the final partner to join VTR. He was extremely charming, his hair cut with precision, always razor sharp. He had a perpetual grin on his face, maybe because he'd had the satisfaction of sleeping with almost every assistant at the company.

Then there were the brokers. Adam Sharpstein was my assigned broker. He reminded me a bit of Mr. Potato Head, as he was badly balding and sported a bushy mustache. His huge belly folded over his pants, obscuring his belt, and as such, he had a repulsive tic of sorts, constantly hitching his drooping pants up. He always looked a bit schlubby, as he didn't see the point in wearing overly expensive, flashy clothing like most of the other brokers, who spent their money as soon as they made it. When Adam got mad, which was fairly often, he wheezed and his face reddened to an alarming shade, and spit gathered in the corners of his mouth, foam flecks flying when he spoke. I was constantly having to disgustedly wipe down my desk when Adam came around.

As a friend of Greg's, Adam had been ushered into VTR without having to cold-call. We had always heard that some people cheated on their Series 7 exam by paying someone to take it for them. We wondered whether Adam was one of those people. Before the advent of digital everything, it was far easier to manipulate systems in your favor.

But even though Adam exuded privilege—his wife's father was a president at a big corporation and they had deep pockets—he also seeped discontent. Even though, or perhaps because, his wife was extremely wealthy, Adam was always working incredibly hard, trying to make as much of his own money as possible. The other brokers didn't like Adam, who never dropped cash at the strip clubs or indulged in expensive vices, and who was, if not ragged, certainly unkempt. He wasn't like the rest of them, spending addictively and with abandon; he had a wife and kids to support, and he didn't fit the archetype of the ostentatious Wall Street broker. He didn't belong, and almost everyone there viciously wanted to see him fail. They talked shit about him constantly, cracking fat jokes around him, calling him a greedy Jew, saying that he would sell his own mother and children if it meant he would make a buck.

Maybe it was because other people at the firm didn't believe I belonged, either, at least not until I started making bank, that I didn't dislike Adam. At least not for the same reasons as the other brokers. If I disliked him at the time, it was because he felt that he worked harder than anyone else at the firm and didn't mind saying so. He was paying for me to be his cold caller and pushed me as hard as I could go so he could get his money's worth, which at the time was a slog, but in hindsight it was solid training. Though, while the other brokers would buy their account openers and cold callers who showed promise certain gifts to motivate them further, Adam never even bought me a cup of tea. The upside was that I never felt like I owed anything to him, which was how I preferred it.

There was Noah Hoffman, who came from a wealthy family, but who had fallen down on his luck because of extreme substance abuse and who couldn't rely on his family to bankroll him anymore. Noah liked to pitch clients by hiding under his desk and whispering to them. You could always tell Noah was pitching when you saw his empty desk, the phone cord snaking toward the ground.

There was Mark Stanza, who was short and bitter about it. He pitched clients by berating them, which occasionally worked but, more often than not, didn't. He would blow up whenever he lost a trade, becoming a foul fucker and behaving like a massive dickhead to anyone who had the misfortune to cross his path after a client passed on his pitch.

Abel Ackerman was a friend of Ari's—he, Ari, and Matilda, the head sales assistant, all grew up together in the city as kids and had seen it through together to VTR. Abel had integrity, unlike a lot of the other brokers at the firm—he never entered into any shady dealings and was content to make a smaller, aboveboard sale than a whopping illegal one. He just coincidentally happened to consort with crooks. Abel was an anxious guy—he'd constantly crack his neck and nervously grab at and rearrange his balls every few minutes. We all became well acquainted with the workings of Abel's digestive system and the guys respectfully never overlapped his bathroom time because everyone in the office knew that Abel would take a dump at exactly 8:35 a.m. every day. He'd stand up, newspaper tucked tidily under his arm, wet wipes in tow, and head decisively toward the bathroom for his post-coffee shit. As regular as clockwork—good ole Abel.

Aldano Cruz, a caller turned account opener turned newbie broker, was clearly very smart and one of the hardest workers at the firm, which the partners respected, and why they actually gave him his books, even given that he was Latinx. That said, they didn't like the way he spoke—he had a slight speech impediment and, because his family was originally from Honduras and he grew up in the hood speaking street slang, he had an accent that the partners thought investors wouldn't respond well to. We would often hear one partner or another yelling at him to "OPEN YOUR MOUTH." Partner Levi actually offered to pay for a speech therapist for him, but Aldano wanted to work it out on his own. You could often hear him practicing enunciation at his desk, with "position" being one of the most difficult words for him; it came out as "puoh-ci-cion."

Jameson Logan, the aforementioned screamer who was a scary asshole to his callers, was really all bark and no bite, I came to learn. His drug of choice was quaaludes. He was actually a bit pathetic, constantly getting taken by the strippers at VIP's in Manhattan, buying a car that he couldn't afford, giving him more agita than pleasure. He was in one perpetually long bad mood because he and his girlfriend, one of the sales assistants, were almost always fighting. It was always the same shit, that old song and dance: He'd come creeping into the office, tail tucked between his legs, coke residue fallen on his rumpled suit, the faint smell of a stripper's cheap perfume lingering on him. He would come bearing an iced coffee and a bagel for the girlfriend, placing it gently on her desk, his posture slumped and contrite. She would glare at him in loud silence, her eyes communicating untold betrayals. Jameson would stupidly try to start a conversation with her, but she'd wave him off, affronted by his presence. He would slink away slowly, *but* after he disappeared, she'd pick up the coffee without looking at him and drink it, at which point Jameson, who'd been watching from afar, would regain his vigor, stride over to the cold callers, a spring now in his step, and be ready to give us all hell.

With the girlfriend troubles over, he'd announce, "Guys, hang up your phones! I don't give a fuck who you're talking to!" If we didn't hang up fast enough, he'd march over to the unfortunate soul who'd been too slow, rip the phone off the desk, cord flying, and throw it against the wall as hard as he could.

"When I tell you to hang up, HANG UP!" he would roar.

Then he would interrogate us about our leads, even though it was only nine a.m., and if someone didn't give him an answer he liked, he'd tell them to get the hell out of the office and go home, that he would decide whether they still had a job by tomorrow morning.

While I was at VTR, I watched as Jameson slowly backslid, transforming from a self-proclaimed hotshot to a down-on-his-luck broker who'd clearly lost his touch. The partners, needing him to be useful, put him permanently in charge of all of the cold callers, which meant a lot more yelling courtesy of his obvious, deep-seated insecurities. The yelling always triggered me, putting me in mind of Fab, and I had to make a concerted effort to push my trauma aside to focus on the job.

It wasn't too long into my tenure at VTR that Jameson was assigned to the callers. One morning when he was running a meeting for us, Jameson paused in the middle of his sentence to point at his tie.

"Do you see this tie?" he asked us, eyes roving around searchingly. This was clearly a hypothetical question, but I took a look anyway. Seemed like a normal tie to me. Paisley pattern, navy blue, silk. Nothing special.

"This tie," he continued, "cost a hundred dollars." He paused to survey the room, which was silent, apart from a hacking, phlegm-filled cough from someone who'd probably stayed out too late the night before. We were all used to Jameson's theatrics and just wanted him to hurry up and get to whatever the hell his point was.

"But I paid a hundred and fifty dollars for it!" he continued. "You know why?" He let the question hang in the air like a stale fart.

"Because I CAN," he roared, before bulldozing through the rest of the meeting.

These guys truly were parodies of themselves.

❧

The sales assistants were all female, unsurprisingly. They were integral to our business, as they were responsible for accounting for the hundreds of thousands of dollars or more coming in and out of the firm daily, as well as keeping track of the brokers' trades, their buy-and-sell orders, and stock positions.

Matilda presided over the bunch, and she was the only assistant to have taken the Series 7, though she didn't trade; the partners had her take it to help facilitate tasks they needed done around the office, and having an assistant with such accreditation was handy. I liked Matilda a lot, and it puzzled me to see that she was dating Brad Ambrosi, the head recruiter at our firm. Remember him? Remorseless asshole and proud of it.

Sonia was Adam's assistant (and later, when I'd climbed the ladder to broker, she became mine) and she looked a little bit like Jennifer Aniston in the early *Friends* era. She was smarting over a recent divorce and was constantly toeing the line between frosty and civil with everyone she came across. She couldn't be outright bitchy because assistants never knew who would be promoted and they'd be called upon to assist, so she compromised by being coldly polite. In what was perhaps a postdivorce rebound, or, rather, *series* of rebounds, she had slept with a number of brokers in the office, including partner Ari. To top it off, she had also slept with Brad who, at this point, had been dating Matilda for years. Sonia and Matilda remained friends for decades after leaving VTR, so it was particularly painful for Matilda to find out from a mutual friend that Sonia had been sleeping with Brad while they dated. Backstabbing was to be expected in this business, though, even when it came to matters of the heart, so Matilda may not have been all that surprised, as tender to the touch as that pain point likely was.

Jessica was a tall blonde with a high nose bridge who always seemed to be impeccably—and expensively—dressed. She had an admirer who was a friend of Greg's who would drop by the office at least once a week with an orange Hermès box, which usually held a scarf or some other bourgeois accessory. She insisted loudly to the office that they were only friends. Still, she wore much more than what she could have bought off an assistant's salary. She always wore one of those scarves around her neck, which put me in mind of the story of the girl with the green ribbon. She always wore a green ribbon around her neck until one day, when she was old and sick, she told her husband to remove the ribbon. As soon as he did, her head fell right off. Probably pretty jarring for the husband. But even though I had my suspicions, I'm fairly certain Jessica's head was more or less firmly anchored to her neck.

We could never have functioned without the sales assistants, and yet they were paid only thirty thousand dollars a year, pennies compared to what the brokers made. And it's not like their jobs were without stress—if they didn't intake money for a trade made, it was just as much their asses that were on the line. In some regards, their jobs were just as or more important than their brokers'. Sure, pulling off a big trade was always worthy of a round of raucous applause and perhaps a round of celebratory coke to be passed from broker to broker. But just because you made the trade didn't necessarily mean that your big bucks were guaranteed. The sales assistants were responsible for following up with the client to ensure that the trade actually went through—plenty of clients would get cold feet and it was up to the honeyed voices of the sales assistants on the other end of the line to help their broker ensure that the client didn't renege on the deal. When money hit accounts, the sales assistants would swivel their chairs around in the direction of their broker, yell out the last name of the client, and proclaim, "Money's in!" It was only then that a broker would heave a sigh of relief. They might momentarily remember to be grateful to their assistant for helping to net their whale, but that gratitude would quickly dissipate as soon as, say, that assistant bent down to pick something up—the broker would never waste an opportunity to make a smirking sexist comment out of the side of their mouth to their neighbor at the desk next door.

Because Matilda held seniority over all the assistants, she was constantly frazzled—you could feel the nervous energy radiating in waves off her body, no more so than when IPO time came around. The air around Matilda crackled with the electricity of her anxiety then and we knew we had to tread carefully with her. She did most of our worrying for us, sweating it out during our risky maneuvering of IPOs.

She was right to be stressed, though. An IPO, if you recall, is an initial public offering. An IPO occurs when shares of a private company are offered to the public for the first time. Shares of the company are sold to an institutional investment bank, as well as to individual investors. The IPOs that we chose to pitch to our clients almost always somehow just happened to be ones in which VTR was the lead underwriter. Convenient! Why? Because being an underwriter means that the institution—whether bank, insurance company, or in this case, our investment firm—guarantees payment to a client or investor in case of financial loss and accepts the financial risk for liability arising from this guarantee. Not that we were doing so out of the goodness of our hearts, of course. Being the underwriter, we were able to slyly sell the stock with our commission included and make a killing doing so. We'd make even more for ourselves and our clients by flipping the stock immediately—this was short-term, rapid-fire trading that, if executed with speed and luck, could make quite the quick profit. Investors who had participated in previous IPOs with us had tasted favorable returns and were hungry for more. They'd quickly come aboard with us again, hoping for the next hot commodity, which, because the market was so much in our favor, would often be delivered to them. With each success, our clients would double down and invest even more heavily with us, compounding dizzying dollar amounts that could—and did—make our heads spin. We were in a bull market, meaning that the securities we were trading were either indeed on an upswing or were expected to be. Bull markets could last for years, and when I was at VTR, we were bull all the way, the bull swinging its horns upward, driving our profits higher and higher.

VTR, like Stratton before it, wasn't the only one in on the IPO game, of course. The IPO market was hot in the nineties, particularly when it came to Internet start-ups. Ever heard of the dot-com bubble? Yeah, that—we were in the thick of it, cowboys riding the wild speculation that cropped up during the popularization of the World Wide Web, of scratchy dial-up, of "you've got mail," of those fucking brilliant AOL mailers, beseeching you to sign up with their innocent-looking, brightly colored discs. I specifically remember the tide turning with the IPO of Netscape Communications. In 1995, the stock went public at twenty-eight dollars a share and, after only one day of trading, was at seventy-five dollars a share, and climbing. And 1996 was looking even better—it was shaping up to shatter the previous record for the most raised dollars from IPOs, which had been set back in '93. Yahoo!, Lycos, and Excite, among others, had all just gone public and, armed with that information, we used it to our advantage, luring investors in on the promise of www dot money. The partners told us that they hadn't seen anything like this before—the IPO craze was making some of the most prudent investors throw caution—and dollars—to the wind. We frantically tried to keep up with this feeding frenzy, pulling investors on deck like silvery, flopping fish by the dozens. Most had never participated in IPOs before, which is where we smelled blood and licked our lips. These guys were sitting ducks waiting to be fed a story, eager to invest with an emotionally delivered, rather than a logicked, by-the-numbers pitch.

The thing is, this job was not for most people. Whether you are in the game as an honest professional or as a thief, it's a hard-ass job. You can be responsible for potentially making or breaking a person. There were times I felt adored by my clients and times I felt true scorn oozing over the phone, but nothing fazed me either way. Yet you'd also have people in the business like Abel Ackerman, who was a nervous wreck, constantly on the shitter when stocks were down or he had to deliver bad news. He probably dabbled in every drug known to man (as most did) to numb himself daily, with GHB, whippets, and nitrous being his main drugs of choice. Not everyone can knowingly have investors buying into an offering or stocks that the firm is manipulating to line its own pockets (and yours)—you have to throw your conscience into your car's trunk and drop it off a bridge because it is a dangerous liability. I was a willing acolyte and in the beginning I didn't even realize that the firm was training me to traverse such a slippery slope—that realization would dawn on me later. You could not succumb to the pressure. If your client's portfolio was at a loss, so what? It was the risk the investor took—there were no guarantees in this business. That said, the optimism that my mother ingrained in me had me believe that we would make our clients money. In the beginning, I believed in the companies we were pushing—the offered cheap stock was affordable. People always want to get in at the bottom. The rewards far outweighed the risk. Clients were doing business with us because they wanted the rush and excitement of sudden wealth. We were something special, bringing you investment ideas that had the potential to trample everything else in your portfolio. How many people at this time who didn't have millions in the market could get access to IPOs, secondary offerings, private placements? No, what we were doing was, in fact, giving them the gift of opportunity. At least, that's what I told myself.

There were those that we at the chop shops fondly nicknamed "IPO whores," the investors who already knew a bit about the game and who would open accounts with various shops in an effort to get their grubby little hands on as many IPOs as possible. The whores would usually start with a small portfolio and build positions with our house stocks in the hopes that they would get allocated shares when deal time came around. At the end of the day, VTR was a chop shop and the whores were our bread and butter—we couldn't have pulled off our IPOs as successfully with-out them, as they built up much-needed hype around our offer-ings before they went public. Landing an IPO whore was fairly simple, as they were already eagerly awaiting your cold call. Early into the call they would indicate extreme interest and, knowing that this meant you had a whore on your hands, you would get the attention of your broker as quickly as you could, signaling silently to another caller to grab your broker as you stayed on the line. If your broker was on the phone and couldn't make his way over to you, then another broker, usually a loose partner of yours, would run over to assist. You would then hand the phone over to the broker and watch the dance begin. This happened to me a few times, and when it did, Shappy would bound over, pumping his little legs, wheezing and going red in the face to get there as quickly as he could. He'd snatch the phone and the lead card from me to take over and try to land the client. As much as I wanted to make headway with Sharpstein and the partners, I loathed his presence at my desk. When pitching, he'd foam at the mouth and spit would fly everywhere, across my phone and all over my desk. I could smell the memory of his rancid breath and whatever it was that he had eaten earlier on my phone, so I took to bringing alcohol pads to work and wiping my phone down discreetly after he'd had his way with it.

Whenever a broker came to the cold caller side to pitch a lead, everyone put their phones down and stopped whatever it was that they were doing. The brokers demanded silence so that there would be no background noise, which meant none of our usual yelling and slamming phones down. But even more so, we cold callers wanted to take every opportunity we could to watch and learn. We were both mesmerized by our brokers and also hoping just a tiny bit that the person on the other end of the line would rip the broker to shreds, just to see how the broker would take it and rebound . . . or not. On the other hand, it was always a good look if the lead you had found turned into an account opened right on the spot. It made you look good to your broker and the partners, and would help make your case for why you should cross the invisible line from the cold callers' side of the room to the brokers'.

The highs that we achieved from trading in a bull market were better than drugs or sex, and it made us feel invincible, as if we were gods looking down on the earth, manipulating those below according to our whims. The thing is, though, at some point, bull markets have to make room for the bears—those pessimistic, lumbering bears that swipe their paws downward, pushing profits lower, and turning gods back into mortals.

Chapter 13

MOSQUITOES ARE RELENTLESS—SWAT ONE AWAY and it will come back, undeterred, to bite you again and again, leaving angry red welts that you can't soon forget. It feeds off you, gorging itself, and it will not stop until you are forced to kill it, squashing its little insect body against your arm or thigh, smearing your own blood across your skin, a streaked reminder that it stole from you.

The men at my firm—and, I'll hazard a guess, everywhere else on Wall Street—were mosquitoes. It's too bad I couldn't squash them with a simple, sharp slap. They were shameless and they never missed an opportunity to sexually harass me and every other woman in our office. I kept my head down and never would have complained about it, but what if I had wanted to? Who would I have gone to? If you tried to bring the issue up with management, which consisted entirely of men, you were branded a tight-ass who couldn't take a joke or a compliment. Some of us women were *lucky* to even be paid such attention.

We couldn't report complaints to the HR department because our company didn't have one. The odds were truly stacked against us given that we were in a male-dominated field in the nineties—toxic masculinity was a phrase that was not yet in the public consciousness—and the objectification of women was so deeply entrenched that frankly it was expected of you if you were a man. If you didn't ogle a woman or talk about her tits out of the side of your mouth to your desk neighbor or you missed an opportunity to grab an ass, what were you, gay, or a mama's boy? Come on, men were supposed to act like men!

At the time, it seemed to me that both men and women knew that men were taught to go after what and who they wanted, and if they just persisted, they could often win a woman over. No is actually just a slow yes. So even if something felt uncomfortable or wrong, what could you do? You just had to put up with it if you wanted to keep your job and climb the corporate ladder.

I noticed, too, that the men had different styles of harassment; some would be blatantly up in your face while others might be more subtle, and still others might even get artful with it. All were inappropriate. A few among many that I encountered:

The Professional

By "professional," did you think I meant that the guy was respectful to me in any way? Ha! No. I'd often have men repurposing pitch lines from our cold caller playbook, as if I couldn't see what they were doing and hadn't used these very lines on investors myself. They ranged from dull plug-and-play lines to more creative riffs. My favorite retort when one cold caller propositioned me with the awful, "Cin, just give me a shot, and I guarantee that you will enjoy the dividends," was looking over at him slowly, picking up my phone dramatically, then slamming it back in its cradle as hard as I could. Let's just say that corny-as-fuck lead didn't work out for him.

The Pervert

Alan Richardson was a fellow cold caller who arrived at VTR almost three months into my tenure there. He was older and attempted to play the role of sophisticated gentleman, arriving to work every day in a suit and a possibly fake British accent that I think he used to mask his true Caribbean accent. He had a smile that never reached his cold, calculating eyes, and he often bragged to anyone who would listen that he had been the top cold caller at his previous firm, but was forced to leave because the company had not kept its word regarding a deal that they had made. He constantly cracked dirty jokes to me and the girl who sat next to him, accompanying each grimy quip with a laugh, as if that would excuse him from blame.

Early one morning, I trudged into work and saw Alan sitting at his desk, laughing to himself. It was a strange sight given that he wasn't speaking to anyone and if you were a cold caller, you likely had nothing to laugh at—your day was probably going to suck.

Mystified, I turned to him and said, "That's a good way to start your morning because in a few minutes someone will be cursing you out."

Alan replied with a complete non sequitur.

"Yeah, and these are some great photos—here, this one is my favorite."

He leaned over his desk and handed me a greasy Polaroid. I glanced down; it took me a second to register what I was looking at, but then the nauseating feeling of disgust washed over me. The photo showed a disembodied hand holding a penis. Ugh. Before the golden age of smartphones with cameras, Snapchat, and porn sites, there were pervs who would be happy to share hard-copy dick pics via washed-out Polaroids and out-of-focus prints from a one-hour-photo kiosk.

Alan winked, and pointed out that the ring that the hand in the photo was wearing just so happened to be the same ring that he was now wearing on his hand.

I grimaced. "Why are you showing this to me?" I asked.

He chuckled again. "We are here all day and you probably get lonely, so I just wanted you to see that it's nice and clean and ready."

I had seen enough unwanted penises in my life—I wasn't impressed. I threw the photo at him and shrugged.

"Way too small for me, no thanks," I said, before turning around and picking up my phone, giving him the cold shoulder.

The next morning, I had beaten Alan to the office and was at my desk when he walked into the Pit and made his way over to me. He triumphantly threw another Polaroid onto my desk.

"The one I showed you yesterday was when I had just gotten out of the shower. In this one my dick is dirty, but nice and hard," he said, smiling lasciviously at me.

Without missing a beat, I said, "Great! I'll be happy to share this with the sales assistants, and I'll pass along your message."

At that, he blanched. He knew that if I passed this along to the sales assistants, he might get in trouble. Not because the company was looking out for them but because a few of the sales assistants were dating brokers and if they caught wind of Alan's dick pics, they'd take personal offense and take it upstairs to the partners, who could blackball him if they wanted to. He backpedaled swiftly.

"C'mon, Cin, I was being funny. It was just a joke!"

I stared at him coldly.

"Alan, this is not funny and we are definitely not friends. So the next time you ever think about being 'funny' with me, I *will* share with the other ladies, and I'll make my own jokes that you really won't like."

He walked away quickly, realizing I was deadly serious, and never spoke to me again.

The Caretaker

One guy liked to cop faux concern for me, constantly asking me if my back hurt and if he could help me out with anything. Why? He was worried that because my breasts were so big, they had to have been hurting my back. Gee, thanks.

The Fruit Vendor

My own boss, Adam Sharpstein, loved to ask me what fruit my breasts put me in mind of—were they closer to melons or were they more like pears? They couldn't possibly be peaches or plums because they were too big for those, of course. Whenever he'd bring up the dreaded fruit with me, he'd clutch his own chest—given that he was so fat, his own breasts were not small—and shake his handfuls at me. I'd always mumble an "I don't know" and walk away before he could see my irritation. I wouldn't grant him that.

❧

It just wasn't worth it to show the men that you were bothered by their lewd comments or hooting jokes. It was just as much a test to see if they could get a rise out of you as it was to see if you were down for some action. When I couldn't ignore the harassment, I'd sometimes even laugh along with the men who were volleying bullshit at me, just to make it go away. There was simply no way to respond to every inappropriate act—I never would have gotten my work done if I had tried. I was propositioned constantly, not only by other cold callers but by account openers, brokers, and investors. It never stopped. And neither did I. I focused only on making my way to the brokers' side of the room. Later, when I'd become a broker, I talked with a few I'd become friendly with, and they admitted that they had felt somewhat bad about the sexist and racist treatment I had received. I disdained that, though—I didn't want anyone to feel sorry for me because if they did, that meant that they didn't think of me as an equal, which was insulting to me and didn't give me the credit I deserved. If I could make money with the best of them, why did it matter? I wouldn't let preconceived notions about race or gender hold me back. At least, that's what I felt at the time. My mother had taught me I could do anything in America, and back then my eyes weren't open to the systemic barriers holding back women and BIPOC. I felt that I had *gamed* the system, sliding into a job without a college degree. I figured that nothing came for free so if I had to deal with certain insults and jabs, so be it—some amount of abuse was to be expected. I just paid my dues differently.

The other women at the firm were treated similarly. Some put up with it like I did. Others, likely feeling pressured to give in to the men's demands, acquiesced and slept with them because they felt like they had to in order to advance or to receive their yearly bonus, to not be ousted from the company entirely, or because the men intimidated them into it. Or maybe a combination of all, sadly.

Sex oozed all over the office and extended to the upper echelons, of course. Once a week, Tie Girl—we never knew her name—would visit the office. She would hand sell expensive ties, usually costing between one hundred and two hundred dollars, to the brokers, and she had no shortage of business. After disposing of her wares, she would make a beeline to a partner's office, closing the door behind her. Shortly after, the blinds would go down and we were all sure we knew what was happening in there. Tie Girl always made sure she was paid for *all* her services.

Tie Girl was one of many. There was a constant parade of

strippers and sex workers in and out of certain partners' offices and nobody batted an eye. They usually came under disguise as masseuses. A lot of "massages" were had in those offices . . .

Some liaisons were never officially confirmed, but given some of the sales assistants' designer handbags and jewelry that were gifted by the brokers over the holidays, it was reasonably assumed that there were sexual dalliances at play. Sex among the staff was so commonplace that I never thought to question these interactions and whether they may have been coerced or what kind of power dynamics were at play between the two parties. I figured that these were consenting adults doing what they needed and wanted to do, for their own reasons, and it was none of my business. I was simply an observer and didn't want to get bogged down on my way to brokership.

❧

The double standards between the men and women of the firm were glaring. The sales assistants were always expected to look expensive and neat, with not a single hair out of place. Somehow, even though they were paid chump change, they were strongly encouraged to wear designer brands to represent the prosperity of the office. Some of the assistants were gifted generously by their brokers, but I'm not sure what the others, who, for example, assisted cheapskates like Adam, did to score Burberry, Hermès, and Gucci. (For the longest time, I wondered what stick was up the ass of the sales assistant who came into the office almost every day flaunting a prominent "H" belt cinched around her narrow waist. For the life of me, I couldn't figure out what was so special about a cheap Hugo Boss belt. When I upgraded from Ann Taylor and started shopping for luxury brands for myself, I finally realized that Hugo Boss belt was actually an Hermès belt that would have cost me three weeks' cold caller pay. Oh.)

Even if the assistants had been invited to a raucous party

with the brokers the night before and encouraged to go wild, they were expected to be back at the office the next morning by eight a.m. at the latest, looking impeccable as always and ready to get down to work. Brokers, however, could slop themselves in, coked out and jittery, some of them wearing the same suit two days in a row, bellowing about the drugs and hookers and bottle service they'd engaged in the night before. One day, one guy came in so fucked up that he sat at his desk with sunglasses on and with an open umbrella perched over his head. People did weird shit and it was so common that nobody ever commented on it. All the brokers had their moments. Even if they wore five-thousand-dollar suits and twenty-thousand-dollar Rolexes, they still looked like they'd just rolled out of bed without washing their faces or brushing their teeth. Those who didn't want to repeat an outfit either kept spare suits at the office, crumpled at their desks, in case they were out partying the whole night and didn't make it home to change, or they would order their caller to pick up a new shirt from the nearby department store, Century 21.

The extravagance of it all both mystified and excited me. Perhaps the most fundamental difference in how I saw the world versus how the privileged white brokers saw it was through food. At home, I'd been taught never to waste anything—so it was eye-opening to see brokers buy a bagel and throw half of it away, order two lunches and only touch one. The callers would often ask the brokers for their leftovers, which the brokers would wave their way. I was too proud to do that, though. I almost always brought my lunch from home, or if I ordered a plate of chicken, rice, and beans from the Mexican-Spanish food truck that idled outside the building, I'd eat half for lunch and save the other half for dinner. At $2.50 a plate, that meant I was only spending $1.25 per meal. I had to think this way given that my salary was so low as to be almost nonexistent. But the brokers threw cash around with abandon. A small example, but it was telling for me: Downstairs in the building's café, the brokers would order a bagel and coffee every morning. If this cost them three dollars, they would pay with a ten-dollar bill and give the barista *seven dollars* in change. Every day. And they would do the same for their afternoon coffee and snack. At fourteen dollars a day, five days a week, that was seventy dollars a week—about a third of my weekly salary.

Of course, this wanton spending extended far beyond morning bagels. It was common to hear the brokers on the phone, ordering a new car for an assistant to pick up. Yes, a car!

"The Porsche needs to be in the forest green, not the sage green, you understand?" was a phrase it was entirely possible to overhear. And of course, this casual ordering of luxury items as if ordering a pizza extended to customized Rolexes and Breitlings, designer clothing, anything that the broker decided in that moment that they just *had* to have, even if they decided to discard it the following week.

One late Friday afternoon, I looked up to see a group of brokers and a couple partners shooting the shit together, jostling each other, loud as ever. Not a big deal. Then I heard, *Let's do it!* accompanied by cheering. What was it they had decided? Oh, you know, just swing by the Olympics. Yep, you heard right. They had decided on a whim to order a private jet and fly to Atlanta, which was hosting the 1996 Summer Olympics. Why? Because they could.

VTR was a glorified frat house, missing only the keg stands and beer pong stations—though of course hard liquor and blow could be found in almost every broker's drawer. If a broker wasn't cracking a sexist joke at you, it was only because he was too busy picking his nose, scratching his balls, or participating in a farting contest with someone else. You could rest assured he'd circle back to ogle you or make a snide comment about your breasts.

One of my favorite people in the office was a cold caller who was promoted to broker like me. His name was John Buckmaster, though we all called him Buck. He wasn't an ordinary cold caller recruited off the streets. He had connections: his girlfriend was a friend of partner Levi's wife, and he was ushered in without having to suffer the hazing of Brad Ambrosi's vein-pulsating wrath. He mostly eschewed coke in favor of weed and had recently gotten arrested for possession, so his father, who was supporting him, told him he needed to get a job or he'd be cut off. Buck was always high and always laughing about something. He was good at breaking the tension that always hung in the air.

Buck sat close to the sales assistants and his eyes were constantly glued to their pod, straining to see the outline of a bra strap, like most of the other men in the office. Because Buck was a shoo-in and curried special favor with Levi, he was allowed to keep a small fan on his desk. As big as the Pit was, it was crowded with bodies, rank with alcohol-infused sweat and BO, and hot as a swamp, so Buck constantly had the fan going. One of his favorite activities was to point the fan toward the sales assistants in an effort to waft his smelly farts over. It was his way of saying "fuck you" to the assistants, who thought they were better than him, a lowly cold caller. When you saw Buck laughing with the fan pointed at the assistants, you knew that he had just let something foul fly.

Of course, Buck wasn't the only one guilty of bodily emissions. The brokers were so dirty and disgusting that the partners had to make regular announcements pleading with the men to try harder to keep the bathroom clean, and that if they took a smelly shit, to please light a match because it wasn't fair to the poor, unsuspecting fucker who had the misfortune to enter the bathroom after them.

The brokers took their morning bathroom routines seriously, whether it was for a post-bagel evacuation or for some solo exploratory time. If a broker was in the bathroom for more than a few minutes, the others would waggle their eyebrows and inevitably someone would remark that he was rubbing one out to start the day on the right foot.

After sugar-sweetened coffee was slurped, after their bodily business affairs were conducted in the bathroom, the brokers, feeling rejuvenated, would set upon us cold callers, listening in on our first pitches of the day, ragging on us if they felt we were being too soft. Screams of "You suck!" and "Wake the fuck up!" would ring out in the boardroom. "Sleep when you're dead" and the more pointed "If you need to jerk off to get going, then do that before you get here" were also common refrains. Nothing like humiliation and fear to wake you up first thing in the morning.

The partners would hold their morning meetings in the boardroom for everyone to hear, and they often would devote a few minutes to hearing a pitch from a cold caller that they would pick at will. With usually around a hundred people at a time lasered in on the cold caller, it was an absolutely terrifying experience, and we always slouched down, desperately avoiding eye contact, hoping against hope that we wouldn't be picked to pitch. Sometimes the brokers would volunteer their callers as tribute, confident—even if the caller wasn't—that they could do a good job and curry favor for the broker. Partner Levi was usually in charge of the morning meeting pitches, and he would act as a sometimes malevolent emcee of sorts, throwing out comments over a microphone. If he was in a bad mood, which was fairly often, he'd wave away the brokers and point to someone, screaming out, "YOU! Get the fuck up and pitch me!"

If you happened to be picked, you'd take a big gulp of air and say your prayers because, depending on how you performed, this could be your last pitch *ever*. If you stumbled or stuttered or just weren't quick enough on your feet, Levi would yell out, "Get those fucking marbles out of your mouth this morning! How do you think you can get on the phone like this, sounding like you are scared of your own shadow? Sit the fuck down, you piker! Or better yet, get the fuck outta here. You don't deserve a desk here." The cold caller would sit down in deep shame, and it was anyone's guess as to whether Levi was serious or not—sometimes he was, and the caller really would be fired on the spot. At other times, his attention would waver and he'd forget about your abysmal performance, and you'd live to see another tenuous day.

One morning, as we all took our seats and the partners wrapped up their meeting, preparing to go into pitch mode, I felt something shift inside me. I cast my eye over the Pit, taking a critical look at those around me. Any casual conversation that had sprung up was quickly petering out and the callers were beginning to fold into themselves, anxiety seeping out of their pores and saturating the air. I could feel the fear welling up inside me, too, but this time, it felt different. It was a catalyst, a jolt up my spine; I was being called to action. I asked myself what I would get out of sinking in my chair and hoping that I'd be passed over in favor of some other unlucky caller. This pattern would just repeat itself ad infinitum and I'd be stuck in that same chair, glued to my phone, hoping to hit my lead count until I burned out. No, screw that. I didn't need to let Levi or the other brokers control my narrative.

I watched for a moment as Levi scanned the room, ready for the kill. Before he could pounce, and before I even knew quite what I was doing, I stood up in a rush, my sudden movement sending my chair hitching back like a startled animal. I cleared

my throat and looked Levi straight in the eye. Without breaking his gaze, I said loudly, "Levi Bing, please—tell him Cin
Fabré is on the phone."

Audible gasps rang out through the Pit and a fury of low
whispers filled the room. I knew what everyone was thinking. *What the hell is she doing?* Not only had I boldly volun-
teered to pitch, but I had unapologetically challenged a partner
of the firm. This had never once happened in the history of
VTR. As messy as the firm could be, there were strict ways of
doing things and everyone who worked there knew their place.
Nobody stepped out of line because fear and ridicule ruled with
an iron fist. I was over it. I had been there for three months
and I hadn't received my books yet, and I hadn't seen any other
callers, even those who'd been there longer, receive their books,
either. I knew that we were just as capable as these asswipe
brokers—we just needed a chance to prove it. We'd faced far
more shit than these white boys ever had. We could play and
we could win.

I took a deep breath, my heart in my throat. Everyone, even
the sales assistants, watched in rapt silence.

Levi looked stunned for a moment, clearly taken aback. He
looked over at the other partners, who gave him a collective
shrug, then he swiveled back to me. A slow smile broke out
across his face and he licked his lips. Game on.

"Who's this?" he said back to me.

There was no going back now.

"This is Cin," I said, immediately shouting *fuck!* in my
head.

Levi smirked.

"Cin *who*?" he shot back.

"Cin Fabré," I said. What a stumble, such a rookie move. I
took another breath. I wouldn't let this trip me up. I forged on.

When you're filled with fear, your hearing hollows out and

your vision narrows. Your memory of events becomes patchy and dreamlike. So I don't recall the exact wording of my pitch, but I remember pacing the aisles like a tiger, back and forth, as I hit Levi with everything I had. I was scared, but I was confident I could do it.

I know I was good, better than good. I was great. I finished out strong by saying, "Remember my name—it's Cin Fabré at VTR. *Have a good day.*"

At that, my legs turned to jelly and I sank into my seat, relieved I was finished, even if I'd just gotten myself fired for insubordination. The room was deathly still for what felt like hours but was probably only a few seconds, and then it erupted into triumphant noise, everyone stomping their feet and yelling. Levi boomed over the microphone, "Give this girl a round of applause!" and a cacophony of cheers swelled around me. Those who were near me all ran over to clap me on the back and congratulate me.

Levi continued on the microphone. "Guys, this girl just put you all to shame. She's a girl and has more balls than most of you! That's the difference from wanting it and just trying to make it in this business. She wants it! A fire has been lit under her ass! How many of you want it? How many of you came to work today saying, 'I'm going to kill it and get ten leads today and I'm going to make five hundred dials'? Or did you come in to bitch about how you can't get anyone on the phone and how you were only able to make three hundred dials? There are no excuses! If you don't want it, you won't get it! Listen up! All you assholes cowering in the corner like a bunch of pussies, hoping I don't call your name—take this as your fucking lesson. You need to get to your desks and jump right into it and start pitching. Now get the fuck on the phone and get some leads!"

From that day on, everything changed. I was newly empowered, no longer deflated by the constant ribbing I got from the brokers and partners, didn't care anymore if I got hung up on ten times in a row by grumpy, shit leads. I knew I could make it and that the firm would have to take me seriously. In fact, my stunt transformed how the partners structured their pitch sessions with cold callers. They now required callers to volunteer to pitch the room, and if you didn't, then you were labeled a pussy and you wouldn't be allowed to represent VTR.

This announcement was made by Levi the following day, with everyone congregating together in the boardroom. Now that I had found my voice, I intended to use it. At the mention of being a pussy if you couldn't hack it, I yelled out, "I AM a pussy!" The room went quiet—I seemed to have cultivated the unique skill of creating silence—and Adam looked at me like I was out of my damn mind.

Levi paused and looked at me, smiling slightly. "Yes, yes, you are."

I wanted everyone to know that I was a pussy and proud of it.

Chapter 14

I HAD VOWED TO MYSELF THAT I WOULD HAVE MY BOOKS by the time I had hit three months at the firm, the minimum amount of time you had to be there to receive them. I was chafing to get them, but the brokers never seemed to give their cold callers their books. I hadn't seen *anyone* get their books since I'd gotten to VTR, and it was suspect.

Looking back, I'm amazed at how naive I was, to think that if we callers just followed protocol, we would be promoted in due time because, well, because that's what the rules said so it had to be so. Callers could float around firms for years, lured to different offices on the promise that such and such firm would *actually* issue them their books. Of course, all the boiler rooms operated in the same way—they wanted the dirt-cheap labor of the cold callers to generate leads for the brokers so they could open accounts and profit. The firms could make more money without having to share it if they took advantage of the cold callers, who, again, were largely from marginalized communities. Most burned out without ever getting their books, resigning themselves to finding jobs outside the industry. Some of the callers who had left VTR actually shared that it was one of the more equitable firms, believe it or not. They told me horror stories about the other firms. One kid told me the FBI raided his firm and he was never allowed to go back and get his personal things. Another shared that the firm he'd worked at had flaked at paying the callers multiple weeks in a row. When the callers found out that they were about to be stiffed for another week, they mutinied and threw their computers out the office window, the boxy machines sailing down to the street below before smashing into a million little pieces. Callers would show up to work and their firm would be shuttered without warning. Some were instructed by their brokers to beat up other callers if the broker felt that caller needed to learn a lesson. On a hurried lunch break one day, I'd gone outside for a small bit of fresh air, and I saw a caller from another firm running for his life, a small mob of men in hot pursuit behind him. Turns out he'd knowingly handed his broker a bunch of wood leads—a very good way to get a black eye and blackballed from the business.

At VTR, wood leads were handled with public fury and expletives, Jameson Logan–style. That is, until Stewart. Proclaimed the new superstar by the brokers at the firm, Stewart was amazingly and improbably getting ten leads a day, every day. Of course the brokers used Stewart's count to shame us, telling us we weren't working hard enough: *Just look at Stewart! He can do it so you should be able to do the same, you piker!* I smelled bullshit in the air, but I kept my mouth shut. Sure enough, a few weeks later, they all changed their tune when his broker attempted to open accounts based off his leads. Wood. Every single one of them. Not one was legitimate. Cue the verbal flogging and firing in front of the entire company. This one was particularly brutal, even by VTR standards. But the sheer gall the kid had to throw that much wood at his broker like that meant it was merited. Just another day at the office.

The next morning, I walked into the boardroom and headed to my desk but stopped short when who did I see but Stewart, sitting meekly at his desk, phone in hand, already dialing. Huh.

I figured he had given a sob story to his broker, who had chosen to take pity on him and let him stay. Whatever, it wasn't my business.

One by one the brokers stumbled in from their morning bathroom visits, smeary bagels and coffee in hand. Once everyone had assembled, we began the morning partner meeting. This time, Jameson Logan walked the aisles of the Pit, demanding that each cold caller tell him how many leads they had secured the day before. Four, seven, three, eight, six, and so on. Then he got to Stewart's desk. He paused, clearly confused. *Didn't we fire this asshole yesterday?* you could see him thinking to himself. He pointed at Stewart.

"What the fuck are you doing here?" he asked.

"I'm cold calling," Stewart replied, vaguely gesturing toward his phone.

Jameson's eyes narrowed. "You were fired for passing wood. You don't work here anymore; you need to get the fuck outta here or I'll throw you the fuck out."

Stewart was seemingly impervious to Jameson's threats. He dramatically raised his palm up into the air for all of us to see.

"You see my hand? You see how it's not shaking? I'm not afraid of you."

Jameson flushed an ominous shade of red and looked ready to strangle the kid. But before he could take another step toward him, Stewart shoved the hand he had been holding high into his messenger bag, rooting around for something. The room fell quiet and then—

He's got a gun! someone yelled suddenly. Pandemonium broke out and everyone stampeded toward the exit, falling over themselves to escape Stewart the Caller's deadly wrath.

This wasn't an overreaction. People were receiving beatdowns on Wall Street all the time; burnt investors would attempt to barge into offices to retaliate. There had even been a homicide or two at brokerages in the last decade. It was the Wild West out here and a shooting wouldn't be entirely out of the ordinary.

While I scrambled to get away, I had enough time to think bemusedly, "If he takes anyone out, he'll definitely go for the brokers first," and, "At least we get a break from the phones for a minute."

Jameson stayed cemented to his spot while everyone rushed to get away. As I looked back, I saw Stewart take his hand out of his bag, his thumb and pointer finger making the gun sign.

He smirked. "Oh, I was just getting a pen. I didn't scare you, did I?"

Jameson was downright apoplectic and everyone else stopped in their tracks, breathing ragged sighs of relief, nervous laughter escaping involuntarily from some. We were all pissed. Not cool. Jameson called on the two biggest men in the room to cart off the little fucker and throw him into the street like the garbage he was.

From that day forward, VTR applied a tad more finesse to firings. Brad Ambrosi would stalk up the aisles of the Pit to whisper in a caller's ear and they'd leave the boardroom together. A desk neighbor, recognizing the telltale signs of a firing, would pack up the caller's few things in a small cardboard box and bring it downstairs, and that would be that. We took to calling Ambrosi "Grim" in homage to the Grim Reaper, as he was always faithfully delivering bad news.

～

At nineteen, so feverishly eager to make it on Wall Street, I meanly scoffed at those who hadn't yet found success. I chalked it all up to a lack of motivation and hard work on their part, and I knew that things would be different for me, ignoring the systemic inequalities right in front of my nose.

My broker Adam was no different from the other brokers in terms of holding people back for his own advantage. I was damn good at sending leads his way, only giving him a wood lead every so often. He didn't want that sweet stream of leads to dry up, which is what would happen if I became a broker and struck out on my own. That is why, whenever I brought up the subject of getting my books, he would punt the conversation to something else. He always tried to keep me in my place. When he wasn't commenting on my breasts, he was lobbing racist questions my way—could I tell him whether it was true that Black people loved watermelon and fried chicken, whether Black guys really were hung, and did I come from a single-family home? He would frame these offensive questions and comments as jokes, that convenient facade of racists and misogynists everywhere, erected to demonstrate that he was laughing with you, not at you—he wasn't *actually* racist; he couldn't be because he was Jewish. He and the other brokers assumed I knew where to score weed and that I was smoking it all the time (never mind that Buck, a white guy, was the biggest pothead at VTR), and that I, and every other Black person at the firm, had to naturally be good at sports. I wasn't the only one to experience racism at the firm, of course. That was thrown at every nonwhite person at VTR. When the cold callers returned from lunch, the brokers would sometimes yell over to us, "Don't get the 'itis!," "'itis" being short for "niggaitis," meaning being too full to be productive and work. They thought it wasn't racist for them to use this term, but it didn't belong to them and it definitely wasn't okay. People were specifically targeted, too. Brad Ambrosi, for example, once had Emilio Pereira hold up a newspaper mugshot in front of his face and do a side-by-side comparison, looking horrified the whole time. He kept looking back and forth, making Emilio increasingly uncomfortable until he let out a big laugh and said, "Naaaah, I guess that ain't you," before walking away. We picked up a copy of the paper in the lobby later and saw that the guy was wanted for armed robbery. Emilio was horrified but didn't say anything because he was afraid Ambrosi was going to fire him. It ate him up inside so much that he quit shortly after this incident.

The horrific blend of sexism and racism that was thrown at me was so blatant and all-consuming that if someone else had told me they'd experienced what I had, I probably wouldn't have believed them. One afternoon, a broker stopped me as I was heading back to my desk. Brokers didn't typically associate with callers more than they had to, especially with a caller who didn't belong to them, so I heaved an inward sigh and said, "Hey, what's up?" I knew that whatever came out of this guy's mouth was going to be hot, smelly garbage.

He asked me solicitously how my calls were going that day—as if he gave a fuck—and I tersely told him, "Fine." Then a shit-eating grin appeared on his face. *Here we go*, I thought.

"You know," he said, leaning in uncomfortably close to me and lowering his voice, "if things don't work out for you here, I, uh, I can help you out."

I arched an eyebrow. "Oh yeah? And how would you do that?"

He grinned like the Cheshire Cat. I always hated *Alice in Wonderland*—too trippy, too many drugs.

"See, I know the owner of VIP's," he continued. VIP's, as we called it, or The VIP Club if you could be bothered for a few more syllables. It was . . . a strip club.

"Yeah, I could put in a good word for you—you know they're always short on Black chicks." He laughed—just a joke!—but his eyes were cold.

I didn't miss a beat, though.

"Oh, that's right! I heard that's where you met your wife. Can you find out what she used to make on her best nights? Or better yet, is she still there? Maybe she can show me the ropes!" I laughed right back at him. It was true, too—his fiancée had been a stripper, though she wasn't in the biz anymore.

The broker's smirk went sour, and he sarcastically responded with a slow "ha-ha, very funny." He walked away and mostly left me alone after that. Guess he couldn't take a joke.

～

Back to Adam. These kinds of conversations happened most often with him, and they were tiring and demoralizing so I tried not to engage with him when he inevitably brought up such harmful bullshit. I would just shrug my shoulders and not give him the satisfaction of a response, and he would eventually move on. Every so often, he would make a show of mentorship, offering me suggestions on how I could improve my pitching, but mostly he centered the conversation on himself, telling me exactly how he was building his war chest at the firm, leaning on his cold callers and other brokers to help him, as he wasn't actually great at landing clients. He appealed mostly to farmers and blue-collar sorts who had managed to amass money. He lost his confidence when talking to more seasoned investors and experienced businessmen; he would fumble and squeal and let them rattle him, all but guaranteeing a lost lead. When this happened, he'd look over at me as if it were somehow my fault, which enraged me—he'd just wasted a valuable connect that I'd worked so hard to net for him, that sweaty pig.

Adam almost always relied on the other brokers to feed him lines. If he managed to hold on to a big lead for more than a couple of minutes, the other brokers would line up by the phone on the wall that connected to his line, taking turns with the phone and feeding him line after line in an admirable effort to save and land the lead.

Even though other cold callers thought I was wasting my time as Adam's cold caller, it was a valuable experience watching him pitch. He taught me what *not* to do, which really was just as helpful as learning what to do.

As much as Adam tried to stymie me, he couldn't keep me

from my books. After my fateful pitch to Levi, I had the support of the partners; they wanted to see what I was capable of, and I was more than ready to show them. They couldn't outright direct Shap to give me my books—only a caller's broker could make that decision, as it was the brokers who paid for their callers and were considered their property. (Yes, we were actually considered their property!) But Shappy had designs on becoming a partner one day and he knew that he'd be lauded as a team player if he gave me my books. I'd shown promise, and if I were promoted to broker, then I'd be contributing to the company's bottom line, which, more than any kind desire to see me succeed, was what the partners really wanted.

At the end of another grueling day of calls, Shap had me stop by his desk. He didn't waste time making small talk—he wasn't that kind of guy; that is, unless that small talk involved how big my breasts were. Acting like he was busy with some papers on his desk, he avoided eye contact and begrudgingly told me I'd better start studying for the Series 7 if I ever wanted to become a broker. He finally was going to give me my books so I could move forward. My time had finally come.

Chapter 15

THE BROKERS HAD THEIR OWN HANGOUT SPOTS around Wall Street, and the cold callers had theirs. There was no overlap. The callers always convened at the same places: Rosario's, a cheap Italian red-sauce joint, complete with red-and-white checkered oilcloth tablecloths and recycled bread baskets; the beaten-up, two-dollar food truck that was always faithfully parked at the corner of Wall Street and Broadway; and the check-cashing place that would overflow with cold callers come payday.

We would meet at lunchtime and after work to swap war stories, like who had gotten the harshest beatdown of the week or who had managed to land a whale for their broker. We all exaggerated, but it was true that our biggest whales could make our brokers a hefty six-figure commission in one go. We'd talk reverentially about the same few callers we knew (or, more often, had heard rumor of) who had made it through the trenches to get their books and pass the Series 7 to become an account opener and then, finally, broker. We collected these stories like unique specimens in jars, taking them out again and again to pore over, examining them for anything new that might offer us fresh insight on how we could do the same.

Some callers, though, were apprehensive, worrying out loud

about the tense responsibility of running a book, as it was known—keeping a lucrative client base up—and making your numbers each month. You could see the fear in their eyes when they brought up hypotheticals of being sued by clients, or getting attacked if they lost the wrong person's money. You always knew which callers would never even reach the milestone of getting their books, much less becoming a broker.

When I told our group, which was milling around the food truck, getting handed dirty water dogs and packets of mustard to squiggle on their buns, that I had gotten my books, there was no resentment, hidden or otherwise—it was always a celebration if one of our own got a step closer to the big leagues. I think one of the callers even treated me to a hot dog, which wasn't nothing when most of us had to scrounge around for enough change to buy ourselves a slice of pizza or a coffee.

My books (unglamorously called the Series 7 Exam Practice Guides) were a symbol of all the riches and ease I was about to inherit, and I liked to lovingly caress them, running my hands over their smooth, glossy covers, flipping through hundreds of pages filled with dense definitions and explanations of all the minutiae of the finance industry, from buying and selling to market regulations to ethics. That said, studying itself was the absolute bane of my existence. I didn't learn until my midthirties or so that I had undiagnosed ADD, which of course made studying almost impossible without proper treatment. Besides, how was I supposed to even know how to study? I had spent my years of school scheming to get out of tests and papers instead of buckling down with books, narrowly graduating, probably because my ADD made it hard for me to focus in the first place.

VTR had an airless conference room that it allowed its callers to study in after five p.m.; that is, as long as we had made our lead count for the day. Most days, I preferred calling over studying, which tells you how much I loathed it. Back then, there were no cheat sheets or CliffsNotes available to snag online. My days were consumed with studying concepts that I'd never heard of in my life—never once at VTR had the brokers attempted to teach us callers anything about trading options, even though we were supposed to persuade our leads that our options were the best! What the hell was a "put and call"? What did it mean to recommend to clients that they keep options in multiple sectors? It was all a foreign language to me, so I resigned myself to rote memorization, hoping to spit answers back out undigested at test time.

After each workday, I'd shuffle to the windowless conference room, which always smelled like old soup, and crack open my books, trying to transmit information into my head. Almost anything had the power to distract me. An errant noise of a chair scraping, a door closing, a broker yelling—and I was spinning out. I struggled to absorb the information on the page, having to read and reread a single sentence many times over before it made sense, and sometimes not even then. Did I need water? Maybe I needed water. If so, I should go grab some and maybe while I was at it, I should see who's on the phone. And so on, and so forth.

It never even occurred to me to reach out to ask Sharpstein for help, or to try to form a study group with others preparing for the Series 7. I snarled at anyone who tried to distract me and was given the nickname of "bitch on wheels." Fine, I didn't care.

After slogging through calls and studying on the weekdays, I worked weekends at Cohen's to supplement the pittance I was earning at VTR. On my lunch breaks and on slow days, I'd try to sneak in more studying while my manager wasn't looking. It was brutal. For the following three months, I studied my ass off and barely managed to pass the practice tests that the books supplied. Shit.

The next tool in my arsenal was Tony DeCicco, a.k.a. Tony D

a.k.a. Mr. Wall Street. He was legendary. It was said that if you took his prep class, you were guaranteed to pass—almost everyone on Wall Street taking the Series 7 enrolled in his class. Tony was an improbable teacher, but I respected him—he was born in the Bronx, just like me, and he'd made it as a broker and then an educator with his wildly popular test prep course. He knew how to hustle. In his lifetime, he was said to have helped eighteen thousand financial advisers. Years later, he would actually cohost a show on CNBC called *Staten Island Hustle* in which he doled out financial wisdom and schemed to dream up new moneymaking hustles with his Italian businessman buddies, mafioso style. His motto on the show was, "We're Italian. This is the way we are."

Tony was a character straight out of *Goodfellas*—if I closed my eyes, it was as if I had Joe Pesci muttering in my ear about wiseguys. He was larger than life and the cuff links he had on every day were even bigger than that. The gold watch he wore was gaudy, weighing his arm down, and it looked to be bigger than the width of his wrist. He had a couple of moles on his face, which put me in mind of the Godfather himself, Robert De Niro. Tony's hair was, of course, slicked back, and I imagine that he thought shorts were a sin to be expunged in confession—it was always a suit for him. His shirts were open at the neck, plunging at least one button more than most men would dare to go. He topped it all off with a stylish matching pocket square.

Tony made it clear to us all that we were hopeless schmucks but he was going to whip us into shape, bada bing bada boom. Failure was not an option because that would reflect badly on him, and you did not want to disappoint Tony. It's not like he'd put your body through a meat grinder for Sunday sauce meatballs or dump your carcass in Jersey marshland, but still. You got the sense that he could make your life difficult on or off Wall

Street if you messed with him or his near-perfect pass rates. We got the message loud and clear that if you weren't ready to take the test, you better think long and hard about moving forward with it.

Tony's class was an intensive seven-day cram. While taking the class you were not to go to work—it was studying and Tony all the time. His class was held in a cramped room with buzzing fluorescent lighting overhead. We all sat obediently at desks while Tony stood at the head of the classroom in front of a blackboard, occasionally pausing to scratch out a point in chalk.

In Tony's classroom you did not speak unless you were spoken to, or else. We learned to keep our traps shut. That is, except for one kid who didn't get the memo and interrupted Tony in the middle of his lecture. Tony was a no-nonsense guy who liked to tell it like it was so he was forthright with the guy.

"Kid, if you don't keep your pie hole shut, I'm gonna throw my stapler at you," he warned him. That put the guy right for a couple of days, until we made it to Friday and a few decided to reward themselves with a lunchtime beer. Mr. Loquacious's lips loosened with the addition of several beers and he interrupted Tony again, who, to be fair, had warned the kid. Tony paused in the middle of his sentence, walked calmly to his desk, grabbed his stapler, and chucked it as hard as he could at the idiot. It missiled rapidly through the air and very narrowly avoided hitting the guy in the head, the stapler exploding into the wall behind him and impressively dislodging a chunk of plaster. I gave the throw a near-perfect score of nine out of ten, deducting a single point only for the ejection of staples upon impact. It seemed to me that this wasn't Tony's first time throwing a stapler. He then kicked the kid out of class, barring him from ever returning, and resumed teaching without disturbing a single hair on his shellacked head. We all snuck glances at each other when Tony wasn't looking—did that really happen? Yes? Okay, guess we'll keep going, then . . . !

With Tony's help, I learned the ins and outs of the Series 7, and if I didn't fully understand all the concepts at play, I did now have a passing familiarity with most of what the exam covered, from blue sky laws (state laws meant to protect investors from securities fraud); to the multiple, varied accounts that brokers had the power to open on behalf of a client; to types of mutual funds available. It was a lot.

Before taking the Series 7, we had to take what was called the Greenlight exam. I suppose the guy responsible for naming the exam wasn't feeling particularly creative that day—finance and regulatory bros often aren't. In order to be greenlit to take the Series 7, you had to pass the Greenlight, which was basically an unofficial Series 7. I ended up scoring an 80, which didn't enrage Tony, so I figured it was now or never.

The morning of the Series 7, I gave myself a silent pep talk to shake the nerves away. I wasn't going to let this exam intimidate me. So what if I didn't ace the practice exams and took shit notes and had no real market experience? I could do this!

At nine a.m. sharp, I offered up a prayer to St. Tony of Staten Island and sat down with about fifteen other hopefuls at a test-taking center off Wall Street. No bubble sheets—the exam was entirely digital, which was revolutionary back then. We were placed in privacy cubicles to avoid cheating, and we took the test on boxy computers that ran Windows 95, the sound of clicking mice and slowly loading programs the only noises breaking the taut silence in the room. The exam was a whopping four hours long; I had never before focused so hard in my life and I attacked it with everything I had.

When I got to the final question of the exam, the program informed me that once I clicked "submit," I would be finished and my exam would be calculated automatically. My stomach did flip-flops, though I supposed it was best to find out your fate sooner rather than later—no need to extend the torture. My hand hovered over the mouse as I debated the final question and then I said to hell with this and clicked the submit button.

The next five seconds while the program tabulated my score were some of the longest of my life. And then, BAM, there it was. A glaring, ugly number flashed on the screen: 67. I had failed the exam by a measly three points. Fuck.

All the steam that I was running on left my body in one long, deflated sigh. I was defeated. I stayed motionless, sitting at the computer, staring at the 67, which stared right back, taunting me. I don't know how long I sat there but by the time I looked away, the light from the screen searing its afterimage on my retinas, quite a few people had gotten up and left the room.

I numbly gathered my purse and stumbled out of the building to find a pay phone. I had to call Adam and tell him I'd failed. Fuuuuck. I walked up to the nearest pay phone and deposited a quarter from my pocket. This was not how things were supposed to go. I'd imagined calling Adam to smugly let him know I'd passed the exam; I'd already placed myself at a new desk on the other side of the Pit, no longer with the scrum of cold callers. Adam, that self-interested asshole, would lord this over me. I could already see him shaking his head in faux disappointment, secretly elated that I'd failed, content to take satisfaction in someone else's misery.

I sighed again and dialed—at least I was good at that—and heard the muffled crunch of a phone picking up on the first ring. I knew it, I knew Adam was hovering by his phone, waiting for me to tell him I'd failed.

I told him I'd gotten a 67. That I wasn't coming into the office the next day. I could tell he was shocked—I had never missed a single day in my time at VTR.

Fuck this job.

Fuck this firm.

Fuck Adam.

Fuck my coworkers.

Fuck the shitty pay.

Fuck the long hours.

Fuck the industry.

But most of all, fuck this fucking test for standing in my way and blocking me from doing great things.

I wasn't going to go back to VTR—I absolutely was not going to take that walk of shame and sit back down in the caller section, which I'd vowed never to return to. Everyone would know—the partners had announced that morning to the company that I was taking the Series 7. And they'd announce before the close of the market if I'd passed. When no announcement came that day, they would all know that the bitch on wheels had failed. I couldn't bear feeling people's eyes boring into my back and hearing their stupid snickering.

Adam listened to me spiral, letting me finish without interruption. Finally, he spoke up.

"Cin, you failed. Okay. Big deal, it happens. Do you *really* want to quit when you are so close to the finish line?"

I was stunned. I had expected him to be a prick and to revel in my misery like a pig in shit. As economical as his pick-me-up speech was, it worked. Whether he encouraged me so that he could keep siphoning off my talent or because he actually wanted to see me succeed, it didn't matter. I sorely needed validation, for someone to tell me, after all the punches, the sexist and racist comments, the flying staplers! that I should keep going. Mr. Potato Head himself had shown up for me.

The next morning was excruciating. I had already told my mother and Catalina that I had failed and that I would need to study harder, delaying me for at least another month, building leads for Adam, not for myself—that was a kick in the gut. I went straight to my desk, avoiding eye contact, and began dialing furiously. I knew some of the other cold callers were almost glad to see me sitting with them. Of a lucky few who had gotten their books, most had failed and hadn't rescheduled their exams. They were relieved to see another member join them in the Losers Club. No thanks.

My calls weren't going well—I sounded like shit. I felt eyes on me so I looked up and groaned. The very last thing I needed was Brad Ambrosi, the Grim Reaper, to contend with, but there he was, charging straight toward me. I steeled myself, ready for some sort of assault. But he pounded my desk with his small, meaty fist and exclaimed, "FABRÉ!" He was glad I was back; apparently he didn't want to see me quit.

There was a thirty-day waiting period before I could take my test again and I was going to do everything humanly possible to cram as much knowledge into my brain as I could. My days sucked. I was behind on my rent payments and was overworked and sleep-deprived.

I decided to move in with Catalina and her family for half the week so that I would have a shorter commute to and from work and be able to squeeze even more studying into my days. Mondays through Thursdays I stayed with Catalina. I'd plod up the stairs to Catalina and Kenya's little apartment to study—they had their own floor in the house, with a bedroom, a bathroom, and a tiny living room with a mattress that I studied and slept on. After a couple hours of studying, delicious cooking smells would begin wafting up the stairs and I would head back down for dinner and stuff myself silly with Dominican food. But apart from eating with the family, I didn't see them, and Catalina knew to leave me to my own devices—I cloistered myself and studied until my eyes crossed and I fell asleep. I would study after dinner, go to bed at nine p.m., and leave the house by five a.m. to do more studying in VTR's conference room. It was brutal.

I did allow myself to occasionally let loose and go to clubs on the weekends with Catalina and our friends, and I got a nice boost from telling them how I was going to make it on Wall Street, as they supported me wholeheartedly, not doubting me for a second—and if they had, they knew I wouldn't give two fucks because I wouldn't allow their negative energy to infect me. Inevitably, though, I would pass out at a table despite the booming music and the allure of alcohol and dancing because I was so sleep-deprived. It put me in mind of when I lived in the projects and was terrified of sleeping because of the roaches—my mother once found me asleep standing up in the shower, the water hitting me full blast. It was impressive, really.

As I trudged through what I hoped would be my final weeks of cold calling, I secretly began amassing promising leads for myself. Was that wrong to do? Of course. But Sharpstein could never close on the best leads I brought him—he always mucked things up, wasting them. The week before I took my exam for the second time, Sharpstein appeared at my desk, his doughy face red with anger.

"Why did you tell me this was a LOCK?" he screamed at me. ("LOCK" leads were ones we deemed the most promising.) He clearly had messed up again. Shappy furiously tore the lead up and threw the tattered bits into my face before storming off. He had, of course, made sure to do this after lunch when everyone had returned to their desks so that they could all witness the scene.

I didn't get mad, though. In my eyes, he had just given me permission to keep the best leads I could find for myself. I carefully taped up the LOCK lead that he had thrown at me. It was mine now.

Chapter 16

THE ONLY TIMES I SAW THE BROKERS OR THE PART-
ners chill out were when we were in the Hamptons or
at a strip club. It was then, when they weren't feeding
off each other's Always Be Closing energy, that they'd let loose
and kick back. Admittedly, the drugs and alcohol helped with
that, too.

A few months before, the partners had announced that they
would be holding a Hamptons summertime bash for everyone
at the office, including even the callers and account openers. I
couldn't believe that the callers were being invited—none of us
had ever been to the Hamptons before. When I imagined the
Hamptons, I thought of pristine white beaches, unmarred by
broken bottles or used condoms, which is what the beach at
Coney Island was littered with. I had heard that Jordan Belfort
had his own helicopter to fly from the city to the Hamptons
whenever he wanted, and the partners at VTR all had houses
there. I assumed the furniture in these houses matched the sand
of the beaches there, outfitted in soothing tones like smooth
beiges, buffs, and oatmeals. Nobody had to worry about lining these couches with plastic—they'd either have their house-
keeper clean any vulgar stains that popped up or they would
simply buy a new one of whatever it was that had been sullied.

Since the announcement, we had all been feverishly awaiting the party, which would be held at one of the partners' houses. A few months before, New York City had been hit with one of the worst nor'easters on record. We kept the party in our minds as the snow melted and we had to contend with gray slush that would seep into our cracked boots and the rain that dumped on the city every spring.

By the time summer showed its face, some of the callers were so antsy to be out of the office that they quit the firm to stake out their own spots at Rockaway or Coney Island daily. I was eager to see what the Hamptons were all about, as mythical as they were, what with brokers all over Wall Street either owning houses there or fashionably renting every summer.

I piled into my beat-up Acura with Max, a fellow caller, and my friend Jose. Amazingly, almost suspiciously, the partners had said that our friends were welcome to join in the festivities if we wanted to bring them. Not only were account openers and callers invited, but we could bring our degenerate friends with us? It didn't quite add up to me, but I know that the partners loved to spew bullshit about everyone at VTR being a family, though you could see even as the words left their mouths that this was just lip service, convenient for quelling rebellion among the oppressed. Maybe they wanted to be able to point to something concrete if someone in our circle actually complained. I didn't mind—it meant I could show my friends exactly why I was killing myself for two hundred and fifty dollars a week, could have them mingle with the successful brokers that I knew I'd be part of soon.

We made our way from Queens to the Hamptons, Max filling us in during the long, congested drive on all the goings-on at the firm, who was sleeping with whom, who had been the latest to be busted for shady dealings, the newest drama at the strip club. He kept his eyes and ears open and was always full of valuable nuggets of VTR gossip. Max, along with another kid, Diego, were the main pickup boys for the firm's drugs. They'd be given anywhere from $750 to $1,500 in cash per run to pick up pills at a regular old CVS or Rite-Aid. One of the brokers had found this pre-signed pad near a printer at Staples, of all places. Max and Diego would spend their days going from pharmacy to pharmacy getting these scripts filled. This was, of course, before New York implemented the Prescription Monitoring Program to avoid abuse of this kind.

For the pills that Max and Diego couldn't pick up with their fake prescriptions, Buckmaster would valiantly step up and pose as a patient to score a legal prescription, getting a cut of 10 percent for his haul. Once a week or more, Buck would head to Bowery in Chinatown to see Dr. Lee and claim he had back pain. If Dr. Lee tried to prescribe him Vicodin, he was told to say it hurt his stomach so that he could score Percocet instead. Buck would pay a couple hundred dollars in cash for the visit, in return getting a prescription for a hundred pills to fill at a pharmacy. Unfortunately, after a few times, Dr. Lee recognized him. . . . No problem, though! Buck just gave a different name and a different ailment each time he went. Dr. Lee probably heard the same story fifty times a day but as long as he could feign ignorance, he'd hand off a script like a grocery list.

And if pills weren't your thing, or the aforementioned technique wasn't paying off fast enough, you went to Tony the Tiger, a Jamaican dude who always made his deals at TGI Fridays on Broadway. Tony was known for having the best top-shelf cocaine, and brokers at all the firms used him. When you were doing business with Tony the Tiger, you knew you had elevated your game because you would definitely be on the hook for thousands of dollars. I saw brokers in the throes of drug addiction selling their cars and jewelry, borrowing, or stealing, to get their Tony-grade fix.

But back to Diego. Diego would also make the occasional run to the strip clubs before they opened, armed with a bag full of Rolex watches, pills, and sometimes straight cash, from various brokers taking care of their girls. (Buckmaster, not Diego, was in charge of buying Rolexes for the guys at the firm. He'd source them from a Hasidic guy at a tiny kiosk in one of the hallways of Penn Station, snagging amazing "bargains" such as a Presidential Rolex that could cost up to a hundred thousand dollars for only twenty-five thousand. Not bad.)

Diego was on a first-name basis with all of the managers at the strip clubs, and these managers would always offer him a drink and a wink when he made his "care package" deliveries. Some of the brokers would shell out up to two hundred thousand dollars for their girls every few months. It mystified me that they would do this for women who weren't even their significant others—because they, of course, already had girl-friends, fiancées, wives.

With this knowledge of Diego and Max's "professional activities," I had Max empty out his pockets and swear to me that he didn't have anything on him before he got into my car that day. On the way, I noted how even the highways were nicer around here, the roads smooth and free of trash. As we got closer to the party, I saw that each mansion was nicer than the last. It was as if we were cramming an architecture course into one car ride—I noted columns and porches and overhangs, tidy gray shingle-style houses next to modern glass boxes. Many were at least partially hidden by what I later learned were topiaries, towering privacy shrubs, which felt both classy and white as fuck to me. When I was able to glimpse the houses' driveways, I saw cars that I'd only read about before—special-edition Porsches, Bent-leys, Benzes, and more. I loved it. This was solid research for when I had enough to buy my own S-class something or other.

When we finally pulled into the enormous driveway, I was

already thoroughly embarrassed by my poor Acura, which had always done its best for me, but it was so out of place next to these six-figure cars. I didn't have to worry too much, though, because once I reviewed the parking directions that VTR had given us, I realized that we weren't supposed to park in front of the main house anyway. We were to park off to the side next to what looked like servants' quarters with all the other callers' cars . . . and probably the help's. I felt it was for the best, though. It would be bad if my bumper fell off and some broker's wife saw me struggling to reattach it in the driveway.

Jose, Max, and I slowly walked up to the mega-mansion, gaping. At least they didn't require the callers and account openers to use a separate entrance. Passing through the heavy double front doors, I stood up straighter; I felt like I'd already made it. I had worked my ass off to earn this invite, hadn't I? I deserved to mingle with the brokers.

What I didn't realize, though, was that the partners weren't inviting us out of the goodness of their hearts. They'd bleed an investor out of all their savings, leaving them destitute and on the street if they had to in order to make their cut—of course they weren't being nice. This party, as glamorous as it was, was a de facto job fair. All the bigwigs had to do was open their doors to their callers' friends and offer them some appetizers in exchange for their souls. They were able to recruit their next battalion, the soldiers who would smile and dial until they burned out, more casualties of Wall Street. Holding this little party "for" us was cheaper and far more efficient than putting ads out in the papers, going to real job fairs, and having their callers source their friends "from the ghetto" one by one. It was like shooting fish in a barrel. They couldn't give anything without taking further from us, their cash cows. They weren't just selling us a dream, they were selling our people, too. It was dirty and gross and brilliant. Unfortunately for them, they wouldn't be recruiting my friend Jose anytime soon—he was a white kid who was college educated and had a job lined up in aviation. Too bad. Jose was more than happy to take advantage of the unlimited drugs and alcohol, though.

Max disappeared and Jose immediately made a beeline for one of the many bathrooms in the mansion; he intuitively seemed to know that there would be blow available, and, yep, when he reemerged he had a jittery new pep in his step. He nudged me jerkily and let me know that there were white party favors in the bathroom if I was interested. I had no idea what he was talking about until he smirked and thumbed his nose, not even bothering to lower his voice to say, "You know, the powdery stuff."

We walked through the mansion, watching as well-dressed people openly snorted coke on the back of their hands and cut lines with credit cards on tables. If they weren't doing coke, they were popping pills like candy or passing around joints to whoever walked by. If, for whatever reason, you decided not to partake in whatever drug you could dream up, there was alcohol practically flowing out of the taps. It didn't matter that we callers were all underage—this was, apparently, our night, and anything we wanted was ours for the taking.

Jose and I slowly weaved through throngs of partygoers and made our way to the backyard—really, the back lawn, which was only one part of the huge outdoor compound, stretching on far beyond what my eye could see, neighbored by the ocean, the crashing of the waves drowned out by the revelry in front of us. There were basketball and volleyball courts, an enormous pool, fountains, and a patio complete with firepit and TVs. The patio held white cloth-covered tables that groaned under the weight of all the food laden on top. Did the brokers eat like this every day? No wonder they were shitting their brains out in the bathroom each morning!

Kept warm in silver chafing dishes, there were fat lobster tails and medium-rare steaks piled high; different kinds of pastas swimming in sauce; fried chicken; shrimp cocktail; caviar; briny oysters in pearlescent shells on ice; lox dotted with capers and red onion; corn on the cob floating in butter; salad; baked potatoes steaming in their jackets. There was an entire table devoted to dessert, with a huge sheet cake spelling out "VTR Capital" in icing; brownies, cookies, pies, chocolate-covered strawberries, and lemon bars.

A memory from high school hazily rose up in my mind, a teacher telling us about the Romans who loved to eat so much that they would vomit just so they could eat more. *The Romans would have had a field day here*, I thought to myself.

A bartender stood at attention near the buffet, ready to mix drinks. Beer, wine, and champagne were up for grabs nearly everywhere. None of the low-wage earners had ever seen anything like this spread and were taking full advantage, making trips to and from cars to stash sweating beers, wrapping up as much food as possible in napkins and plates to take home, hiding treats in purses and bags, whatever could be found to hold this bounty. Could you blame them?

The crowd, which had to number at least two hundred, milled around, but the place was so big it didn't feel packed. Some compared Rolexes and bragged to one another about their latest sale, while others tanned in bathing suits in the hot sun, hairlines slick with sweat, or splashed around in the pool, or alternated between drugs and drinks.

Jose went off, nervy and in search of more cocaine—he was already well on his way to shit-faced. I chose to hang back by the buffet, picking at a plate of food and dipping my toe in the pool. I would have to drive our asses back so I was taking it slow, and I never did drugs anyway. Plus I had just gotten my hair done so I wasn't about to ruin it by jumping in the pool. (I'm sure the brokers wouldn't have understood what was happening if I did—us Black people didn't swim, right?)

"Hey, Cin!" someone yelled. I looked over to see Brad Ambrosi of all people waving me over. He was outfitted in khakis and boat shoes; he still looked like his sweaty little self, but he was smiling. I walked over to him and he introduced me to a few brokers I had never met, white guys with white teeth and white polo shirts, looking very much at ease with themselves. In this sense, the scene never changed, just the characters.

"Cin is kicking ass, guys," he said, to my complete surprise. "She's going to do big things when she is on her own." The brokers glanced in my direction and nodded, but I wasn't paying attention to them. I was basking in Ambrosi's praise, which was far better than lobster and champagne.

I excused myself while I was ahead and found the nearest bathroom. It was so fancy that there were multiple toilets enclosed behind frosted-glass doors. As I picked a stall and went in, two women walked out of another. One woman had bleached, white-blond hair, which stood in contrast against her deep tan. The other was a brunette with reddish highlights; she had gone further than the blonde and tanned herself into oblivion—her skin looked like leather. Both were wearing dresses with plunging necklines and dangerously high stilettos, and I couldn't figure out whether they were strippers, girlfriends, or wives. From what I'd seen of the brokers' women, they sometimes looked interchangeable.

After I peed, marveling at how soft and thick the toilet paper was, I stepped out of the stall to wash my hands at the marble-veined sink. The women were still there, whispering and giggling to each other. Then, a sharp knock sounded at the bathroom's entrance door. The blonde rushed to the door and peeked out, and a disembodied hand gave her something.

"Where do we want to do it?" the blonde asked her companion.

Holy shit, they're about to have sex in here, I thought.

The brunette grinned. "Let's do it on my ass," she replied. That cracked them both up. I busied myself with washing my hands, trying to appear as if I wasn't listening intently to every word of their conversation.

The brunette lifted her dress to reveal that she wasn't wearing any underwear. She bent over the bathroom counter facing the mirror, her perfectly toned and tanned ass out for public display. She smiled into the mirror at the blonde, who uncapped what I could now see was a little vial of what I presumed was coke. She poured a line of powder from across the brunette's tailbone to the beginning curve of her ass cheeks.

"Don't move," Blondie said.

She then quickly snorted the whole line, her face buried in the brunette's ass.

"That tickled!" the brunette said, laughing.

I tried not to stare at what was happening right in front of my eyes, but it was impossible not to. It didn't matter, though; I may as well have been invisible to the women.

Brunette then pulled her dress down and scanned herself in the mirror, fluffing her hair and wiping a smudge of red lipstick off her teeth.

"Let's go find Bruce and finish what's left with him," she said to the blonde. The blonde nodded and pecked the brunette on the lips. Never have I ever dried my hands so slowly in my life.

They walked out, arm in arm, laughing, still having never once looked in my direction. I waited a beat, trying to process what I'd seen, then opened the bathroom door, which brought the party rushing back to me at full volume. *Have fun, Bruce*, I thought. Squinting in the bright sunlight, I caught sight of Max, hamming it up with some of the other cold callers.

Max was a short, compact guy who was in a perpetually good mood and who was very easily excitable. He had a cute baby girl named Ruby and he liked to say that he boxed in case he had to protect her. Because he had so many potentially damaging secrets on a number of the brokers, he was virtually untouchable. After he proved to be a reliable source for blow and other drugs, he never had to pound the phone as hard as the rest of us. He was also never fired for being late or a no-show, which would have merited a public execution if it were anyone else. He didn't limit his transactions to the brokers; he offered his wares to the callers as well, constantly pushing drugs on us and letting us know he had a connection to anything else we might want or need. I didn't mind Max, as he was more or less harmless, but he could talk even me into doing things for him, and I considered myself the smooth talker. That's why I found myself giving him a ride to the Hamptons, though it was on the condition that he couldn't bring drugs into my car and he had to chip in for gas money. I wasn't about to get busted at a traffic stop and I wasn't running a nonprofit, either.

I waved to Max and headed back to the patio to try to network with the other guests—eyes always on the prize. The next time I saw Max, I didn't actually see him—I heard him. Or rather, I heard people who saw him.

"OHHHHHHHH," a roar went up on the beach-facing side of the patio where a small crowd had gathered. I walked over to see what was going on.

"Shit, well, that's the end of that," a broker said. I looked out onto the ocean, but all I could see was a miniature Max, bobbing in the ocean, waving frantically at us.

I asked someone what had happened, but they didn't really know.

"One minute the guy was on the Jet Ski, hitting the waves, and the next it was gone," he said, mystified.

"Max was gone?" I asked.

"No," he replied. "The Jet Ski."

Nobody quite knew how it was possible for one person to sink a Jet Ski in the ocean, but apparently Max managed to do it.

He never told me, or anyone else for that matter, what actually happened, he just copped a mile-wide grin and stayed quiet about it. All he would say was that he was somehow bucked off the Jet Ski and the next thing he saw was bubbles rising to the water's surface where the ski had immediately sunk, like the *Titanic*. Pretty sure it wasn't an iceberg, though Max's antics always involved some amount of ice, if you know what I mean.

Max was only about fifty meters out from shore so he frontstroked back to the beach, where he took a sweeping bow, and everyone who was watching broke out into loud whoops and cheers. I was completely bewildered. These people were egging on a guy who'd just destroyed something that cost thousands of dollars! But to them, it didn't matter. They could just buy another one—ten grand or so wouldn't put them back one bit. To them it would just be a funny story to recount over cigars at Angelo & Maxie's off Park Ave.

The party accomplished what it was supposed to—I was impressed by the gaudy wealth in front of me. But it also reinforced to me that there was nothing special about these people— shiny privilege had been handed to them automatically. Their hard times growing up would likely have been better than any of the callers' best times. They didn't know what it was to scrape by, had no idea of the dark things we would have done for the same opportunities they were afforded on the other side of the room. It's tragic because we all could have been so much more. They used their minds to manipulate, to machinate; we used ours to survive, to hustle. What could they have done if they put their minds to goodness? What could we have done if we had been given goodness?

I felt it was time to go so I went inside to collect Jose. I'd already mouthed to Max that I was headed out as he toweled off on the beach. Inside, the party was still going strong, alcohol flowing and music bumping. There was coke strewn about on almost every surface—everyone was hitting it hard and passing it to the next person. Doors were closed and the occupants within weren't doing anything to hide the animal noises they were making. I turned my head just in time to see a guy on a couch pull the bikini strings off the two girls who were sitting on top of him. He slapped their asses and loudly told them, "I know you want this fat cock." Yeah, right, he probably had the smallest dick in the place. I scowled. I hated those types— you know they got off on humiliating women and proclaiming to everyone how much money they made, exaggerating their income and their inseam.

We left then. Jose and Max were both obliterated, which was for the best. I wanted silence as we drove back into the city so I could replay the day's events in my head. The brokers could keep their cocaine and their Jet Skis for now. I wanted something different for my life. In this moment, I had something priceless—the glittering lights of the city at night as we crested over the bridge back home.

⌖

What was home for me these days? I rarely saw my mother, Phil, or Glifford, as I was so busy hammering away, cold calling and studying. I would faithfully call home and speak to my mother, but she would discourage me from coming home too often.

"Sendy, you must focus on your work right now, that is what is most important," she told me. Occasionally, I'd go home for dinner, asking Phil how school was, trying to draw Glifford out of his shell without success. The resentment and anger that I previously held toward my mother had melted away by now, and I didn't argue. Besides, even if I had wanted to see my family, I just didn't have time for it. Catalina and I also didn't talk much in this period, and I was too numbed by work to miss her or my other friends too much. My own apartment was cold and sterile. I suppose someone else might have felt lonely or isolated, but I didn't. If anything, this solitary lifestyle gave me the momentum I needed to keep pushing forward for better. Half of the week I sat at my kitchen table in my apartment, a single lamp illuminating my practice exam, as I tried to stuff vocabulary and numbers into my head. The other half of the week, I sprawled out on Catalina's living room mattress, alternating between staring at my books and at the pointy popcorn ceiling, telling myself that this time I would hustle and that I could—I would—succeed.

Chapter 17

SOMETHING WAS IN THE AIR—WE COULD ALL FEEL IT. The cold callers would sit down at Rosario's for greasy pizza and exchange rumors like state secrets. More dubious chop shops were opening with alarming speed, and with them, the SEC and NASD (National Association of Securities Dealers) were shutting them down as quickly as they could, citing their stock manipulations and devious sales tactics. We would exchange lead cards, tired out from efforts at our firms, but new to others, and give them to our brokers for a "discounted" price. The brokers never questioned where we got these lead cards. We did this because our own leads were drying up and we needed to get creative and show our bosses that we were still on top of things, still making things happen. Everyone was calling the same people—the seven-figure white male business owners across the United States—and we were getting less and less return as these people got angry and demanded that they be taken off our call lists. They knew our game.

VTR could read the writing on the wall and knew it needed to switch tactics fast or it would end up dead in the water like so many other boiler rooms that had gone belly-up. The solution came, improbably, from John Buckmaster, serial prankster and weed connoisseur.

Buck had friends in town visiting from across the pond in the UK and they planted the seed of an idea when they asked him, *Why don't you try out the UK?* He was stumped. Why had nobody thought of this before?

It was astonishingly simple, it was beautiful, it was something the other shops weren't doing, or if they were, there was plenty of room for us all to play nicely. Buck made a few trial calls to the UK and found the recipients open and *very* polite, much more so than the Americans who would slam the phone down on you, cursing your mother to an early grave.

Armed with this intel, Buck marched into partner Greg's office and pitched him his UK idea. Greg had the final say on who was pitching what at the firm but he was intrigued. He told Buck to lead the charge and ordered everyone new UK lead cards. The game was on.

We began our campaign and even though it seemed far too simple to work, it did—for a time. The news of the Jordan Belfort scandal had not traveled the waters and gained the same punchy prominence that it had in the United States, so UK investors knew little about our high-pressured sales tactics, not having encountered them before, at least not in this context. As far as these investors knew, VTR Capital was the same kind of institution as a Merrill Lynch, a Charles Schwab, a Paine Webber. Plus, their pound was worth more so investing was only a third of the price for them. *Cha-ching.*

This all unfolded while I was in the process of getting my books and studying. On top of *that* pressure, our new office hours now started at six a.m., to account for the time difference between the United States and the UK. Asses in desk chairs by six sharp. I was excited, though. I was tired of battered leads and wanted a go at these puzzlingly nice leads who somehow never swore at us. The US market was alluring to them, and even if the British did not entirely trust us Yankees, they would still hear our pitch out without interrupting us, and would often first invest the minimum of one hundred shares, twenty-five hundred dollars, then perhaps twenty-five thousand, then fifty, then one hundred thousand. Later, as the other chop shops caught on and began ringing the UK, the Brits would catch on and stop investing, but they were still always nice.

Being what we believed to be one of the first chop shops on Wall Street to try this out, the partners wanted us to maximize our chances for success: If you weren't in the office by six a.m. latest, you would be at risk for getting fired.

It was out the door by four a.m. for me, and because the other callers who lived in Queens didn't have cars, I rounded them up and we carpooled to work. Even though at that time the streets would largely be deserted and the sun wouldn't even be thinking of showing its face yet, my madcap dash to work was a chaotic blur of activity, all at breakneck speed.

Inevitably, one of the carpoolers would hit the snooze button and I'd be forced to idle outside, my patience wearing thinner than Shap's hair by the minute. One of the backseaters would be forced to bang on their door and drag them out, still half-asleep, eyes crusted with grit. It was a race to get to the office on time and I drove like a demon, revving up to ninety miles per hour on the FDR Drive and fixing my hair between stoplights, moving on to lipstick and mascara once my hair was done. I was not about to be fired because someone in my carpool overslept. I didn't think that I was *that* bad of a driver—I had learned to weave expertly between taxis, braking hard when I needed to and speeding up if I saw an opportune gap in a lane—but my crew and my brakes begged to differ. I had to replace my brake pads twice in one year and my riders regularly feared for their lives. I drove on the outer lanes of the highway just in case the bumper of my Acura fell off, which it sometimes did. No problem—I'd screech to a halt, jump out, put it back on, and continue with the commute.

With the injection of UK cash, the cold callers were amped—we didn't need coke like the brokers to stay hyped. We were feeding off the energy of the ignorant. Sometimes by lunchtime, I'd have my lead count for the day. In that case, I'd either surreptitiously dial more leads and keep the good ones for myself, or I would spend the next few hours in the conference room studying for the Series 7 before heading back to Catalina's house for dinner with her family and then back to the books again.

The firm obviously didn't give the callers a pay increase for the longer hours. The partners told us we were *lucky* to be calling overseas, that when we became brokers ourselves we would appreciate and in fact be *grateful* to them for the discipline that they had instilled in us, and that moving forward, anything in life could be considered a cakewalk. Besides, they said, joking but not joking, we should be used to "slaving" away—didn't our ancestors work on plantations?

I suppose they were partly correct—working seven days a week, five days at the firm, starting at four a.m. and ending around nine or ten p.m.—I vowed that I would never work this hard again, that moving forward I would never have to. The hours were literally killing me: One evening, exhausted after another seven-day workweek, I was driving down Queens Boulevard doing everything I could to stay awake, pinching myself and talking out loud. But exhaustion won over, and she's a real malicious bitch because she convinced me that it would be safe if I just closed my eyes for a second, a long blink, really, just so I could give them a quick rest. I soon woke up to a man in a white van, honking at me furiously in loud, hyphenated beeps, his headlights streaming through my windshield, lighting up the interior. He was on the opposite side of the road and I was headed straight for him, drifting dangerously across lanes. I was so close I could see the panic on his face, his mouth forming silent, panicked screams. I quickly grabbed the steering wheel and swerved back into my lane just in time to avoid a future that would have included mangled metal and zero chance of ever becoming a broker, or anything else, for that matter.

Thankfully, my Series 7 retake was approaching. This time, I was scoring solidly in the 80s on the practice exams, though I worried that it was only because I was memorizing answers, rather than fully understanding the concepts behind the test questions, and that method hadn't worked for me the first go-round. The first time I'd taken the test the partners told me that it didn't matter if I understood—that most of what was in our books was useless for our purposes; we were never going to, say, trade on margin, or diversify a client's portfolio with a broad range of conservative products. Penny stocks, secondary offerings, private placements, and IPOs—these were our bread and butter. We would never recommend to clients that they sit twenty years on Disney and Home Depot, hoping the stock would split or that they would get thrown dividends. That wasn't sexy.

My test was scheduled for December 4, which was my high school friend Nina's birthday. I asked her to make a passing grade on my exam her birthday wish. I would take all the luck I could get.

Chapter 18

On the morning of the exam, I decided not to cram any more studying in. I didn't think I could fit any more finance facts into my brain—it was already overflowing. I choked down some breakfast, dry toast that caught in my throat, and I did my best to relax. Because I didn't want to deal with city parking, I left my apartment to drive to Catalina's house and left my car in the driveway and Catalina's mom gave me a ride to the 7 train, which I took into the city, transferring over to the R, which would take me to the Financial District. It was cold that morning, one of the first freezes of the season, and I found comfort in the familiar, the warm steam rising from the grates, the nails-on-a-chalkboard screech of stopping trains, the close scent of overheated bodies in winter coats mingling with the unique, indescribable smell that is the New York City subway underground.

The doors opened with their automatic *thunk* and I got onto the train, which surprisingly wasn't crowded for a weekday morning, my gaze settling on the pattern of alternating yellow and orange seats in the car. A voice filled with salt-and-pepper static yelled out something unintelligible on the intercom, probably announcing the next stop. I hoped that someone would sit beside me. I actually liked it when people would hunker down next to me in the winter—I would scoot closer so that I could absorb some of their warmth.

At the next stop, a dark-haired Latinx man took the seat next to me, and I was filled with the urge to tell him everything; maybe it would straighten out the chaos in my mind and dial down my nerves. I explained to him the high stakes that were at play for me—he clearly had no idea what the Series 7 was, but that was okay, I just needed an ear. He kindly wished me luck anyway, which is what I was looking for, just a little sympathetic connection. While it's true that New Yorkers have the reputation for being cold and unfriendly, to me we're just busy people. I have ultimately found that when you need something from the city and her dwellers, she will deliver. Small, quotidian moments like this happen all the time—you just need to look for them.

I said goodbye to the man and got off at my stop, deliberately walking up each step of the stairs, instead of rushing and skipping like I usually did, always in a hurry. Before I headed into the test site, I called my mother, looking for one last bit of reassurance. When I told her I was about to take the exam, she told me, "Sendy, say a prayer. Ask God to take the test for you."

I really didn't think God was going to stop whatever it was He was doing up in heaven to come down, kick His sandaled feet onto the desk, and whiz through the test for me. But I knew better than to question my mother's faith—I believe that she was attuned to certain things that others weren't. I asked her to explain.

"It's simple. You need to say out loud, 'God, please take this test for me today.' Just do that."

I told her I would. And I actually did, not caring if anyone heard me. I walked into the building, sat down at my computer, uttered one more prayer to the Almighty, and went at it. Four hours later, I was again faced with that terrifying "submit" button. I felt tempted to go back and change my answers—I had screwed up the Options section ("option" being how you might buy or sell a stock at a fixed price, and there were, well, a lot of options for doing so) the first time, and I didn't feel any more confident about it this time around—I was still bewildered by options, and the brokers had told me not to focus on them because they were a smaller part of the exam. But I felt good about the other sections. It was now or never. I submitted my test and closed my eyes while the computer cranked, processing my score. Taking a deep breath, I slowly cracked one eye open and took an apprehensive look at the computer.

SEVENTY-THREE.

I was stunned for a moment, not comprehending the number on the screen. Then it all came rushing over me at once. I passed! I was licensed! I forgot that others were still taking the exam and jumped out of my chair, which fell over with a loud crash in the quiet room, and let out a small yell of victory. The test administrator sitting at the front of the room peered at me over her glasses and raised a finger to her lips to shush me, but she was smiling. My outburst could be forgiven.

I raced out of the classroom and called my mother, who thanked God and reminded me that He would do great things for us if I would only put my faith in Him. I frankly didn't hear much of what she was saying because I was in such an elated stupor. Then I called the office and gleefully gave Sharpstein the good news. He was genuinely excited for me—maybe because he was sincerely rooting for me, but also because while cold callers were a dime a dozen, good account openers were invaluable. I was walking on air—the people passing in front of me were blurs, the sounds of the city muted. Did I just do what I had set out to accomplish? I was a fucking broker at twenty years old!

At the time, I don't think I fully understood the ramifications of passing the exam. Yes, of course I knew that it meant I could formally move forward as a broker, but I had not yet fully absorbed what achieving this milestone would signify for my career in the years to come. I was a young Black woman who came from the Patterson Projects in the Bronx. I had been beaten by Fab, and yes, by my mother, yelled at constantly by both. I was too scared to go to sleep in our cramped apartment because of the roaches that would come out of hiding to crawl all over me. Before we moved to Queens, I witnessed violence on the streets daily. I didn't have money for extracurriculars or books of my own. My mother didn't believe in the benefits of therapy, much less mental illness, so none of us—Phil, me, and Glifford in particular, could access a therapist for the trauma we'd undergone. I didn't have the means to go to college without being buried under a mountain of debt. I had had to deal with the systemic racism and sexism and generational poverty that accompanied these life circumstances, scraping to get here. And yet I would now be working alongside some of the most brilliant—if crooked—minds on Wall Street as an equal. This was real, no longer a pipe dream. I had found my seat at the table and then, with time, I thought, I could one day offer someone else a seat.

I didn't know what to do with myself next—I couldn't contain my excitement and was bursting at the seams to tell everyone I knew that I had passed the exam. I wanted to celebrate! But all my friends were either in school or at work. I picked the pay phone back up and called Nina to wish her a happy birthday and to say thank you for her wish because it had helped. Then I took myself home on the train, though getting anything done was nearly impossible. I was far too amped up. I tossed and turned during the night, picturing my arrival at the office, smiling at the imaginary victory lap I would take, graciously accepting apologies from all the brokers who had fucked with me as a lowly cold caller, who hadn't believed in me.

The next morning I got to VTR early. I stepped into the building with the knowledge that I was doing so as a real, live broker, that I had the same right as the other brokers to be there and take up space and nobody could take that away from me. I puffed out my chest as I walked down the hallway—this time on the left side, which the brokers and partners used—and made my way to the Pit, arriving to high fives and congratulations from all the cold callers. They would now be talking about me in their sessions at Rosario's or huddled around the food truck.

As I had nothing but leads to take from my desk, transitioning over to the brokers' side was easy—I just picked up my cards and walked to the other side of the room, where I sat down at an identical desk and chair. Perhaps that sounds anticlimactic, but the energy on this side felt different, more electrified. It was thrilling.

Sharpstein walked over and gave me a quick congrats before bringing it down by reminding me sternly that I needed to work harder now than ever to open the twenty required accounts that would allow me to forge ahead solo and work for myself. He didn't need to worry—I was burning to get out from under his thumb. Our morning meeting was the first that I had ever looked forward to. With the callers already sitting at their desks, and the last of the brokers trickling in, yawning and making their animal noises, I felt the anticipatory energy that always preceded these meetings build within me. Roll call—check. Pitches—check. And then for announcements. No "keep the bathroom clean" warnings this time. Levi got on the microphone.

"Ladies and gentlemen, I need to call Cin Fabré to the front," he boomed. All the heads in the room immediately swiveled toward me. I could see some of the callers looking puzzled. I walked up to Levi at the front of the boardroom, keeping my expression as neutral as possible. I was going to keep cool.

"Cin had to pack up her desk this morning," Levi yelled, pointing to the callers' side of the room. Eyes bored into me.

"Cin had to pack up her desk because she is moving on over—SHE PASSED HER SERIES 7!"

The entire room broke its silence then, people roaring and whooping, their thunderous applause washing over me. I had made it to the other side and you'd best believe I wasn't ever going back.

⚬

One day later, VTR held its annual holiday party at the Millennium Hotel downtown near the World Trade Center. I dusted off the December snow that had collected on my jacket and headed inside, the warmth of the hotel immediately enveloping me. The lobby was decorated for the holidays and the mood was festive and cheery, bursts of laughter coming from the lobby bar, hotel guests dressed up in their finest, heading out to dinner and a Broadway play.

This time I was in the mood to let loose and celebrate my licensing. I brought along Jose, who I'm sure was hoping to score more free coke, but unfortunately for him, this was not that kind of gathering. The brokers showed up with their wives, who, up until this point, I didn't even know actually existed. With all the ogling and sexist comments and bragging about goings-on at the strip clubs from the guys, I figured that most of them were unentangled. I did many double takes when the brokers introduced me to their significant others—I didn't recognize a single one of them—none had been present at the Hamptons party. I suppose it was convenient to leave them at home, you know, what with all the strippers, sex workers, and their girlfriends on the side in attendance there. It probably would have been a bit awkward.

⚬

The brokers had made admirable efforts to clean up—no rumpled, lipstick-stained shirts from the night before, no ties slung sideways, no coke residue fallen on pants. Everyone wore pressed shirts, ties, and jackets; pocket squares bloomed from chests. Sharpstein stood stationed next to his wife, pants sagging as always—hey, they were more formal and he'd found an iron. Junior broker Noah Hoffman looked like an entirely different person—amazing how much a shower and a change of clothes could transform! They were all on their best behavior, too. For once nobody propositioned me, which was a Christmas miracle.

In order to get by at VTR, I knew I had to abide by the code of silence, the bro code. I wasn't about to enlighten these women that their boyfriends and husbands were sleazy pieces of shit, that they had wiped away the sneers that were usually on their faces and replaced them with innocent smiles. Yeah, innocent as wolves around sheep. I might not be giving these women enough credit—they may very well have known exactly what their men were up to but because they were being taken care of, they looked the other way. Maybe it was world-weary cynicism, but I had seen too much at the ripe age of twenty—I knew everyone had an angle and I felt sorry for no one. Their baggage was entirely on them.

There was another huge buffet, all the meats, fish, pastas, bread, and salad you could ever want, more than enough to feed the couple hundred partygoers. I gorged myself and this time I drank, happily slinging back whatever anyone offered me from the open bar, accepting their congratulations and dancing under the huge chandelier that glinted above the dance floor. There was a live band, playing nineties stuff like Pearl Jam and the Spin Doctors—white people music, but I didn't mind—my mom played rock in our house when we were growing up. They were playing for me—this was my night. We ended the evening with cigars, a VTR tradition, and I watched as our smoke curled lazily toward the ceiling, content to enjoy myself for once. I knew that come Monday, my work would begin in earnest.

Chapter 19

THE FIRST FEW WEEKS OF CALLING AS A LICENSED broker were a complete blur. I was determined to get to twenty accounts as fast as I could and leave Sharpstein and his watermelon-and-fried-chicken bullshit behind. I had never had coffee before in my life and I wasn't about to start now—I was riding high off the thrill of being able to call myself a stockbroker. Just two years before, I didn't even know what the stock market was, was selling stolen lunch tickets to make a couple extra dollars. I was in danger of not being able to graduate with my high school class of '94. And now I was on Wall Street. It was surreal. I practiced pitching on the train, in the shower, in my car, at Catalina's house during family dinners, and over and over again to my friends until they couldn't take it anymore. Then I'd pitch to myself in the bathroom mirror.

I was determined not to stay in the purgatory that was being a broker's account opener. Yes, you were of higher status than a caller—you had passed your Series 7, but you couldn't or didn't want to engage with investors on trades—so you only opened accounts for your broker, who would do the actual trading, the closing of deals with clients, which is what saw the real influx of cash into the company. I had seen firsthand what happened to account openers who couldn't cut it and who became mired in the quicksand of mediocrity. They were angry and embittered bastards. Marco Ricci was one of them. He was partner Levi's account opener and his lackey. As a caller, I watched as he failed to close on account after account, decaying into something poisonous and twisted. He did drugs like so many others at VTR, but it wasn't the drugs that had him on edge. It was the failure that was always nipping at his heels. His eyes bugged out of his head from constant yelling, and I often wondered if they would be able to pop back in or if they'd stay like that forever. He slid from being Levi's number one, his clear favorite, to being number two, as UK mastermind John Buckmaster ascended the ranks to become Levi's number one. Buck was easygoing and liked by both sides of the room. He did drugs but was discreet and Levi knew he could trust him with his business. This enraged Marco to no end and he branched out from bitching out Levi's team to everyone else. He never missed an opportunity to remind us that he was better than us callers; he always put us in our place. We could all smell the stink of vulnerability on him, though, and we had no respect for him. He was probably the most hated person at the firm after Brad Ambrosi and Sharpstein.

Once, after he had learned from someone that I drove to work every day, he walked up to me. I braced myself.

"You have a *car*?" he asked sneeringly. I nodded.

"Yeah, I did happen to have a life before this, Marco," I said.

"What kind of car is it?"

"An Acura Legend."

He looked like he'd just been forced to suck on a lemon. "Oh, yeah, *your people* like those kinds of cars." I stayed silent, refusing to take the bait.

"You probably have the kind of rims that spin, too, don't you?" he prodded.

"Nope, just whatever came with it," I said coolly, swearing at him in my head.

He walked off to go bother someone else. This was how he usually conversed with the callers, disdain dripping from every word that fell out of his mouth.

His anger was endemic to the business—it festered in most people who were talentless but who had gotten hooked by the allure of Wall Street, gotten in the door because they were more often than not white men. Anger was the outlet for their frustration, that or drugs, alcohol, sex, or a combination of them all. They numbed themselves so they couldn't feel. There was darkness that came with this business. The question was, how much of this did I want? I knew, after growing up the way that I did, that I didn't want to be controlled. When I walked into the boardroom and saw Marco and people like him foaming at the mouth in a rage, I again saw Fab. He was with me every day in the Pit, walking with me to my desk in the morning and out the door at night. I thought I had gotten on Wall Street to leave him behind. I wanted to be the one in control, but the specter of Fab was ever present, always bringing me back to Patterson Projects, on the floor, Fab standing over me with a belt in his hand.

Along with all my enthusiasm for my newfound career, I did have nagging doubts in the back of my mind whenever I was reminded of Fab. I did my best to push them away. Besides, Marco got what was coming to him.

Despite being such a piss-poor closer, Marco decided to break away from Levi and go it alone. He gave up his salary as Levi's account opener and dropped to three hundred and fifty dollars a week with his draw against commission. He had something to prove and I could see that his jealousy of Buck was eating away at him. There was no way he could hold all of that inside him and move forward, I thought.

So I was surprised when, soon after, Marco netted a whale. This trade was one that could change his life and propel him forward—he had closed on an incredible fifty thousand shares with one investor. When the trade was done and he hung up the phone, the room erupted into cheers. He'd finally broken his cherry. I figured, though, that even a blind squirrel will find a nut every once in a while.

Marco was grinning ear to ear, and he went out for a celebratory smoke with some of the guys who clapped him on the back and grabbed his neck, rubbing his head with their knuckles. He did it.

It did turn out to be a career-defining moment for him. Two days later, the investor reneged. Marco went pale when he heard the news. He desperately tried to save the deal and had one of the partners get on the phone to try to resuscitate the trade. The partner was able to get the investor to agree to open up a joint account to pay for the shares. But when he was asked the name of the joint holder, the investor said, in a deadpan voice, that the man's name was Jesus. Yes, Jesus Christ, as in the son of God. The partner had put the investor on speakerphone so everyone in the boardroom, silent and listening intently, heard that Jesus had decided to invest in the market. I guess he wanted to speculate beyond loaves and fishes.

Marco left soon after, and we never heard from him again.

I held Marco up in my mind as an example of what I could never allow myself to become. I put my head down and pushed. I hadn't thought that I could work harder than I already was, and yet I somehow found an untapped reserve of strength that I didn't know I had. I came into the office every morning at five a.m., and usually stayed until ten or eleven p.m., pitching Australia and New Zealand, where we had recently expanded our efforts. All that people knew there were secondhand stories of investors who had made millions off speculating in America, and they wanted in. They had never heard the phrases "chop shop" and "boiler room," and I think it wouldn't even have mattered if they had. The promise of making big bucks blinded them to risk. Of course, eventually, the facade would come crashing down, when enough people had been "churned and burned," as we called it, and we exhausted our leads in these far-off places, just as we had in the United States. But that was off in the misty future—right now it was my time to seize opportunity by the throat.

Busting my ass soon paid off and I hit gold. I opened my first account with an American guy; he was the CEO of a paper company, and he purchased a hundred shares of US Air. The tradition at VTR, as at other firms, for opening your first account was that you would walk to the front of the boardroom, all eyes on you, and a partner would ceremoniously snip your tie. The only problem was that I . . . didn't have a tie. Everyone was flummoxed because I was the first woman to get this far and they didn't know what, if anything, they should cut.

"Take off your bra!" someone from the back of the room shouted.

I had drilled it into myself that I needed to be a good sport so the thought actually crossed my mind that maybe I *should* take my bra off for a snip. It would certainly give the brokers something to talk about and I wanted to be one of the guys, down for anything. But my breasts were, as Shappy would have been proud to note, almost the size of watermelons, and they would be flopping around for the rest of the day if I went ahead with that plan. Scratch that. I needed my bra, and really, that would be such a waste—bras were so damn expensive.

In the end, partner Ari just shook my hand and handed me a hundred-dollar bill. There were always at least a few hundred-dollar bills taped up on the whiteboard at the front of the boardroom to give to anyone who opened an account. It was a great motivator—watching people walk up there, grabbing hundred-dollar bills, made you want to be that person, to crush that person, and open up even more accounts than them. Snatching one of those crisp hundred-dollar bills off the board was the best feeling in the whole world, and conspicuously marching up there multiple times a day put the other brokers on notice that you were killing it.

Cracking that first account was exactly what I needed to get my flow going. I started opening up accounts left and right. I even opened three accounts in one day and got Knicks tickets from the partners plus the cash for my handy hat-trick.

Opening an account put everything I had learned to use. After snagging the lead, getting an investor on the phone a second time was hard enough. Once you had his ear, well, that was your cue so you better not fuck it up. He—always "he," remember—had decided to give you his undivided attention to hear your pitch, and if you were not able to convince him with all the desperate urgency you could muster that he needed to get involved *right this minute*, then you were toast.

As I pitched more, I became increasingly comfortable interacting with these men I had never met, whom I was trying to convince to give me hopefully six figures on a risky investment. I never sat down when I pitched, and I always made sure that they could hear exactly how excited I was to be bringing them this opportunity. Some leads would let me give my pitch just to be nice; then they would say they weren't interested and would hang up. Others would play along and let me pitch, then ask what the minimum was to open an account (a hundred shares of a stock), at which point they'd shut me down. Finally, I had the guys who would take me to the mat and, yes! would open. You never knew with complete certainty where a call would go—it could last ten minutes and be a winner or drudge on for an hour and be a waste of time.

If I knew I was close to getting the guy, I would sometimes sigh, acting exhausted, and say, "Mr. Jones, why are you beating me up so badly for just a hundred shares? It's eighteen hundred dollars and you and I both know I'm not making any money on this trade." I'd pause to let that sink in for Mr. Jones then continue, sounding annoyed that I had to spell things out for him.

"Obviously, sir, my motivation is not to continue making five dollars on every trade I facilitate. Frankly, I would never waste my time or yours like that. What I want to do, and what I know is most beneficial for you, is to set you up with our firm and bring you ideas that will, unfortunately for him, blow your other broker out of the water. So, Mr. Jones, please stop busting my balls because I know it's not about the money." Here, I'd pause again for dramatic effect, but not long enough for him to get a word in.

"You don't have to hide it from me. I know what this is about—it's that you aren't comfortable with me or my firm. You are not familiar with us. Hey, I get it—I might feel the same way if I were you. But that's exactly why I'm willing to start you off with a hundred shares of US Air, which I know, for a guy like you, is peanuts. Look, we both know you are not going to get rich off of a hundred shares, even if the company is bought out tomorrow. But what I do know is that if the stock does exactly what I say, you will never second-guess me again. A hundred shares and the next time we have something we know will knock your socks off, you will take us a bit more seriously and you'll take a real position in the company." I'd take a breath and knock the guy out with my final blow.

"Take the hundred shares just for now. The only thing I ask for in return is that next time you will never make me work so hard to make you money. Is that fair?"

There were a million ways to close the guy. One that I used for a majority of accounts was the "stop-loss order" move:

"Mr. Jones, are you familiar with a stop-loss order? No? It is a market order to execute the sale of your stock at a specific price below what you paid for it. It's what we call a safety net—it limits your downside risk. Hypothetically speaking, you purchase two hundred shares with a three-point stop-loss order. And let's just say, again, hypothetically speaking, I'm an idiot and I am wrong here. For the record, I don't think I am or wouldn't be on the phone with you right now [*insert cheesy laugh*]! But just say I am and you lose six hundred dollars. Honestly, if I lose you six hundred dollars, am I going to put you in the poorhouse? Ha ha, of course not! You probably spent that much on dinner and wine last night! On the flip side, if I am right and I make you a few hundred dollars, I don't think you're flying me in first class and buying me a lobster dinner, are you? But what this trade will do is to serve as a benchmark for future business. It will show you that I am the type of broker who can guide you into the market at the right time, but *even more importantly*, guide you *out* at the right time. Guide you in and guide you out, and put dollars in your pocket. You give me this one small shot on two hundred shares with a three-point stop-loss and all I ask is that next time out we work bigger and better on a level I know you're more capable of. Fair enough?"

～

If I felt like I needed reinforcement, I would also use the line, "Give me a one percent vote of confidence and I will earn the other ninety-nine percent."

Cheesy? Yes, but most of the guys loved it. If they weren't going for the cheese, then I would switch up my game with a witty rebuttal. Because if you could get a guy to laugh, you were in.

Even when an investor said "yes" to me, I didn't breathe until the money was in. I was walking on a tightrope, tiptoeing through the paperwork for the account to verifying their positions in the market to the very end when payment was due—they could go through all the motions just to finally renege on the deal when payment was due. I didn't want to be a Marco Ricci. Nobody wanted to be a Marco Ricci.

That said, I never knew anyone to take a hit and pay for it. If the firm would have tried that with anyone, the sap would have been better off quitting and disappearing rather than paying what likely would be a very sizable debt.

That first trade, the stock you opened the account with, was never big enough to pursue any legal action against an investor if they didn't pay and the stock was down from their purchase price. It actually made the brokers uncomfortable if a first-time investor immediately opened on a big share ask. It was a rarity, so when it happened, it immediately put us on guard. Were they part of the SEC or NASD? Were they trying to catch us doing something shady? With the activities we got into, our firm was definitely not looking to have additional eyes on us.

As much work as we put into netting the lead and opening the account, we put just as much into making an investor cough up. The sales assistants were our frontline soldiers. They would leave the investors ominous messages informing them that they would be restricted from trading for a fixed period if they didn't pay, or, if that didn't work, that they would be put on a list in the industry that showed they had reneged on trades and weren't creditworthy. Sounds scary, right? It wasn't true, but it would often get investors to pay up. And if *that* didn't work, or an investor reneged on a second trade, the assistants would threaten investors, letting them know they would be blacklisted on Wall Street and would never be able to trade again. Again, totally false! But it sure helped us get to payday.

Chapter 20

IN THE BULL MARKET, I WAS BULLISH. WHENEVER I picked up the phone, I'd bark out, "FABRÉ!" I needed investors to know I was busy and had zero time to waste on their whining and complaining. You're calling to request the sale of your stock? Not happening. You had better be calling me to ask how to wire more money into your account. Nothing else. No asking for an update, no bitching about your stock being stagnant. Oh, and if you said you needed your money back? I didn't care. You need this money so your kid can go to college? That didn't faze me. *So what!* I'd yell back at the investor. *Your kid can go to community college—he's going to fuck around the first year or two anyway, partying all night and sleeping his classes away. By the time he gets serious about school, I will have made significant gains in your account and you can send him to any private school you want.*

Any other excuse they threw at me—surgery, divorce, saving their business, payment to their mistress for blackmail—I threw right back at them. I'm your new mistress, bitch—you pay me. You need to keep me happy. You better be thinking about me when you open your eyes in the morning and when you close them at night. I am busting my ass to make you money (or so I thought), and a little downturn in stocks makes you nervous?

If you liked the stock at five dollars, then you better fall in love with it at three. You want something guaranteed, get a CD. You wanna make real money, you gotta spend real money.

That said, I also knew how to offer them a bit of honey to make it all go down easier—that was part of emotional selling; you needed to know when to reel it back in. Most of the brokers didn't know how to make their clients feel special, feel protected. All they knew how to do was yell, curse, or ignore them. I learned about my clients' families, what was happening in their lives. I gave them a false sense of security, that I would give them notice if their investments took a nosedive. At twenty, I didn't fully understand the machinations at play within VTR; I thought they would be safe buying big positions in our stocks based on our recommendations. No one at the firm ever seemed to get upset that their clients weren't making money. The other brokers and I would have to tell clients "I lost a hundred K, two hundred K, half a mil," and it was no sweat off anyone's backs because we'd already gotten paid on the client's loss. We would advise people to take out mortgages on their homes and liquidate their savings and they would still lose with us. The guys would laugh when this would happen, saying, "His wife is probably going to leave him!" or "I guess he has to come out of retirement!" It was a joke to them—the bigger the investment, the funnier it was. I didn't find it funny. This charismatic about-face, switching from sycophant to trickster, also reminded me of Fab. These men were all wolves in sheep's clothing, desperate to satiate whatever void was inside them, refusing to hold themselves accountable to anyone.

That also meant to one another. There was no loyalty in this business. Partners turned on one another, stealing clients. Ex-colleagues would call your clients when starting up a new firm to woo them away from you, bashing you and your company in the process. Some might even call up a broker at another firm and give them your client's details so they could have the other broker open an account and ACAT it. "ACAT," or "Automated Customer Account Transfer," simply transfers your securities from one firm to another. During the three-day transfer period, you would feverishly try to convince your client not to do it. The bitter taste in your mouth would sour when you found out who the other broker was who tried to inherit your account. That said, we were all on both sides of an ACAT. After all, it was just business.

Being the only woman at the firm did give me a leg up in some regards, as I turned clients' lasciviousness to my advantage. They would think they were being sly, asking me hypotheticals that weren't—if they came to New York, would my boyfriend or husband mind if I showed them around? I'd give them vague responses, telling them that everyone who knew me knew that my clients always came first and I didn't need anyone's permission to show them a good time. It was a game that I played well. They'd tell me that they liked my New York accent and loved the way I ordered them around, calling me naughty. They'd confess in hushed tones that they hadn't told their wives that their broker was a woman, as if this were some kind of illicit affair. White guys in suits were the default on Wall Street; as a Black woman, I was the special exception to the rule and it was in your best interest to listen to me because if you didn't, you might never get a chance to hear my voice in your ear again. Emotional selling like this was—and is—everything in the business. It fuels the market to this day. I could praise and emasculate a man at the same time. Our emotions ran high and our interests were intertwined. I wanted the men to trust me and I didn't want to let them down.

VTR stoked misogyny not just among the men but with me as well. They trained us to believe that the investor's wife was enemy number one. Whenever a client would balk with a "Let me speak to my wife about this," I'd laugh and say, "Leave your wife to pick out the socks you're going to wear. You can leave us to pick your stocks." If he protested further, I'd scoff and say, "What do you need to talk to your wife about? Does she call you whenever she's buying groceries or getting her hair done? Let her stick to what she's good at and you stick to what you're good at—making money. Scared money doesn't make money!" We were like a pack of wolves—if you couldn't go for the kill when the time came, we turned on you. If you'd heard me talking on the phone, you'd swear it was the 1950s, not the 1990s. I threw out these lines likely thousands of times and not once did anyone stand up to me and say, "Sorry, my wife and I make joint decisions."

My mother made the financial decisions in our household—I watched as she hustled and became the primary breadwinner for our family. But I followed VTR's script. I knew I was being derogatory toward women, and back then I truly didn't care. I reasoned with myself that I was proving that if men could do it, women could do it better.

We were all content to follow VTR's script as long as it pulled in money for us, which it did handsomely. And why wouldn't we? These pitches were sourced from Stratton Oakmont and our tactics were the best in the business. If a client didn't want to listen, well, there goes the fucking door, and I hope it hits you on the way out. In fact, VTR actively discouraged us from reading papers like the *Wall Street Journal* or *Bloomberg News*, gave us speeches about how these outlets were shams that pushed the same old stocks making the same predictable gains. It was mighty convenient to purposely keep us uneducated so that we wouldn't ask pointed questions. Where else but these chop shops could someone be given access to become a broker within six months flat at nineteen years old and start taking home fat commission checks without knowing a single thing about investing?

That ignorance came in handy for when I reliably pitched the same questionable stocks for literally *years*. We had a useful pitch involving US Air, the now defunct airline, that netted hundreds of accounts for me; it had landed me my first account. I pitched it so often at VTR that I truly believed what I was saying despite the fact that there was no evidence to support my claims. I could rattle it off in my sleep: "Mr. Jones, do you happen to know who Stephen Wolf is? He was the CEO of Republic Airlines and responsible for the successful merger with Northwest Airlines, which was the largest merger in aviation history! Mr. Wolf also orchestrated the buyout of the Flying Tigers, the world's largest cargo carrier, by FedEx where he was the CEO at the time. He single-handedly turned the company around and made it profitable again under his watch. He is now the CEO of US Air and we believe he is at it again with a United Airlines merger."

I dared investors to interrupt me, dared them to say no to me. I crafted the pitch with such precision—it sounded so well researched and safe—that they simply couldn't say no. I won with it time and time again for the next four years. It was also how I landed my first whale. I was able to close on a whopping thousand shares of US Air with an Australian investor who was eager to enter the American market, even with his dollar trading at .66 to our dollar. This set off a volley of incredulous comments from the brokers—"You got him on the first close?" and "Let me know if you need any help with him." But I certainly didn't need any assistance from these leeches. They just wanted to partner up and snatch the client from me, slowly siphoning off my contact with the investor and transitioning themselves to be the primary contact until, poof, one day, the other broker would be fully in control. No thank you, assholes.

While I was busying myself with building my book of clients, VTR was digging itself into a hole with our investors. Unbeknownst to me at the time, we were pumping and dumping massive amounts of one of our house stocks, Compare Generiks

(COGE), a dietary supplement company, to investors, stealing their profits while the stock went south. We needed a miracle, and fast; otherwise, people would soon catch on to our shady dealings and we'd have an SEC raid on our hands.

Enter Noah Hoffman, a junior broker at the firm and meek as a mouse. He had recovered from heroin addiction a couple of years before joining the firm and had a glassy-eyed stare about him that made you think he'd seen some serious shit. I had never heard him pitch out loud—he actually liked to cover his mouth while he was talking to investors on the phone. Still, it was rumored that he was a silent killer.

Day by day, the partners became increasingly anxious as the COGE situation grew more dire. They paced the halls and snapped at the callers like never before. The last thing that they—or any of us, really—expected was for Hoffman to be our soft-voiced savior. I just happened to look up on a Tuesday and there was Hoffman, standing at his desk with his hand over his phone. This was the most animated I had seen him, though by our usual standards he'd qualify as a corpse. I sensed something in the air so I kept my eyes on him. I watched as he gently placed his receiver back in its cradle and calmly wrote up an order ticket, handing it to his assistant. Then, without a word, he walked out the door and didn't come back.

It was only when partner Greg got on the mic that we learned what Hoffman had been up to. "Give a fucking round of applause to Noah Hoffman, people—he just made a *one million* share purchase for COGE!" The relief in Greg's voice was apparent. With one purchase, Hoffman had just saved the entire company. Well, that's a slight exaggeration, but there would definitely have been a mass exodus of angry clients from VTR if he hadn't pulled this off. With this share, the stock price went back to trading near its previous high, despite our best efforts to swindle people, getting them all to buy the bad stock, driving it into the ground until it was worthless. With this move, we could show clients that they had gains—on paper, at least. . . . They would likely never see cash, as they'd suffer another loss in the future. So VTR could breathe easy. For now, at least.

Hoffman's trade also set off a chain of events that would cement my career as a power broker moving forward. It would also find me getting caught in a habit that so many brokers adopted: Make the money and, only after you've been paid, question the purchase . . . but not too hard and only if you have to.

After the COGE news broke, I hurriedly rang all my clients to encourage them to buy more—it's what VTR had taught us to do. One of my clients, Alfred Davies, a UK businessman, was impressed and offered to introduce me to his friend who had deep pockets. *Yeah, sure*, I thought.

"Okay, Alfred, I'm waiting for his call. Just tell him that this stock won't be at this price forever," I said, not expecting that Alfred, who was a modest investor, would know anyone worth my time. I promptly forgot about Alfred and his anonymous friend until a couple of weeks later when my phone rang and I picked it up without thought.

"Hello, Cin?" a constipated British voice said in my ear.

"Yeah, who is this?" I asked.

"This is Alfred Davies's friend. My name is Charles. He said I ought to give you a ring."

I figured I'd launch into my standard US Air pitch to see if my trusty default could land whoever this was. I had barely finished my spiel when the man told me he would take a thousand shares. I made a mental note to thank Alfred. Not bad, Alfie.

As I filled out the new account form with "Charles" on the line, curiosity got the best of me and I asked him what he did for a living.

"Oh, my family and I own Man U," he said.

"Man U?" I repeated. That didn't ring a bell.

"Yes, Manchester United," he replied.

I still had no idea what he was talking about so I played it cool and acted like I knew exactly what this was.

On an account form, there is a field that you must complete for the holder's net worth. When we got to Charles's net worth, I asked him to estimate, and he replied with "Conservatively, it would be one hundred million pounds." *Holy God.*

I didn't flinch.

"What's that in US dollars, you'd say?" I asked coolly.

I hung up the phone and stared bemusedly at my desk for a few seconds. Then I dropped my ticket for the US Air purchase with my sales assistant Sonia and sat back down. After all, I had more work to do.

Partner Greg called me into his office just a few minutes later. He constantly monitored the new accounts and he'd seen the form I'd just turned in.

"Uh, Cin, am I reading this guy's net worth right or did you accidentally add in extra zeros?" he asked, peering up at me from his desk.

"Nope, that's correct. He owns Man U, whatever that means," I told him. Greg stared at me, frozen. I waited for him to say something but he didn't, so I shrugged and walked out.

A few minutes later, Greg's voice piped in on the office-wide speaker system.

"Boooooys and giiiiiiirls, Cin has just opened the whale we wait our entire lives for. Her client is worth almost TWO HUNDRED MILLION DOLLARS! Get out of your fucking seats and give her all the applause because she is giving you all a run for your fucking money!" he screamed.

The office went wild. It was pandemonium.

"How the fuck did you get him as a client?"

"Cin, do you need help?"

"You gotta second trade him as soon as that money hits, Fabré!"

"Cin, do you want to go out tonight?"

"Cin!"

"Cin!"

"Cin!"

Charles. Charles was Charles Martin Edwards, the primary shareholder of Manchester United, one of the most popular football teams on the planet. Yes, that Manchester United— the English football club originally founded in 1878 when the United States was a pimply teen; the football club that had won more trophies than any other club in history; the football club at the top of the Premier League; the football club worth hundreds of millions or even billions depending on the year. Charles, chairman of the Man U board, was the real deal. (So much of a real deal that he followed all the conventions of men in finance—he was later accused of hiring sex workers while on company business.)

❧

When that money hit, I never looked back. I had legitimized the company almost single-handedly—who wouldn't want to work with the brokers who handled the owner of Manchester United? I pitched furiously and I closed again and again and again.

When I received my first commission check a couple of weeks later, it was for thirty thousand dollars (the first of many five- and six-figure checks). I paid my landlord all the back rent I owed her, then I paid off the balance of an expensive watch she had been paying for. I was nowhere near finished, though. Jameson Logan took me to his jeweler on Long Island and I bought a two-thousand-dollar Cartier watch. I took Catalina and her sister Kenya to Cancun for a long-overdue vacation, one of the first I'd ever taken. It was exhilarating to finally, *finally*, take some time off work to spend it with my favorite people.

Catalina's father, as domineering as ever, almost didn't let her go on our trip to Mexico even though she was a grown adult at nineteen years old. But because I was taking Kenya along, too, he relented. Kenya was the goody two-shoes of the family, and I suppose that their father felt that she could chaperone and keep her sister out of trouble, which he was always certain Catalina was bound to find. Kenya, in turn, faithfully reported her findings to her father, which often caused friction between Catalina and Kenya. But if Kenya's presence on the trip meant Catalina would be able to go, she'd deal with any paternal consequences later.

We stayed at a hotel near the beach, all of us piling into one room together. Our first evening there, we went clubbing, dancing up a storm and drinking tropical cocktails with abandon. I found myself on the dance floor near a costumed, spandex-clad Batman and Robin, and didn't question why, exactly, they were there, choosing to revel in the surreal, slightly dizzying fun of it all.

It wasn't until I paused to take a breather and grab another cocktail that I saw Catalina walking toward the exit, leading a mysterious figure out of the club by the hand. Kenya, huddled beside me, immediately started making noises of concern, but I shrugged it off. Catalina was an adult, even if her family didn't treat her as such—she'd be okay.

We didn't reunite with Catalina until the next morning when she sauntered into our hotel room, where Kenya and I were having breakfast.

"Damn, girl, you're just getting in?" I raised an eyebrow at Catalina and smiled. I was glad she had decided to take full advantage of vacation to have some fun.

"The beach is really nice," she replied coyly.

Kenya spluttered. "But we haven't been to the beach yet!"

Catalina giggled. "I was there last night . . ." She trailed off.

Kenya looked ready to interrogate further but I interrupted them both, holding up a copy of the English-language newspaper that had been delivered with breakfast.

"Diana, Princess of Wales, 36, Dies in a Crash in Paris," I read solemnly from the front page, which was plastered with photos of Diana, Charles, her children, her partner who had been in the car with her. We collectively sighed, sobered for the moment, and Catalina's nighttime liaison was soon forgotten in the wake of the tragedy screaming at us from the headlines.

⌁

When I returned from our trip, I moved to a one-bedroom apartment in Battery Park directly across the street from the office. I wasn't going to waste any more time on a commute when I could be at work making deals. Living in an apartment where there was little danger of roaches was a godsend, too.

I was twenty years old. I had used up almost all the funds from that first check. But money wasn't a problem. There'd be more where that came from.

Chapter 21

THE YEAR 1997 A.C. (*AFTER CHARLES*) WAS ONE long party. Or at least it felt that way to me—day blurred into night back into day in one uninterrupted rager. If you couldn't find me at the office, which was rare, then I was likely with the other brokers at a strip club. Some companies may employ trust falls as team-building exercises. VTR paid for its employees to get lap dances.

Once I became a broker and landed Charles, I was officially brought along to go to Scores, VIP's, and Tens, which the boys considered to be the best strip clubs in Manhattan. If I didn't go, I would have been *that* girl again. There was no room for me to say, *Hey guys, could we maybe hold one party that* isn't *at a strip club?* I couldn't tell them, *Actually, no, I'm not always comfortable getting lap dances from these girls that you keep sending over to me and no, I don't want to have sex with them while you watch.* I wanted to be able to say, *I feel kind of awkward seeing you go to the back room with a girl to fuck her when I know I'm going to see your wife at our next holiday party or when she drops by the office to bring you cookies.*

And yet they were more than comfortable asking me about my sex life and whether I'd ever seen a white dick and oh, did I maybe want to see theirs? Because they'd be more than happy to volunteer. How generous!

It was par for the course for the guys to drop twenty K in one night, getting anything—and anyone—they wanted. It soon began to feel completely normal to sit in the VIP lounge at the club, holding in my hands thousands of dollars that the partners had given me as funny money to make it rain and pass out to whoever might have caught my eye. We bought champagne worth hundreds of dollars a pop just to shake up and shower all over each other. Why? Because we could. The hottest girls in the club would do X-rated things with the brokers just short of having sex with them at our table so that they could curry favor and join us, sampling the bottles of top-shelf liquor and white party favors that were in constant, unending supply. And I wasn't exempt from the attention. Girls would rub me up and down and shove my head into their chest so I could motorboat them. They'd lean in close so I could smell their cloying perfume and whisper in my ear that I had free rein to do whatever I wanted to them. Some of them used me to get attention, hovering over me with their nipples dangling in front of my mouth, looking over to make sure that the brokers were watching the show. The girl with the biggest ass in the place would sashay over to me and bend over, having me shove my face in her thong. This didn't turn me on—I had basically shut all my sexual urges down to focus on work. Nobody caught my eye, man or woman. The only thing that turned me on was power. The brokers would cheer us on, throwing bills like it was their own private show. I think they enjoyed my presence, but I believe they were also trying to unnerve me, to have me tell them I was uncomfortable so that they could exchange looks with each other and mouth, *You see? I knew it.* Or, it could have just been that they were so incredibly high that they didn't care that I was witnessing their debauchery.

It was intoxicating to know that you really were the VIPs of the entire club—you could feel others' eyes on you, watching enviously. Regardless of lines, we were immediately privately ushered inside the club by the bouncers. Even the celebrities we occasionally saw didn't get the same level of treatment.

I tried not to think about the guys' constant objectification of the girls, *of me*. And the girls didn't seem like they were unhappy. A few who spoke to me in between dances told me that they were saving up to go to college. When I told the guys this, they laughed uproariously like I'd just told them a knee slapper.

"Cin, that's a fucking line. They're here to find a sugar daddy and be a kept woman. That's why you keep their mouths busy so they don't talk. Besides, why would they go to school when they can make more money on their backs?"

They'd shake their heads, amazed by my apparent gullibility, then they'd hand over a thousand dollars to their girl for that night and walk to the back room so that they could do things together in the dark. In turn, I'd shake my head at them. It seemed to me that everyone was in it for something, each party getting exactly what they wanted without pretense, manipulations exercised both in the strip club and in the office.

❧

When summer arrived, we hit the Hamptons. "Summering" was a new concept for me and I discovered that I liked it. I rented a house with Abel, Jen, our compliance officer (all she ever did was try to keep the brokers out of trouble), and a few others. The house was in Quogue, officially a village within the town of Southampton, but far out enough that the stuck-up blue bloods didn't necessarily think of it as part of the Hamptons. For us new money folk, it did just fine. Our house wasn't as grand as the partner's Hamptons house that I'd visited the previous summer, but it was still lavish—gray-shingled with turrets and balconies, multiple basketball courts, a huge pool, and, obviously, a mess of drugs and alcohol.

We'd drive out of the city on Friday evening after dinner, along with the rest of Manhattan, it felt like, getting to our house at around nine p.m. Then we'd freshen up and I'd sling back some drinks while the others snorted coke, and we'd head out. We got invited to wild private parties and everyone kissed our asses. If we weren't partying with the rich and famous— professional athletes, very wealthy businesspeople, and trust fund babies—we were in the VIP sections of exclusive clubs.

The one time Abel, Jen, and I got denied entrance, the bouncers looked us up and down and pointed at us to wait in line. Fortunately, one of the partners happened to come out of the club for a smoke and saw us standing there. He walked over to the bouncer and said in a dangerously calm voice, "Remember their faces and don't *ever* make them wait again." The bouncer, who towered over him, cowered and meekly said, "Yes, sir." As we walked past, I cut my eyes at the bouncer and gave him a look that said, "Yeah, motherfucker, you better remember my face."

It was rare for me to see Black people out in the Hamptons. I chalked it up to the likelihood that they just didn't want to party with drugged-up, supremely boring white people. Seriously, the dance floor was always empty! What a waste of space. Our crew was always a good time, though, livening things up wherever we went, getting wallflowers out onto the dance floor, or if we couldn't do that, content to dance with each other. Nobody in the Hamptons ever treated me with hostility, but I did get a lot of curious looks always accompanied by the question, "What do you do again?"

I received that same look and query when I was stopped in my new Mercedes coupe by the police. I had been driving buzzed and got pulled over. When the cop knocked on my window, he gave me a long look, then whistled and said, "What do you have to do to get a car like this at your age?"

I just smiled and said, "I got my Series 7 license and I sell my ass off." I flipped out my wallet. "Here's my card—call me if you ever want a job."

I didn't get a ticket that night. I was invincible.

↩

Invincibility came at a price. I obviously enjoyed the crazy profits, but it was starting to dawn on me that what we were pushing didn't seem to be benefiting clients in the slightest. And yet, despite this, VTR kept urging us to get investors to take bigger positions in our losing stocks. We were all making money at the expense of our clients, who we were supposed to be serving but were fucking over in the most magnificent fashion.

Around this time, it leaked that one of our account openers had gotten curious about one of the companies we were hawking. He decided to Hardy Boy it and located the company and paid it a visit. When he got there? No company. It was just a P.O. box. The account opener left a week after this discovery.

I had always thought the market was about buying and selling, push and pull, up and down, but not, it seemed, at VTR. All we did was buy house stock for clients. Selling was a no-no. If you did sell, the stock would tank significantly even if only a small number of shares had been sold. This made no sense to me. How does selling five thousand shares of a stock cause the stock to decline by thirty percent?

When this happened, one of the partners would get on the loudspeaker and scream that the stock was cheap and we needed to buy, buy, buy. As I continued to open new accounts, I started to see a pattern forming. We held our position until our next IPO. As long as you didn't sell, you were okay. Back then, pre-Internet, there was no tidy way to track your stock daily unless you called us or you had a Quotron, the first electronic stock tracker, a bulky machine that everyday people certainly didn't have in their homes. As a result, the investor couldn't see what was going on and relied heavily on us to advise them, believing that we would steer them true.

Yes, I should have realized what was going on, that what VTR was doing was highly illegal. But I was only twenty and had no formal education beyond high school. I certainly had cloudy suspicions, but I didn't put the puzzle pieces together. I just knew that I wanted to make my clients money and it wasn't happening at VTR.

❧

It was George Liebman who opened my eyes. He was a junior partner at the firm and we had hung out a few times, as we were both friends with Buckmaster. He did big business so it was a huge blow to the company when he suddenly left, taking all his clients with him. He was one of a number of brokers who had left recently, and the partners were scrambling to replace them. I figured I'd never see George again but a couple of months after he left he called me out of the blue and invited me to his apartment to talk.

George opened the door, smiling, and let me in. His apartment was in the Financial District and it was nice. It wasn't flashy, but you could tell it was expensive.

I took a seat in a black leather swivel chair, and George sat opposite me on the couch. He looked at me for a long minute.

"Cin, how do you feel about all the people who have left the firm?"

I shrugged. The partners had just told us that they had all had cases of grass-is-greener syndrome.

George sighed. "So you don't think there's anything off at VTR?"

I paused. I wanted to weigh my words carefully. I didn't

know what George wanted from me and I didn't want him to use anything I said against me.

"I don't know, George. I follow the program and I'm really good at it."

George sat forward. "Cin, it's all wrong. The firm is stealing money from our clients, pushing their own companies that they have a vested interest in. Don't you ever wonder why you guys aren't allowed to sell a stock? There's no one to sell it to! If the firm has to buy it back, they will, but it'll be a large loss to your client." He gave me a moment to let this sink in.

"Cin, you were duped. So was I. It's not your fault, but you can do something about it. I think we both have the same goals—we want to stay in this business and make our clients money." He grew animated.

"Look, if I recommend a company and my clients end up losing money, I can still sleep at night knowing that at least I put them into legitimate companies that have earnings behind them."

George spent the next two hours breaking down exactly what was wrong with VTR. My head was spinning but I was starting to get it. Then he shifted into why he'd asked me here.

"You need to make a move, Cin. Fast. If you don't, your clients are going to lose all their money and you'll get sued. Come over to Ladenburg."

I was stunned. Ladenburg was one of the most respected firms on Wall Street. It was over a hundred years old and had thousands of employees. It wasn't a chop shop.

"You've got a job waiting for you, Cin. But VTR is in trouble. You have to move quick. Do you have your book with you?"

I nodded. Of course I did—I'd never leave my book of leads at the office. Those vultures would steal it without a second thought if they found it. But George wanted me to meet the directors of the firm as soon as possible and make a decision by *tonight.* Shit. I calculated quickly. I couldn't keep holding clients off, selling them stocks that weren't performing. I had to get out before we all got burned.

"Okay!" I blurted out, without thinking further. "I'll do it."

George broke out into a wide grin. "That's my girl," he said. Then he shifted back into business mode.

"I'll get you that interview for tomorrow morning. Call all your clients late tonight. You know that they'll try to take them from you. You've got to move fast."

Chapter 22

GEORGE MADE GOOD ON HIS WORD. TWELVE HOURS later, I walked into 590 Madison, a gleaming skyscraper in Midtown. The building had originally been constructed for IBM and seeing its logo stamped on the building gave me confidence. Next door was Tiffany & Co., and a few steps farther were Breitling and Tourneau. This was prime real estate.

I was meeting with David Hersch, the director of the company, and Mark Friedman, managing director of the firm. David had unfortunate Donald Trump–style hair and wore ugly, oversize glasses, but he looked smugly comfortable with himself. His eyes widened when he saw me, but he quickly hid his surprise and stood up to shake my hand. (I would later learn that there were no other Black female brokers at Ladenburg, nor did I ever hear of or see one from another firm.) I didn't mind—George said that he had no doubt that they'd want me. I had Charles Martin Edwards in my pocket. I was valuable and I knew it.

I sat down and, like Brad Ambrosi had done nineteen months earlier when I interviewed with him, put my feet up on Hersch's desk. I leaned back and assessed Hersch, who looked at me incredulously.

"David, tell me why I should work here," I said, arms crossed. He burst out laughing.

"You gotta have a lotta balls to come in here and do that, kid. But I like you and I heard you're good. Let's do business," he said.

Now this was more like it.

"I want an office. I want a seventy-thirty payout for at least six months and two paid cold callers. I need a ten K business budget."

David didn't blink. "Is that all?" he asked.

"And . . . and a car service to get to work and home," I added. David didn't hesitate.

"Done. Can you start today?"

And that was that. It was that clean. I was now officially part of Ladenburg Thalmann & Associates.

What was messier was VTR. Jen, the compliance officer I'd shared a Hamptons house with, called me on the blocky cell phone that I had acquired a few months prior.

"Cin," she hissed. "The partners know. If you don't bring your book back, they will come after you!"

An empty threat, I thought.

Jen directed me to meet her outside the office so I could turn over my book, which was officially VTR property, as I'd opened those accounts there. Not that it mattered. I promptly made copies of my book and waltzed over to meet her. She looked harried.

"They want you to pay after the shit you've pulled," she said, referring to the partners. "Half the brokers up and quit today and they really didn't need you abandoning them in the middle of this."

Apparently, a rumor had broken out and spread like wildfire that the SEC was planning a raid on VTR. Brokers were leaving in droves to avoid getting implicated in fraud. The only thing VTR could do was to try to go after the decamped brokers' clients. And that meant mine, too. They weren't going to go down without a fight. Well, neither was I. I handed my book over to Jen and walked away without another word. The race was on.

❧

As soon as Jen gave my book to the partners, I knew they would be ringing my clients, doing all they could to keep them at VTR. I immediately applied for a same-day passport, which you could do back then, and booked a flight to Manchester, England, leaving in only a few hours. Then I sped home, manically threw clothes into a bag, and ran like a madwoman to JFK Airport. I couldn't afford to miss my flight.

When I got to my gate, panting and drenched in sweat, check-in had already closed. I pleaded with the gate attendant to let me through, trying and failing to summarize in a few seconds why it was so important I make it on the flight. She looked me up and down disdainfully.

"The next time you fly overseas, you must dress appropriately," she said to me, ice spiking in her voice. I looked down at my designer jeans, my expensive tee, and Gucci shoes in bewilderment.

"You're in Club Class. You need to cover your arms," she said disapprovingly.

I rolled my eyes. Whatever. I didn't care if I had to fly naked—I just needed to be on that goddamn plane. Thankfully, she descended from her throne and let me through. As soon as I sank into my seat, I passed out, exhausted, getting into Manchester the next morning. My first stop was a hotel restaurant for breakfast with Michael Whittaker, a new client I had signed up a few months before. Michael happened to own almost all the KFCs in the UK, which of course put me in mind of the buckets that Fab would unceremoniously drop onto the kitchen table when we were kids.

I spotted Michael quickly—he had told me he would wear a red tie to identify himself—and walked up to him.

"Michael?" I asked.

"Yes?" he said, looking startled.

"I'm Cin!" I said. Michael looked taken aback. He went silent for a few moments, then found his voice.

"I didn't know you were Black," he said quietly.

What a greeting, I thought to myself.

"I didn't know you were white," I threw back at him. He didn't know what to do with that one.

"Well, I suppose we should carry on," he finally said, sighing.

We continued with our meeting, then got up to leave. As we headed toward the door, Michael leaned in, as if to offer me a tip.

"Manchester is very small, with only about fifty thousand people. You may be stared at because we aren't used to seeing colored people unless they're on a football team," he said.

Wow. I hadn't actually ever heard a person use the term "colored" before.

"What do you mean by 'colored,' exactly?" I asked him.

"Oh, well, you know," he fumbled. "Colored people like you."

I grimaced. "Michael, if by that you mean 'Black people,' then just say 'Black people.' Who says 'colored'?"

I didn't want to have to educate this man, but at least that seemed to set him straight. He appeared almost apologetic and he promised me that he would come with me to Ladenburg. One meeting down, one to go.

The next day, I met with Charles Martin Edwards, the Man U owner. We had arranged to meet at his office, then head to a game where Man U would play against Chelsea. I was excited—I had heard that the Brits took their football seriously and games could get crazy.

When I arrived, I was surprised to see plexiglass surrounding his office. Charles, or Martin, as his friends called him, gave me a look similar to Michael's. He clearly wasn't expecting someone like me but he rearranged his face quickly. To get past this, I asked about the plexiglass.

"I've only seen this at liquor stores in the hood!" I told him.

He nodded, his face serious. "You can't take any chances with footballers here. I need to be bulletproof."

Apparently, things could get ugly fast with opposing teams. Yikes.

We moved on to business and Martin told me he knew he was losing with me but that he would give me another chance now that I was with a new firm. I had already lost him a shitload of money using VTR's fleecing methods so I was grateful for this lifeline. He promised me a hundred thousand pounds on the spot and told me he'd send more if things turned up. Relief coursed through my body. I hadn't lost my biggest client.

After the football game, I left Charles/Martin to try out a real British pub for myself. I walked over to one of the pool tables in the smoke-filled bar and nodded at a Black man who, like everyone else I'd met in the UK, seemed surprised to see me there. We picked up a game and then another and another. At the end of the night, as we were drinking, I told him I worked in finance. He seemed impressed so I gave him my card and told him to call me. Then he told me he was a boxer. The only boxers I knew of were Muhammad Ali, Mike Tyson, and George Foreman, so I just shrugged and wished him luck with his career as I headed out. He tilted his head and gave a smile like I'd said something funny. In retrospect, I suppose I did because my pool buddy was none other than Olympic gold medalist and three-time world heavyweight champion, Lennox Lewis. Small world.

The next day, I left Manchester to return to the United States. As I walked down the plane aisle to get to my seat, I spotted a familiar face.

"Hesh!" I cried. Herb, "Hesh," was a broker at VTR. He looked over and his face fell.

"What are you doing here?" I raised an eyebrow. I knew exactly what he was doing.

"Visiting clients," he said, not quite looking me in the eye.

"Visiting Martin Edwards?" I asked. At least Hesh had the decency to look contrite.

"Yes," he admitted. He started to turn back in his seat but then he paused.

"You know, Cin, you should be proud of yourself. You're what—twenty?—and you landed this whale and came all the way to the UK to save him. It takes a certain kind of person to push like that," he said.

I thanked him and took my seat. I didn't think that I had done anything particularly special. I was a hustler and I'd be one until the day I died.

Chapter 23

LADENBURG WAS AN ALIEN PLANET. INSTEAD OF BLINDLY following firm mandates like I did at VTR, I was now expected to make my own recommendations to clients. George had promised to mentor me but he disappeared after my first day, never offering me more than a wave as we passed each other in the hallways. Shit. I knew that he had gotten a referral fee for bringing me over and that he wasn't offering me a lifeline out of the goodness of his heart. I buried myself in the *Wall Street Journal* and *Barron's* to try to understand the actual workings of the market but I was lost.

Fortunately, I happened upon Aldano Cruz, the VTR broker who had trouble with enunciation, a few weeks into working at Ladenburg. I didn't know he had made it over until he passed me in the hall one morning.

"Oh, hey, Cin," he said, smiling at me. "I heard you came over, too. Did you see that GE went up this morning?"

A lightbulb went off in my head. Aldano. I would use Aldano.

"Oh, yeah, yeah, I did," I said, thinking on my feet. "But, Aldano, I've been looking for you. I think we should talk."

I led him down the hallway to my office and ushered him through the door. He whistled.

"This is all yours?" he asked, clearly impressed.

"Yup," I said, waiting a beat then—"Don't you want an office like this?"

See, Aldano was smart. He sourced strong recommendations, but he couldn't pitch worth shit. But that was my forte—I pitched and maintained client accounts expertly. We complemented each other's strengths perfectly. On the spot I did what I did best—I pitched him, telling him that we would make an amazing team. And just like that, he was in. While I never would have teamed up at VTR—I could push bad stock all on my own—this was a different ball game and I needed to shift my strategy. Now, I didn't have to worry about making recommendations and I could sleep soundly, knowing that Aldano had my back.

This was the middle of the dot-com era. As long as a company ended in ".com," clients wanted in. I was feeling much more comfortable now that my investors were making money, but I wasn't necessarily averse to padding for a bit of extra cash. Anyone running the Wall Street race is bound to trip up and fall at some point, whether this means doing something illegal in a way that gets you caught or perhaps a stumble that is more insidious, like moving the line on your morals.

More quickly than I'd like to admit, I stopped thinking about my own contributions to the Wall Street way—it would be dangerous to reflect on these things if I wanted to keep going.

So I just *didn't*. I let myself engage in creative math with Aldano. For example, let's say AOL was trading at seventy-five dollars a share. Aldano and I would mark them by up to one dollar on the way in and one dollar on the way out. So, if they owned ten thousand shares at seventy-six dollars and we sold at seventy-eight dollars, on the next day, which included our one-dollar markdown, they would make ten thousand dollars in profit while we would make twenty thousand dollars. While this wasn't exactly aboveboard, we certainly weren't the only ones engaging in this practice. We desperately wanted to get to the next level of our business and snag a big corner office. But in order to do so, we had to gross a hundred K monthly. We had no choice but to turn to churning, which is the act of trading in order to generate commissions. We needed to make twice the amount of money because we were splitting commissions after the firm took its cut. Clients were making hundreds of thousands of dollars at a time investing in these tech stocks, so everyone was making piles of cash. Nothing wrong there, right? Well, the commissions we charged don't exist now. The SEC and other regulatory bodies put a stop to all of that immediately after the tech bubble burst to better protect investors. But the bubble hadn't yet burst and I had more months than not when I was taking home thirty K a month net, saving and spending some, but mostly putting it back into the market to riskily speculate in the hopes of making an even bigger payoff. I was immune to panic, sometimes losing fifty K in one day to make it up the following couple of days. It didn't matter to me—I knew the market fluctuated and I had faith that I would come out in the green.

Aldano and I were so frantic churning that neither of us had time for much outside of work and entertaining clients. Aldano did have a pregnant girlfriend that he lived with but they fought constantly. While he wanted to be a good dad, he had no problem hiding out from the girlfriend in the office; it was no surprise that they broke up. It suited him because all he (and I) cared about was making money and getting that corner office, which we soon did get, one with huge windows overlooking Madison Avenue. If we weren't on the phones, we were strategizing pitches, throwing a ball around with our feet up on our desks. Aldano started slipping in compliments here and there, and I could feel his attraction to me radiating off him. I tried to shrug it off, but it was flattering. And I understood where it was coming from—the high that came from making money together as a team was addictive, and it drew us closer together. I wasn't attracted to him, but I was attracted to his work ethic, attracted to how he could help me build my empire.

Our team of two grew to four as we added two cold callers, in addition to our sales assistant, Tito. Our callers were also imported from VTR, two guys named Mike Sanchez and Jesus Castillo. Sanchez had coincidentally walked into Cohen's just a few weeks before I started at VTR and I had sold him an expensive pair of glasses—crazy! Jesus had actually started out as one of Jordan Belfort's guys years before—he told me that on his first day at Stratton, he had been ordered to pick up Jordan in his Ferrari. An assistant just tossed the keys to this six-figure car at him and let him loose! Jesus unfortunately just couldn't make it as a broker and now he was working for me, opening accounts, which was dizzying to think about.

We then added another cold caller to our roster, making our team a robust five. Unlike at VTR, where callers were never afforded special treatment like, say, being treated like human beings, we would take our team members out to enjoy themselves and to give them a taste of what they could someday hope to have. We'd go wild in company limos, attending Knicks games, popping Cristal on the way over (I didn't even like Cristal that much! But we could afford it, so why not?). Aldano would almost always drink too much, which I took note of but didn't bring up—he was having fun and blowing off steam after a stress-filled day. Nothing wrong with that, right? We never waited in line—I always tipped the bouncers so that we would be whisked to the door immediately and so that they would know that Black girls have money of their own, too, thank you very much.

We offered these perks to our clients as well, taking them to two-thousand-dollar dinners at Asia de Cuba, Broadway plays where premium tickets could cost five hundred bucks a pop, and sports nights. We'd buy them "little" gifts as a thank-you for their business—my go-to was Tiffany because they had nice men's accessories. I often bought five-hundred-dollar cuff links, sometimes multiples at once. While Aldano and I each had expense accounts, our expenses outstripped our budgets. We paid for it all, splitting it between the two of us. For clients we needed to keep content—because we were losing their money—we enticed them with drinks, dinner, and dessert. "Dessert" was a sex worker from the back page ads of the *Village Voice*. I'd usher our clients to a hotel in Times Square where my aunt Hermite—my mom's favorite sister, who'd moved to the United States years after Oline—was head of housekeeping and I could get room discounts, and it was there that their sex worker would be awaiting them. Aldano and I once went to check on a room to make sure that it was up to standard and we made the mistake of walking in on our client already sampling his "dessert." The sex worker wasn't fazed at all—she was such a pro that she only briefly eyed us before getting back to work. We ran out as fast as we could, and our client's hairy white ass has been emblazoned in my memory ever since.

It was also helpful to book massages for clients when they were in town—it kept them happy and when Aldano or another broker took them, they were more liable not to drop their accounts with us, maybe because they felt we had a certain amount of collateral on them. Obviously, these weren't just massages and clients could take their pick from masseuses and techniques. One woman was known for using only her stilettos!

It was just another part of the job, as commonplace as filling out an account form. Knowing now that many of these women, usually foreigners, who I suspected were Eastern European, were almost certainly trafficked is something that weighs on me heavily and I often wonder what happened to these nameless women and whether I contributed to any bad endings they may have come to.

Ninety percent of my clients were middle-aged and older white men and it was assumed that I'd take care of their sexual needs through these kinds of services, especially since I wasn't putting out myself. Clients also made the leap of logic that if I were arranging sexual favors for them, I would be open to sleeping with them, too. They felt entitled to my body because they had invested with me—why would I not pay them back in this way? This ranged from mild innuendo and eyebrow waggling to outright asking me if they were to invest a certain amount of money, would that guarantee that I'd sleep with them.

I didn't particularly care whether they were married or single, but that was another thing I would not compromise on, even if I had been interested—I would not cross that line with clients. It never stopped clients from trying, though, impressing me with finery I didn't know or care about.

One client—let's call him Bob—once threw a party in my honor at his mansion and sent me a cocktail hour menu for my approval beforehand. I had to look up what "prawns" were, and I had no idea what reserve I preferred for wine (when out with clients, I always just blindly ordered the most expensive bottles), so I quickly gave my approval without any further thought.

Canapes on trays, lights tastefully dimmed, his giant house was drippingly expensive, beyond compare even to the Hamptons houses I'd visited. Bob found me sampling prawns and enthusiastically introduced me to his wife—we can call her Jill. I'd hired him a sex worker the week before, and he'd also propositioned me. He gave me a gleeful look as I shook hands with Jill. I could tell that he loved the thrill of such secrets passing between us. There was little risk, though, as I certainly wouldn't tell Jill—as a broker, I'd already been bought. The price of my silence? My very large commission check.

Chapter 24

As Aldano and I continued further intertwining our business lives, we became friends, and then, we somehow slipped into sex. It just . . . happened. I didn't really care about the sex—it was just convenient—we were both available. By that, I mean we were in front of each other practically all the time, touching elbows while reviewing a stock report, popping bottles in the company limo, playing golf, which we'd picked up to help network with clients. Neither of us had time for dating—I'd had a couple of boyfriends in the past, nothing serious, and once I'd become a broker my attention shifted entirely away from romantic relationships; I barely had time to see my family or friends. I was only able to squeeze in time with Catalina, but she was busy, too, working and attending college. Even though Aldano and I really weren't well suited for each other, it somehow made life easier to be together both professionally and personally.

Our liaison went on for far longer than it should have, but in a life filled with extremes, it was a rare, easy thing; that is, until it wasn't. We enjoyed each other's company and were great work partners, but . . . the sex was mediocre at best. We should have stayed friends, but once we started, we didn't know how to stop. We kept our relationship from as many people as we could, only sharing with our closest friends. As our commission checks grew, Aldano bought me increasingly lavish gifts, which to me felt like "keep your mouth closed" presents—Hermès scarves, Chanel bags, Prada shoes. I knew that even though he'd officially broken up with his girlfriend, he was stringing her along, hinting that they might get back together someday. He did this so that the girlfriend wouldn't date other men because Aldano didn't want her bringing them home around his kid.

"Aldano, just tell her," I'd say, not really caring whether she knew about me, but the secrecy made life harder.

Aldano's good mood would evaporate then, and his eyes would narrow.

"Don't you dare tell me what to do!" he would yell at me, which would spark a heated argument, conflagrating the rest of the day.

Around this time, I noticed that Aldano's drinking had become a real problem—he was messy and he'd get belligerent if someone said something he didn't like. I was not okay with this—his temper reminded me of Fab, and I wanted nothing to do with anyone even remotely like him. This clearly wasn't working. It was confirmed beyond a doubt when one night Aldano and I were partying in a limo, headed to God knows where at God knows what time. Liquor was not a problem for me like it was for Aldano, who by now was drinking to excess almost every night. That said, I was the sloppy one that evening. Things soon became hazy and I passed out. When I came to, I was on the floor of the limo and something was stabbing me in the ribs. I groggily opened my eyes to see Aldano toeing me with his boot as if I were some sort of animal. I was furious—I wasn't ashamed that I'd passed out; I felt that Aldano should have been ashamed for treating me like less than a human. The clock on our relationship was ticking.

At the company's holiday party, Aldano got plastered even

though he had told me he wouldn't be drinking that night. He began making a ruckus, going so far as to even rip a few paintings off the walls. I could see senior management raising eyebrows so I very quickly dragged him out of the party and back to my apartment. He was so tanked that the bastard ended up peeing on my bedroom wall, thinking it was a urinal. I knew that this would have to end sooner rather than later.

When New Year's Eve rolled around, I went to Aldano's family's house to celebrate, but he somewhat puzzlingly had invited his ex, too. The entire night she was staring daggers at me. Of course that set off yet another argument between Aldano and me, one thing led to another, and somehow we ended up drunkenly having unprotected sex. It wasn't until three months later that I realized our alcohol-fueled entanglement had gotten me pregnant. Shit. I was twenty-two. I didn't want a baby, and I certainly didn't want *his* baby. An abortion was the only option for me, so I went to Planned Parenthood with Catalina. Aldano had weakly protested at first but we both knew he didn't want another kid.

After the procedure was finished, I looked up at the nurse and asked whether it was a boy or a girl.

"Can't tell, not fully developed," she said curtly, without looking at me, and that was that. I sipped some juice, then left to rest at Catalina's house, my home away from home. Catalina knew about some of the drama between Aldano and me, but she knew better than to ask questions when it was clear I didn't want to talk about it. As the night wore on, though, and I didn't hear from Aldano, I grew annoyed and then enraged when a colleague told me he was partying at TAO. We might not be in a real relationship, but he couldn't even check on me as a friend? I had just had an abortion and here he was drinking lychee martinis and eating Peking duck, getting shit-faced under the watch of a massive Buddha? Fuck that.

Despite Catalina's protestations, I hobbled outside and into a cab, and sped over to TAO. Aldano's presence was confirmed when I saw his car on the street. A red mist descended over me, and I yanked open Aldano's car door using my spare key. I broke out into sobs and got even angrier when I saw my tear-streaked face in the rearview mirror. I let out an anguished shriek and tore the mirror bracket from the ceiling and began attacking the windshield with it. A crack spiderwebbed across the glass and I sat back, surprised at how satisfying that had felt. I couldn't stop now. I beat on the glass as another, and then another crack appeared. I didn't stop until Aldano's windshield was crushed. I regained my breath, wiped the sweat off my forehead, and stepped out of the car to admire my handiwork. Not bad at all.

I rang Aldano and told him to get his ass outside. When he stumbled out a few minutes later, I introduced him to the new and improved version of his car. His face dropped and he started crying.

"You're out partying while I got an abortion?!" I shouted at him. "How dare you fuck with me like this!"

Aldano hiccupped and shuddered. "I don't deserve this. What's wrong with you?" he yelled.

As I stood there watching the snot hit his top lip, I felt the finality of the moment and my anger lifted. I would never have a future with Aldano. He wasn't worth this. We'd keep doing business together, yes. Maybe we'd sleep together, maybe not, but he would no longer rule my emotional well-being. We left together, then, Aldano still sniveling. It would be okay.

And it really was. That night didn't stop us from continuing to gross incredible amounts of money, and out of countless employees, I was rated one of the top ten brokers at the firm multiple times and received a shiny plaque with my name on it. Meanwhile, Aldano continued his descent, showing up to work looking slovenly, being disrespectful to our cold callers, which—given where we had come from—was not okay. If I had any respect left for him, it quickly evaporated.

My checks piled up so haphazardly that I would sometimes have sixty or seventy thousand dollars waiting to be deposited into my bank account, and I wouldn't even notice. I finally felt financially secure and started buying five-hundred-dollar shoes and two-thousand-dollar purses without blinking. Boxes of Prada shoes piled up in my apartment, and some pairs I never even wore. I finally bought myself my own Hermès belt and I was more than comfortable dropping by Gucci and dropping a few thousand in one go. As thrilling as this might sound, the thrill of making myself—and my clients—money was what was most alluring to me, not buying things. Even when I was on my lunch ticket hustle, I knew that I would have to buy myself what I wanted and needed. Buying myself material things— even though these things were much more expensive than what I previously furnished myself with—was something I had always done. It was nice, but nothing special. I simply wanted to be great at my job, make money, to have the ability to protect myself financially if I needed to, and to not have to ever worry about how I would pay my rent. If a Gucci bag happened to come my way in the process, great.

I took Catalina and Kenya on trips with me to the Dominican Republic, to Miami, to warm places where we could order tropical drinks with little umbrellas stuck in them, and on cruises, paying for their expenses.

I had a weekly standing dinner with my friends that I always tried to honor even though I was so busy, treating them all to steak and drinks at Rincon Criollo, a Cuban restaurant.

My first car? A Mercedes that I got through Catalina's boyfriend at Englewood Mercedes. When I walked in, a stockbroker with the budget to pay for it, I noted a few raised eyebrows, but it didn't faze me. Any microaggressions that were targeted at me rolled off me—I simply attributed someone's negative attitude, likely racism or classism, to mere pettiness or ignorance. I *couldn't* see these acts as microaggressions because keeping my eyes closed to these acts was how I survived as a Black woman in these spaces.

I tried to share my newfound wealth with my family, finding reasons to drop by the house where Phil and Glifford still lived with my mom, handing cash over to Phil, who gratefully accepted it, and to Glifford when I could convince him to take any. I would also attempt to take our dog Rusky, now an old man, to the groomer for a much needed bath and haircut, but both Phil and Glifford would protest, which puzzled me until Phil took me aside one day to explain.

"Cin, Rusky is all that Glifford has," he said wearily, sounding far older than he was.

I sighed. I knew what he meant. In the past few years, Glifford had further retreated into himself. He didn't work, and he rarely went outside, preferring to stay cloistered in our mother's house, listening to rap music in his room. The few friends he had made when he was younger had long since stopped visiting, and what little energy he seemed to have was devoted entirely to Rusky, his only companion.

Glifford hadn't really ever seemed happy since we were young kids, and I knew that things had gotten worse in recent years. I admittedly was incredibly self-absorbed during this time, and also stressed due to my job, and I rarely inquired after Glifford. It wouldn't have mattered anyway—my mother did whatever she could to stop me from visiting. She didn't want me coming around the house, scared that whatever darkness had rooted itself inside Glifford might somehow infect me, not allowing me to stay longer than thirty minutes if she was home when I dropped by. She would evade my questions about Glifford when we talked on the phone, waving them away like gnats in front of her face, saying only that Glifford was going through a hard time.

"Sendy, don't worry about him. You don't need to be distracted right now," she would tell me, admonishing me to focus on my career.

Whether or not it was wrong to do so, I took my mother's word at face value, assuming Glifford would sort himself out, even when it was clear to everyone except my mother that he was going through a mental health crisis. Our family didn't talk about depression—my mother didn't believe that it existed.

So I didn't make any overtures toward Glifford and he never reached out to me. Instead, when I did pause to think about my family, I chose to focus on Phil. When he wasn't busy with school, he would occasionally drop by Ladenburg, and I would treat him to hearty lunches, always ordering more than we could eat, imploring him to take our leftovers home with him. One afternoon after we had eaten lunch together, I took him to the Nike store, which was around the corner from my office. I strolled in with Phil in tow and gestured toward the clothing racks.

"Pick out what you want," I said coolly, holding back a smile. Phil's eyes widened.

"What? Really?" he asked, incredulous.

"Really," I said.

We walked around the store, picking up jerseys, socks, sneakers, shorts, pants. I bought Phil enough clothing to last him for years. I knew my mother didn't like to take money from me, so I paid for Phil when I could. Besides, I didn't want my baby brother to wear threadbare clothes, not when I was making real money. And of course, being me, I didn't pay full price—my friend Chanelle worked at the store and gave me her employee discount.

Even with these extravagances, I couldn't entirely shake my roots; I still conserved paper towels, clipped coupons for groceries, and always remembered to turn the lights off in the apartment before leaving. I had moved to a one-bedroom in Astoria even though I could have chosen to live in SoHo if I wanted to. You can't kick old habits and rent was cheap there, plus Queens felt familiar and I was, best of all, close to Catalina.

But the fact that we were trading so much had begun to make management leery. The word on the street was that investors overseas were beginning to take legal action against those employing chop shop tactics who had lost them huge sums of money. Ladenburg had hired about thirty brokers from VTR when it imploded, and the alums had a lot of overseas clientele. The department heads watched our trades more closely and made sure all our paperwork regarding discretionary accounts was meticulously accounted for. On a few trades, the firm's compliance officers even asked us to lower our commissions because of the losses on that particular account. This was a complete about-face from the firm's lax attitude in years past when we were never questioned about our accounts or commissions. Even though we were capitalizing on the dot-com boom like so many others, they felt that the SEC wouldn't take a liking to what we were doing. We had to tread more carefully than ever with the firm breathing down our necks, and we weren't happy about it.

We needed to exert care here not just to keep our jobs but because it was costing us. If we landed a particularly big loss, in order to keep the client happy, we would "take a hit" as it was called, paying for the loss out of our commission checks so that the client would stay with us. This happened to all the brokers at Ladenburg here and there, but the more risks that Aldano and I took, the more hits we received. These hits were usually between ten and twenty thousand dollars each, but one particularly bad hit that Aldano and I had to split was a whopping one hundred and fifty thousand dollars. That one really hurt.

Fortunately, or so I thought, the CEO of Ladenburg, Antonio Chavez, had taken a shine to me. I wasn't necessarily surprised—I stuck out at Ladenburg—I was the only Black woman there, and the only female broker. The only other person of color whom I can recall being at the company was Monique, an Indian American woman who worked in Compliance.

Antonio would often call me to his office to shoot the shit and he had scored me Mariah Carey tickets through the firm's connection to Madison Square Garden. When he handed them to me, he winked and said, "You owe me."

I laughed. "I make the firm good money so I think we're good, no?"

He shook his head, smiling. "I heard you were a ball breaker, Fabré."

"You heard right," I shot back, still laughing.

Antonio's favorable attention couldn't stop the heat from being turned up on Aldano and me, as well as many others in the office. Ladenburg was now being investigated for trading overseas without proper authorization, making those trades technically illegal. Law firms had begun putting ads in the papers targeting overseas clients, offering to go after firms to recoup lost earnings. On top of that, with the Internet growing rapidly every day, the previously opaque market was becoming more accessible to investors who could now check their portfolios online, compare the merits of brokerage houses, and conduct research on potential investments. E-Trade came onto the scene, allowing investors to trade themselves, and why wouldn't they? They could avoid our exorbitant commissions and still make a killing in this dot-com bubble. Investors were quitting their jobs to begin day trading, starting small and ending the day with huge profits.

As 1999 came and went, there was rampant speculation that the dot-com bubble would burst—and soon. The NASDAQ

Composite Stock Market Index, which traded a large number of tech stocks, had risen four hundred percent. Investors were so eager to invest in literally any dot-com company that they overlooked traditional metrics they had used for many years before investing in a company. The price-earnings ratio (PE) was no longer scrutinized—they were confident that if investment banks were fueling speculation and bullish on investment in the tech sector, these companies would eventually turn a profit. Brokers were quitting by the handful every day to become day traders. They didn't need the nine-to-five grind anymore because they were making millions on their own. As for myself, I could trade fifty K to two hundred K a day in my accounts. It was a complete madhouse on any given day in our office. We were constantly glued to our screens, watching a dozen stocks or more at a time. We were afraid to leave our office during market hours because we didn't want to miss any of the action. The warning signs of meltdown were screaming in our faces every day. Older brokers who knew that we were heavily invested in tech warned us to get ready because a crash was imminent. I stayed optimistic because that was my default, but I did begin to wonder where I fit into this scene that I would have done anything to be a part of only a few years before.

❧

To let off steam from all the pressures at work, I took advantage of my limited free time and disposable income and went shopping and attended Yankees games (where I met legendary player Willie Randolph and caught a signed ball that he launched at me). I played golf obsessively—being my own competition appealed to me, and I was always trying to shave points off my scorecard. I also partied more heavily, going from work to the club and right back to work, just like the brokers at VTR used to do—without lap dances, though. One night I attended a party at Windows on the World in the World Trade Center and

I bumped into none other than my boss, Antonio Chavez, on my way out. He suggested that we share a car home, as it was billed to the office anyway. I accepted and we got in.

"Where do you live, Fabré?" he asked. I told him I lived in Queens.

"That's going to be quite a long ride home." He looked at me pointedly.

I shifted in my seat. I had a feeling I knew where this was going.

"Oh, it's fine, I might just take a short nap and I'll be home before I know it," I said, trying to sound casual.

The car suddenly turned onto a brownstone-lined street and slowed.

"Well, this is my stop," Chavez said. I scooted further away from him and brightly said, "Thanks for sharing the car! I'll catch you at work then." He leaned over as if to kiss me on the cheek, his acrid breath on my face.

"Why don't you forget that long ride home and I'll give you a different kind of ride?"

I was repulsed. This man was at least thirty years older than I was, not to mention that he was my boss.

I sighed and decided to face it head-on.

"Why? Why do you want to have sex with me? I'm sure you can get it anywhere you want."

He gave a creepy smile and laughed.

"Well, that's an easy answer. I've always enjoyed light coffee. And you owe me one." He smiled again, but this time it didn't reach his eyes.

He cocked an eyebrow. "Remember Mariah? And those Yankees tickets?"

I wasn't even surprised that he'd brought this up. You couldn't do *anything* in this business without expecting something in return.

Why did I have to make him comfortable with a gentle letdown when he'd made me feel so dirty? I couldn't hold back.

"Yeah, Mariah really didn't put on her best show that night—she had a cold. And the Yankees lost that game so that's just not worth my pussy, sorry!"

Chavez didn't like that response at all and glared.

"Now we're keeping our legs closed? I thought you liked Latino men. I'm Venezuelan," he huffed.

"I like men who aren't old enough to qualify for social security so I think we're done here," I said.

He stared at me, silent, then broke out into a smile.

"Ah, I was just testing you! I heard you were a tough one. That's why we love you so much!" He playfully punched my shoulder. "Have a good night!"

He got out of the car and quickly shut the door, not looking at me as he headed toward his brownstone. I had a feeling that the night's events would come back to haunt me. I was so tired of this—always the same story, just a different character. How long did I want to keep doing this? Was this job really worth the endless harassment and the other heavy costs that came with it? I was starting to think that maybe . . . it wasn't. I sighed and gave the driver my address, laying my head back on the seat rest, trying to get Chavez's insistent stare out of my mind.

Chapter 25

DESPITE THE MISGIVINGS I HAD ABOUT MY INTER-
action with Chavez, I had to put it out of my mind to
deal with more important matters.

My mother had told me she'd had debilitating back pain just
a few weeks before when I'd visited her at her house in Queens,
and she had as nonchalantly as possible asked to borrow some
money so she could get an MRI, as if this were just a trip to the
dentist and she'd walk out with a new toothbrush in hand. Now
she was on the phone with me matter-of-factly delivering the
news that they had found a lump. She had breast cancer.

My stomach dropped but I tried to keep the quaver out of my
voice. My mother was forty-six. She was the toughest person I
knew—I had never even seen her with a cold before.

"We'll fight this," I told her. "We will treat this."

Suddenly I was the one reassuring her—our roles had flip-
flopped and now I needed to be the strong one and assure her
that everything would be okay. I could sense her nod through
the phone, saying nothing, her emotions as efficient as ever.

More quickly than I thought possible, my mother was prodded, assessed, and prepared for surgery in a matter of a few
days.

As we walked into Sloan Kettering Cancer Center for surgery,

I took in the antiseptic smell that hospitals always have, absorbed the energy of doctors and nurses in scrubs moving with purpose, watched the bright light from the ceiling bounce off the tile floor. *We will be okay*, I repeated to myself. There would be no "I" in this fight. This was a battle that we would fight together.

When they wheeled my mother off to surgery, I took one last look at her. She looked fragile and small in her blue hospital gown, the ID bracelet encircling her wrist looking far too big for her.

I stayed at the hospital until the surgery was over, interrogating the oncologist as soon as she came into the recovery room where my mother lay.

"Did you get it?" I asked her. "All of it?"

The doctor looked me confidently in the eye and nodded.

"If there is any cancer left, it's on the microscopic level and we will, of course, monitor. She will be fine."

I let out a sigh of relief. My mother was at one of the top cancer hospitals in the nation. She was in the best hands possible. I turned to my mother, whose eyes had stayed closed while I spoke to the oncologist.

"Did you hear that, Mommy? You're going to be just fine."

My mother didn't reply, just sighed and kept her eyes closed.

The doctor smiled and shook my hand, then left the room to attend to another family desperate for the answer I'd just received.

It was then that my mother opened her eyes and focused her gaze on me.

"I know my body. They didn't get all of the cancer," she said softly. "I can feel it in my bones."

My throat constricted. I didn't want to hear this. She had always had a ghostly sense of knowledge that told her things other people didn't know.

"Mommy, you're wrong. They got it, didn't you hear her?" I asked.

She just sighed again, her eyelashes fluttering against her hollow cheeks.

She would be fine. Everything is fine and everything will be fine.

⚬

The atmosphere at 590 Madison had chilled considerably in the few months since the car ride with Chavez. I wasn't greeted warmly by any of the directors when I ran into them. Chavez never called me to his office again. I wasn't invited to any more private parties as before. Complaints about me started being reported where there had been none before. It felt like everyone outside my team had become frosty with me, even the damn assistants. They could smell blood in the air. Case in point: one morning, nature called so I headed to the bathroom. When I came out of the stall, an executive's assistant exited the adjacent stall. We eyed each other in the mirror as we both washed our hands.

"I love your shoes," she said, pointing to my Gucci platforms.

"Oh, thanks very much," I said, cranking a paper towel from the dispenser.

"Yeah, they're really nice. I remember them from last season," she said, curling her lip. "Did you get them at an outlet or something?"

Barb thrown. I was insulted, less so about being on trend, which I didn't care about, and more because this assistant had the gall to say this to me, a high-earning broker at the firm. This was majorly disrespectful. But whatever, I wouldn't let her see me rattled.

"You know what?" I said, playing along. "You're right. I actually got them at Woodbury Common for a *great* price. On major sale. I love a bargain." Fuck her. I balled up my paper

towel, threw it away, and walked out of the bathroom, not looking behind me to see the girl's reaction.

As if I didn't have enough fashion-related drama in my life,
the company had also instituted a new dress policy that I felt
was horribly sexist. Women now had to wear skirts of a certain
length, with pantyhose. The new requirements listed out for
women ran to about a page, while the men's dress code could
be encapsulated in a couple of sentences. I told HR that I would
not be adhering to a dress code that had not been disclosed
during my hiring. HR did not take kindly to that and said they
would be reporting this to the directors, who would offer an
official response. I knew my challenge wasn't making my position at the company any better, but I was tired of being targeted
as a woman.

I could read the writing on the wall—I wasn't long for the
world of Ladenburg. I started interviewing as quietly with other
firms as possible in case the ax came down on me.

So it wasn't much of a surprise when I was called to Chavez's
office a month or two later. When I walked in, I found the
compliance team present. This wasn't good. I sat in a chair and
waited in silence for whatever they were about to throw at me.

Apparently, I had received a customer complaint about trading without authorization. Even though I had a written record
confirming that I had the power to do so, I would still be investigated for excessive trading on the account, I was told.

Fine, I told them, I would hire a lawyer and fight this. There
was an easy counter here and I deserved a chance to prove my
innocence. I figured Chavez was behind this, and it was true that
he looked particularly smug when announcing that I was being
let go for insubordination. I would have to leave right away.

I got the message loud and clear: *We hope you've enjoyed the
ride, but this is your stop so get the fuck off*, they were saying.
Fine. I left quietly without saying goodbye to anyone, packing

my things and my book, figuring that making a scene wouldn't help with future job prospects.

In addition to the interview circuit, I had recruiters calling me to join top-notch firms, with top-notch signing bonuses and offers. I couldn't fully concentrate on the offers, though. My mother's cancer had returned, just as she had predicted. I urged her to go back to Sloan Kettering, but she refused—after the doctor said everything was out, she'd lost her trust in traditional Western medicine. She didn't want to try chemo; instead, she put her faith in a witch doctor who gave her thick, viscous shakes to drink and herbs to swallow multiple times a day.

Through all this, my mother was still giving me her two cents on my career. I had gotten an offer from a firm based in the World Trade Center, and I wanted to take it, but the morning I was to call back the recruiter to sign, my mother got to me first. Panic was evident in her voice.

"Sendy, don't take that job in the World Trade Center!"

I scoffed. She was constantly calling me to tell me to avoid going places or seeing certain people. She always had hunches that I would listen to in order to humor her. But her urgency here was on a level I'd never experienced. I asked her what was wrong.

"I had a dream and I saw planes crashing into the World Trade Center and a church," she gasped. I incredulously started to repeat her statement but she cut me off.

"Sendy, listen to me! You never listen to me!" she cried.

❧

"Okay, okay, Mommy." I promised her that I wouldn't take the job. I figured with her illness that she was increasingly losing her grip on reality. But if it made her feel so much better for me not to, then I wouldn't.

I had plenty of offers and ended up signing with a large brokerage called Investec Ernst & Co., which had offices all over the world and was based in the Chrysler Building in Manhattan. They wanted Aldano and me to join as a package deal, so even though I wanted to rid myself of him and strike out on my own, I decided Investec's offer was too good to pass up. No micromanaging, a huge office, an amazing commission split, unlimited financial resources for whatever we needed, and an international client base.

Everything in my life was speeding up, though, and I wasn't sure if I was in full control of it anymore. The dot-com bubble had burst, and it was an absolute bloodbath. The excitement of working at a new firm quickly wore off, as our screens glared red with fast-declining stocks. We had no guidance from the senior partners or directors on what we should be doing for our clients and we didn't have enough experience with the bear to avoid mistakes. The account of my Man U owner, Charles Martin Edwards, was in the mere thousands. The stock market was spiraling and so was I.

My mother's health was also in a free fall. She called me one morning to say that she had admitted herself to the Queens Hospital emergency room because she, as she stoically put it, wasn't feeling well.

I dropped everything and ran to the ER, where a solemn-looking doctor informed me that her cancer had metastasized to her liver. He shook his head and told me that this wasn't a good sign. I needed to get whatever she needed to make herself comfortable, as they would be keeping her indefinitely for treatment.

I was in severe denial—this just meant that they needed her for a longer stay to find the appropriate treatment, which would make her all better, I thought.

From the hospital, I called my younger brother, Phil, who was away at college. He was understandably upset, but I told him to try to focus on his studies as best as he could.

I was more apprehensive about telling my older brother, Glifford. Ever since Oline had gotten sick, Glifford, who lived with her, had fallen into a deep depression. He now mostly stayed in the dusty attic of the house, usually only descending the stairs for meals, and sometimes not even then. He often had a wild glint in his eye and I didn't fully feel safe around him, which gave me a lump in my throat to think about. Glifford was my coconspirator when we were growing up. He had protected me all my life, and now I felt scared of him? How had it gotten this bad? I didn't know the extent of his mental illness until last year, when my mother had him hospitalized because she was convinced he was going to hurt himself or someone else. When she told me this I was shocked—I had no idea he had disintegrated like this. When I asked her why she hadn't told me, she simply shrugged in true Oline fashion and said that she didn't want it to affect me.

After our mother's Thanksgiving hospitalization, I paid for Glifford to see a pricey therapist in Manhattan, but he soon stopped going, saying the sessions weren't helpful. I never considered at the time that *I* could benefit from therapy. Therapy was okay for Glifford because he was clearly having some sort of breakdown, but anything short of that wasn't real or recognized in our family. Mental illness was not something to be talked about. Per Oline, you just needed to put your head down and work harder.

After a day in which Oline's pain rated a nine out of ten on one of those sliding-scale pain charts that you often see in hospitals, Glifford despairingly told me he was suicidal.

"If Mommy dies, I'm going to kill myself," he announced darkly.

I felt like I was an observer to everything going on in my life. As much as I tried to hustle and stay on top of everything—it's all I knew to do—I couldn't fix things. I couldn't fix the market. I couldn't fix my mother. I couldn't fix Glifford.

I couldn't even be a friend to my mother when she needed one. Shortly before she went into hospice, I came to visit, bringing her some of the bright fruit she used to love, which now tasted like ash on her tongue from the chemo that she had finally agreed to undergo. She led me to the bathroom and brought us in front of her mirror.

"Look," she said. "Look at my hair."

In her hands, she held her hair, which had fallen out from the chemo, the long, straight hair that she was so proud of all her life, a gift that she felt she had given me.

"Look at me. I'm ugly," she said, a tear rolling down her cheek.

I stood rooted in place, shocked. This entire time that she had been battling cancer, not once had she ever complained or mentioned the toll that the illness was taking on her.

I had never had a real conversation with her before—she was my mother and had provided for me, taught me to be proud of myself, to have confidence and self-respect. But we weren't friends—we never had been close. We didn't know how to talk to each other like a mother and daughter would. And I didn't know how to start now that she was opening up to me and showing me the open wound of her vulnerability. I struggled to say something.

"You're not ugly, Mommy. It's just hair—it'll grow back. You'll see."

I put my arm around her, not as a showing of affection but to get her back to bed so she could rest. I look back now and wonder, *Should I have hugged her?* We were so supremely uncomfortable demonstrating our love for each other in tangible ways like this that I couldn't. I don't know if she wanted a hug in that moment. But I'll always think about how I could feel her bony shoulders biting through her sweater and how maybe I should have wrapped my arms around her just that once.

Once Oline was installed in the hospital, I visited her almost every night, pasting a smile on my face and leaving the hospital with searing headaches. One night she told me she was going to die, just like that. It was always her way to be ordered and no-nonsense. She signed a DNR because she knew I would do everything to resuscitate her if not. She gave me instructions for her funeral—to put her in her favorite dress, to hold an open casket ceremony, to have lots and lots of flowers. She told me to take care of my brothers, especially Glifford, as he needed me. And then for the only time in our lives, she said, "I'm proud of you and I love you." I had waited all my life to hear this.

I went out the double doors of the hospital and was blinded by white-hot pain between my eyes. I could barely drive and I felt like I was going to vomit. I finally understood.

The next day I couldn't bring myself to go to the hospital. I needed just one night in which the headaches didn't take over, one night that I didn't have to think about my dying mother.

"Mommy, I can't come tonight," I told her, the exhaustion weighing heavily on me.

She let out a ragged whimper.

"You're not coming?"

"I'll come tomorrow, Mommy, you'll see me soon," I said.

The anguish in her voice was so sharp, and it still haunts me. I had no idea it would be the last time I would ever hear my mother's voice.

The next morning at work, the hospital rang me. She was slipping fast—it was time.

I called Catalina, who worked nearby, and together we went to the hospital. I couldn't process what was happening—I remember even laughing with her about something. When we got off the elevator, I walked slowly to her room. *Maybe if I take my time, I can postpone her death*, I thought.

At the entrance to her room, I saw a nurse holding my mother's hand. She looked unconscious and was taking hard, ragged breaths.

The nurse looked up, relieved that I'd made it. "Sweetie, she's dying. She's holding on right now, maybe to say goodbye. We think she can still hear you."

I took over, clasping my mother's hand. "Mommy, I'm here. You are not alone, I'm here, it's okay if you want to go. I will take care of Glifford and Philip. I love you. Just let go." I felt her suddenly squeeze my hand.

"Keep talking, she hears you," the doctor said, so I continued.

"Mommy, Catalina is here, too. She wanted to see you to say goodbye."

"I'm here, too, Ms. Fabré. I will look out for Cin," Catalina whispered.

My mother opened her eyes, which had webs of veins running across the whites. Her blood vessels had popped.

I leaned in close.

"I love you!" I choked. She stared straight at me and squeezed my hand, her teeth chattering. She was gone in that second. My mom died on March 16, 2001, at the age of forty-seven.

Chapter 26

THE FUNERAL PASSED LIKE A DREAM. HUNDREDS OF people showed up, including friends and family who traveled from Haiti. The only people who didn't show up were my father and my grandparents, who hadn't been told. Fab was not welcome and, besides, he was in Haiti, so there was no way he would have found out. Not that he would have attended—there was nothing for him to take. He wouldn't learn of my mother's death until years later. My grandparents were in poor health so my aunts and uncles kept the news from them, impressively taking the family secret-keeping to a whole new level.

After her death, I couldn't stop interrogating the pieces of my mother's life. She had always worked so hard and yet seemed so unhappy. She was self-sacrificing to the extreme, going without so we could have what we needed. Even when we were the poorest we'd ever been, she would scrounge for change so she could buy an Entenmann's boxed cake and stick a candle in it for our birthdays. She never said it, but that was her way of saying I love you.

She taught me that I had the right to pursue whatever it was I wanted in life, that I should never hesitate to take a chance, that I should respect myself above all. Her life lessons were always in my head now, playing on repeat. Her words ringing through my brain made work increasingly difficult. Staring at my desk with my eyes hazily unfocused, I realized that perhaps my mother was trying to tell me something. I didn't want this life anymore—I didn't want to make money just to make money. I wanted to enjoy life, to actually absorb its pleasures and its pain, instead of numbing everything with work and partying. In the back of my mind, I knew that I would need to make a big decision about my job sooner or later. I was just too tired to think about it right now.

Checking in on Glifford at the house one day, as I knew my mother would want, he handed me a letter, slightly crinkled, and said it was for me. My mother had written it while she was in the hospital. She confessed that she knew she was dying and that she would be sad that she wouldn't get to be in our lives as we grew older, perhaps got married and started families. But she ended it with, "I will always keep an eye on you." It felt like a sign that she really was trying to guide me to make the decision that I knew, deep down in my bones, I needed to make.

A couple of months later, my aunt Hermite invited my brothers and me to her house in Brooklyn for a Haitian dinner the night before my birthday. Even though Hermite had been my mother's favorite sister, she had rarely interacted with Hermite after Hermite moved to the United States. I had only met Hermite a few times before because while Fab was in our lives, Oline didn't want him anywhere near Hermite or her sister, Paulette. He had a penchant to stare at their chest, I even noticed at a family wedding. Our top heaviness ran in the family.

I was excited to taste the same flavors that my mother so skillfully knew how to create, to feel her love again through my aunt's cooking. I stopped at the house to pick up Phil and Glifford, idling outside in my car, waiting for the two to hop in, but Glifford didn't feel like socializing and begged off.

We headed home, stuffed, with Tupperware bursting with leftovers for Glifford. I dropped Phil off at the house, waving goodbye, then I sat in the driveway, debating whether I wanted to drive to a friend's house or call it a night. But only a minute later, Phil came flying out of the house, screaming and screaming.

"Glifford is dead! Glifford is dead!" he screamed as I tore myself out of my car. "He shot himself!"

Time stopped and I somehow managed to dial 911. An ambulance got to the house in only a few minutes but Glifford was already gone. The paramedics said that he had shot himself most likely a couple of hours earlier. We couldn't go upstairs to see him because the police, which had also been called, classified the room as a crime scene. We stood in the driveway with the blue and red lights of police cars washing over us, turning us into ghosts.

I spent my twenty-fifth birthday identifying my brother's body at the morgue. He had made it to only twenty-six. When I called the funeral home, the director was happy to hear from me. He thought I was arranging to pick up the guest book from my mother's funeral, which I had forgotten about, but he was soon sobered to learn that I was calling to arrange to bury my brother, five months after I had done the same for my mother. Glifford would be buried in the same plot as my mother, with both of their names on one gravestone. Oline would have her firstborn with her always, just as she had in life.

❧

Life continued its surreal painting. I went to Mexico after Glifford's funeral. I had already planned the trip for my birthday, and I needed to get away. I wanted to feel sand between my toes and sun on my face. I didn't want to think about my job, which was weighing heavily on me.

As I walked the beach one evening, the sun was setting in a

magnificent blood-orange sky. The gulls soared through the air, punctuating the sounds of the beach with their salty cries. As I approached my hotel, I looked up at the balcony and did a double take. I saw my mother and brother standing there with their arms around each other, looking down at me. My mother's hair was shining and gently blowing in the breeze, and she wore a colorful dress. Glifford looked relaxed and content, the first time I'd seen him so in a long time. I waved at them and they waved back at me, and I felt that I had now said my goodbye.

Shortly after, on September 11, 2001, I stayed home from work—I didn't feel like going in. I had the TV on that morning and watched as first one and then another plane flew into the World Trade Center buildings. I called Catalina and we stared at our TVs in disbelief together over the phone. Then Catalina reminded me.

"Cin, didn't your mom predict that planes would fly into the World Trade Center?"

I nodded, in shock, even though I knew Catalina couldn't see me. My mother had been right. Her dream, or rather nightmare, had come true. I suddenly teared up, thinking of her concern, how desperate she was for me not to take that job in the World Trade Center. I had to take deep breaths to calm myself down. It was strangely comforting and eerie and tragic all at the same time.

The New York Stock Exchange and NASDAQ would cancel trading that day, a Tuesday, until the following Monday. When we returned to work, we knew that when the market opened we would be looking at huge losses, especially in the travel and hospitality sectors. We could see in premarket trading that everything was red, setting up the close of the day as the largest single-day loss on the NYSE. By the end of the week, trading losses would reach over a previously unimaginable trillion dollars. For about a month I desperately tried to recoup my clients' losses and encourage them to invest in tech sectors that would likely receive government contracts for combating terrorism.

As 2001 came to an end, I reflected on everything that had transpired in one short year. It felt a bit like a train had run over me. I wanted to find something to be grateful for so that I could at least try to look forward to the year ahead. I thought about my mother, wishing she had taken better care of herself instead of caring for everyone else. I wondered what might have been if my mother hadn't tried to hide my brother's illness, if society didn't teach us to be ashamed of mental health struggles. Would he still be with us? I thought of everyone who had been lost on 9/11 and all the words that their families didn't get to share with their loved ones who had died. No amount of money could have bought those cherished sentences. No amount of money could have brought them back.

These thoughts weighed heavily on me day after day. I wanted to do more with my life beyond moving money and writing checks. I didn't want to be too busy to call a friend back. I wanted to go to a bookstore and read all day long in a comfortable chair. I wanted to eat at my favorite hole-in-the-wall restaurant and share a bottle of wine with someone in the park. I wanted to trust people and stop wondering if there was a motive behind any kindness shown toward me. I wanted to seize every possible opportunity that might allow me to tell my family and friends that I loved them.

Nine months after my mother passed away, and three months after 9/11, I walked into the Chrysler Building and took an elevator up to Investec. I sat down at my desk and took a look around my spacious office with its skyline view. There was nothing meaningful here for me anymore. I had given everything I had to fight and stay and be respected in this business, and I had won. I had clawed my way up from lowly caller to account opener to broker, yes, and I had proven to myself that I had value, proven to everyone who doubted me that they were wrong, leaving them far behind to dwell in their own insecurities. I didn't need to keep the fight going to prove anything anymore. I did something remarkable, testing the limits of my resilience, self-worth, and determination. I had conquered Wall Street—I could do anything I wanted. I appreciated everything that the business had given me and I forgave it for what it had taken. I walked over to Aldano and handed him my book. He looked up, confused.

"It's all yours," I said, not waiting for a reply.

⤫

I passed my colleagues, my team, and my bosses without a word to anyone, taking only my Gucci bag. Goodbyes weren't necessary. I walked out the building and into the anonymous crowd on the street, ready for my next hustle.

Author's Note

I WROTE THIS STORY TO INSPIRE AND EMPOWER OTHERS while also shedding light on the goings-on of past and present-day Wall Street. Just as it was when I was working there, Wall Street today is still overwhelmingly white and male with very little representation beyond this narrow identity. I am grateful for the blinders I wore while in the business, as they gave me the opportunity to be on a level playing field without having to experience any crushing self-doubt that I might otherwise have held. I had—and still have—a voice, and I used it to give others a seat at my table—for many, the first seats they'd ever had.

When I grabbed my Gucci bag and left behind my life as a broker, I also left behind my financial security. I had made hundreds of thousands of dollars while in the business in a short amount of time. While I had left Wall Street on my own terms and gained peace of mind, which ultimately was most important to me, I was no longer pulling in five- or six-figure checks and had to adjust my means of living accordingly.

A lack of financial literacy has kept a core demographic of people from achieving generational wealth, health, and equality. Effective money and debt management are, in my opinion, the key to achieving financial freedom. The irony of my own lack of knowledge in this arena prior to working on Wall Street never escapes me: as a result of not being financially literate, I made costly decisions. It never once crossed my mind while on Wall Street that I wouldn't always be in a position to make the type of money that I was racking up while in the business. And while I never made millions like some of my counterparts who were fully willing to gamble away their souls, I did lose a small fortune because I thought that rainy days would never come. It is my wish that now that you have read my story that you keep it going. Teach yourself and others—especially children—financial literacy in any way that you can: by reading, speaking to professionals, enrolling in courses, and crucially, by heeding the warnings embedded in this story.

Acknowledgments

IF NOT FOR MY MOM, OLINE, I WOULD HAVE NEVER BEEN ABLE TO be in a position to write my story. Her language for expressing love was at times tough, but I took what I could and was inspired by her relentlessness to always go higher, to believe that there were never any limits to what you could achieve.

To my brother Glifford, when I read the old birthday cards you gave to me over the years, I can see that you always believed I could do whatever I put my mind to. You had sweet, kind energy that could be read easily in your eyes. I will always miss you. Thank you for being my big bro.

To my baby brother Phil, I am so glad you got the tail end of the better years. You were everyone's favorite and got us all to laugh.

I would be remiss if I didn't mention my father, Poppy. I will always try to remember you coming home with our favorite banana almond ice cream from Baskin-Robbins and with a smile on your face. Life was rough on you and in turn, you were rough on us. I took away from you only the things that help me to prosper in life, and I have made peace with that.

To my "Santos" family! You were the family I would dream of when I was taking the stairs two at a time in the projects, sneakily peeking into neighbors' apartments. I wanted to laugh, cry, and share my triumphs with my family at the dinner table. You gave me all of that and more. Love you all!

To my "Catalina," who changed my life in the most profound ways. To say you have been my biggest cheerleader since the day I met you is a vast understatement. There was not a single idea or thought that I ran by you that you did not support (well, with the exception of me trying out for *American Idol*). You have welcomed me every single time you have seen me for the past thirty-plus years, all with a smile on your face, always so genuinely glad to see me. We all need a Catalina as a bestie.

To "Kenya," the little sis I got without asking. You made sure to always remind me that I had my own house to go home to when I'd start rummaging through your fridge for leftovers. Nothing has changed!

To my aunts, Paulette and Hermite, who shared some of their own stories with me about my mom, some bittersweet, all appreciated.

To my buddy Jose, thanks for chaperoning me and enjoying some perks! Thirty years later and we're still laughing.

To my writing buddy Zain Asher, who shared her own remarkable story recently. Miss you being just across the street from me, but loving our new adventures together out in the world.

To Harper Glenn, a fellow writer, thanks for your patience, willingness to always help, and for just always being cool as shit.

To my therapist Carmy, I will keep talking as long as you keep listening. You have kept me grounded, shared so much wisdom, and put up with me all these years. How could I not thank you!?

To Buckmaster, undoubtedly one of the best people I know. You have always been there to help me put the pieces together, and fiercely loyal to boot. You will always be Buck to me.

To all the people I worked with over the years in the brokerage business, I am so glad to have had that amazing experience with you all, especially those of you from my cold calling days. Truly, I have fond memories. Those of you I spoke with while writing this book who I hadn't spoken to in over twenty years—thanks for encouraging me to do my thing and for voicing your support. It was almost as if we were back in the Pit at VTR all over again.

To the two people who played a crucial role in getting me into the brokerage business unknowingly—my classmate and the female broker who walked into the eyeglass store that rainy day. Thank you.

To my manager, Ben Levine, who saw the vision in my manuscript in its rawest form and never wavered in his belief that this story would get out there and be a success.

To Retha, my editor. Our initial encounter was so serendipitous. The second time we ever spoke I knew that my story would come to life in your hands and we would be home.

To the team at Holt—your shared excitement was expressed loudly from day one. We make an all-star team. Always rooting for you!

Thank you to my literary agency, Folio Literary Management, especially to Frank Weimann.

To the most badass literary agent ever, Katherine Latshaw. It was kismet from the moment we met. I immediately knew there would be a deep friendship between us and that you would always steer me in the right direction. You have the utmost respect from me, always.

To my wife, Irina. I hope there's never a day that you stop believing in me. Your belief in my story was my "go button." You never once doubted that I could do this. You were always so patient when I stayed up for forty-eight hours at a time, writing. I promised it would pay off one day. Thanks for being my Solnishka. Love you!

To my children, Madison, Maddoux, Sienna, and Hudson. I hope reading my story will better explain who I am and why I am. You guys have been so forgiving, patient, and loving to me, more than I could ever ask for. There is nothing that should ever stand in the way of your passions and beliefs. I couldn't have asked for a better crew. Love you always.

About the Author

Cin Fabré is a New Yorker born and raised in the South Bronx and Queens. At the age of nineteen, she joined a brokerage house on Wall Street, eventually becoming a high-earning broker at a top firm, before leaving in search of a more meaningful life. Today, She divides her time between New York City and Europe and enjoys spending time with her wife and four children. *Wolf Hustle* is her first book.

Bringing a book from manuscript to what you are reading is a team effort.

Dialogue Books would like to thank everyone who helped to publish *Wolf Hustle* in the UK.

Editorial
Joelle Owusu-Sekyere

Contracts
Megan Phillips
Amy Patrick
Anne Goddard
Bryony Hall
Sasha Duszynska Lewis

Design
Charlotte Stroomer

Finance
Andrew Smith
Ellie Barry

Marketing
Emily Moran

Production
Narges Nojoumi

Publicity
Millie Seaward

Operations
Kellie Barnfield
Millie Gibson
Sanjeev Braich

Sales
Caitriona Row
Dominic Smith
Frances Doyle
Hannah Methuen
Lucy Hine
Toluwalope Ayo-Ajala